The 2nd Canadian Mounted Rifles
[*British Columbia Horse*]

In France and Flanders

FROM THE RECORDS OF
LT.-COL. G. CHALMERS JOHNSTON, D.S.O., M.C.

The Naval & Military Press Ltd

Published by
The Naval & Military Press Ltd
5 Riverside, Brambleside, Bellbrook
Industrial Estate, Uckfield, East Sussex,
TN22 1QQ England

Fax: +44 (0) 1825 765701

www.naval-military-press.com
www.nmarchive.com

In reprinting in facsimile from the original, any imperfections are inevitably reproduced and the quality may fall short of modern type and cartographic standards.

FIRST EDITION

LIEUT.-COLONEL G. CHALMERS JOHNSTON, D.S.O., M.C.
(Whose carefully kept diary made the publication of this book possible)

FOREWORD

BY

BRIGADIER-GENERAL D. L. DRAPER, C.M.G., D.S.O.

Memories of the War still live. In every Armistice Service, in every Re-union of Veterans, in every Regimental History—we commemorate the Fallen and recall courageous deeds.

The record of the 2nd Canadian Mounted Rifles is an outstanding example to those who follow, in upholding and supporting the full measure of Canadian Manhood. These men were recruited in British Columbia from the ranks of the best Citizens, who valued their liberty and were ready to sacrifice life itself in the cause of Humanity. They came under my personal observation at an early stage of the World War, and later under my command as General Officer Commanding the 8th Canadian Infantry Brigade.

The 2nd Canadian Mounted Rifles nobly played its part in a most intricate and complicated problem during a World Crisis. Their achievement in battle deserves the commendation of all Canadian Citizens.

I am glad of the opportunity in this Foreword to pay my tribute to the officers and men of this Unit who counted not the sacrifice and only felt the urge to serve.

CONTENTS

CHAP.		PAGE
I	Canada and England .	7
II	France and the Trenches	10
III	The Salient and Sanctuary Wood	20
IV	The Somme	30
V	Vimy Ridge	36
VI	Passchendaele .	54
VII	The Final German Offensive	59
VIII	The Last Hundred Days	65
IX	Armistice and Home	73

APPENDIX

I	Decorations .	74
II	Honor Roll of Officers, Warrant Officers, N.C.O's. and Men Killed in Action or Died of Wounds	80
III	Nominal Roll of Officers, etc., Missing or Prisoners of War	94
IV	Nominal Roll of Officers, etc., Wounded	95
V	Nominal Roll of Officers, Warrant Officers, N.C.O's and Men	125
VI	Glossary of Abbreviations	169

ILLUSTRATIONS

	PAGE
LT.-COL. G. CHALMERS JOHNSTON, D.S.O., M.C.	FRONT
LT.-COL. C. L. BOTT	7
ORIGINAL OFFICERS, 1914	7
ZILLIBEKE BUND	10
THE RAMPARTS	10
CLOTH HALL AT YPRES	14
YPRES CATHEDRAL	14
THE TAKING OF VIMY RIDGE	18
ON VIMY RIDGE	18
A SMASHED PILL-BOX	26
MUD AREA IN PASSCHENDAELE	26
PASSCHENDAELE	30
PRISONERS AT PASSCHENDAELE	30
ON THE ARRAS-CAMBRAI ROAD	34
STATION AT VALENCIENNES	34
CANADIANS ADVANCING	42
A VIEW OF DOMART	42
CAPT. J. McGREGOR, V.C., D.S.O., M.C.	46
A VIEW OF BOURLON VILLAGE	46
IN MONS SQUARE	50
GROUP OF 2ND C.M.R. OFFICERS, 1918	58
DECORATIONS, JANUARY, 1919	62
2ND C.M.R. ORIGINALS, 1919	66

THE 2nd CANADIAN MOUNTED RIFLES

PREFACE

At a reunion of the 2nd Canadian Mounted Rifles, held in Vernon, B.C., on January 26th, 1928, the question of the publication of a History of the Regiment was discussed and a Committee consisting of Major M. V. McGuire, Capt. W. S. Wilson and Mr. G. W. Pearson was appointed with authority to investigate the proposal, and, if deemed expedient, to make the necessary financial arrangements for publication.

The above Committee, after obtaining costs from all the leading publishers, and realising that the expenditure entailed in printing a comprehensive History would be great, decided to circularise all ex-members of the Unit to enlist their moral and financial support.

Very little response was received to the circular and in 1929 a further circular was mailed with no better results.

At the end of 1930, Capt. W. S. Wilson had to withdraw from the Committee as he was leaving for England, his place being taken by Major H. R. Denison.

Early in 1931 it became apparent to the Committee that the publication of any extensive History was out of the question and that even for the publication of an abbreviated History, some other method of preparation and financing would have to be adopted.

The Committee therefore approached Col. G. C. Johnston for permission to publish his personal diary which had been loaned for the use of the Committee and which in itself constituted a most complete record of the activities of the Unit, and after pointing out to Col. Johnston that permission on his part would save great disappointment on the part of the ex-members of the Regiment who were expecting publication of a History, the Committee were fortunate enough to get Col. Johnston's consent.

The Trustees of the Regimental Fund were then approached and a loan obtained which in conjunction with the funds received from individual members, provided a total sufficient to proceed with the work.

While Nominal Rolls and other appendices have been carefully checked, errors may have missed correction, and the Committee asks that any corrections or additions for use in subsequent editions be forwarded to Major M. V. McGuire at Vernon, B.C.

Additional copies of the History may be obtained from Major McGuire, or from Mr. H. D. Williams, c/o Bank of Montreal, Vancouver, B.C.

The Committee are deeply indebted to Col. G. C. Johnston, both for permission to print his personal diary and for his great assistance in providing photographs from his personal collection; also to the Trustees of the Regimental Fund and to Major W. Bapty for assistance in financing the work and last but not least to Mr. West and the staff of The Vernon News for their active interest and able co-operation which made the publication possible.

M. V. McGUIRE
H. R. DENISON
G. W. PEARSON

LT.-COL. C. L. BOTT
WHO COMMANDED FROM MOBILIZATION UNTIL OCTOBER 3RD, 1916

Original Officers, 2nd C.M.R., Victoria, B.C., 1914

NARRATIVE

CHAPTER I

CANADA AND ENGLAND

                  In August, 1914, after the declaration of war on Germany by Great Britain and the British Empire, a great number of the militia units of Canada were mobilized and recruited up to strength, among these being the 30th B. C. Horse, commanded by Lieut.-Col. J. C. L. Bott, and the Victoria Inde-
Aug., 1914 pendent Squadron of Horse, commanded by Major Walter Bapty.
                  Orders to mobilize were received from Headquarters M. D. No. 11 on August 10th, and by the 14th of the same month both units were up to war establishment, the 30th B. C. Horse being billeted in various large buildings in Vernon, and the Independent Squadron at the Willows Park, Victoria.

    A telegram sent to the Minister of Militia on the 4th of August by the O. C. 30th B. C. Horse volunteering the services of the regiment was acknowledged with thanks, but no action followed, as it had already been decided that the first contingent should be infantry.

    During the following period a recruiting station was opened and recruits signed up for the First Division. Lieut. C. K. L. Pyman, of the Kelowna Squadron, left shortly after with some thirty recruits for Valcartier. From this time on continuous training was carried out, escorts were furnished for enemy aliens, and guards were mounted at the Internment Camp established in the Provincial Asylum at Vernon and now rapidly being filled with Austrians and Germans.

    In the adjutant's office all details were prepared for turning the regiment into an overseas unit, with the result that when, on November 6th, a wire was received by the O. C. offering him command of the 2nd Cana-
Nov. 6, 1914 dian Mounted Rifles he was enabled to wire to Ottawa a complete establishment of officers selected from the 30th B. C. Horse and the Victoria Squadron of Horse, and so the 2nd Canadian Mounted Rifles became an accomplished fact.

    "A" and "C" Squadrons from Vernon and Enderby became "A" Squadron, 2nd C. M. R., under Major M. V. Allen; "B" and "D" Squadrons from Lumby and Kelowna became "B" Squadron, under Major J. T. Bardolph, while the Victoria Squadron, under Major W. Bapty, became "C" Squadron.

    On December 4th, in accordance with orders issued from Headquarters M. D. No. 11, Regimental Headquarters with "A" and "B" Squadrons moved to Victoria,

2nd Canadian Mounted Rifles

Dec. 4, 1914

joining "C" Squadron at the Willows Camp. During the six months spent at this camp by the regiment continuous mounted and dismounted training was carried on, while sports and entertainments were successfully organized to relieve the monotony of training. Other units in the camp at various periods were the 30th and 48th Overseas Battalions, the 88th Fusiliers, the 50th Gordons, and a Company of the 5th R. C. G. Artillery.

On January 1st, 1915, Major-General Sam Hughes, Minister of Militia, inspected and reviewed the troops, and complimented them on their smartness and efficiency.

May 7, 1915

On May 7th, the Lusitania was sunk by a German submarine. This atrocity particularly affected our regiment, as Lieut. James Dunsmuir, a great favourite with all ranks, who had resigned shortly before in order to join an Imperial regiment, was one of the victims. The sinking of the vessel resulted in an anti-German riot in Victoria, and for several days mounted detachments of the regiment co-operated with the Infantry and the civic police in restoring order.

June 1, 1915

After many months of waiting, impatiently endured, orders were at last received, on the 1st of June, that we were to proceed overseas immediately, and late on the 4th of June the regiment embarked on the Princess Alice, being played down to the boat by the Gordons' Pipers and cheered on its way by dense crowds of Victorians, with whom the boys were extremely popular.

Entraining early the following morning at Vancouver for Sewell Camp, where the First Canadian Mounted Rifles Brigade was to assemble under the command of Lieut.-Colonel Sissons of Medicine Hat, the journey across was devoid of incident, the regiment detraining at various points for exercise marches, and Sewell Camp was reached on the 8th. After a stay of twenty-four hours the journey was resumed to Montreal, where the Brigade embarked on the R. M. S. Megantic during the night of the 11th-12th of June, the steamer leaving the docks at 4 a.m. on the 12th.

On arriving opposite Quebec the Megantic hove-to, and H. R. H. the Duke of Connaught, coming aboard, inspected the regiments drawn up in lines on the various decks. Three very hearty cheers and a tiger were given for H. R. H. as his tender moved away and our voyage recommenced.

June 21, 1915

Calm weather and smooth seas were experienced all the way across, a much more southerly course than the regular peace-time one was taken by the captain. Inspection of quarters, physical drill, medical inspections, games and boat drill at unexpected times, were all in the daily routine, while, as soon as the submarine zone was reached, boats were slung out, machine guns were mounted on the upper deck, and two hundred riflemen were posted on the other decks. Early on the 21st an escort of two

Canada and England

British destroyers met us, remaining until close outside Devonport Harbour, which was reached toward evening. Next morning the Megantic docked, the work of disembarkation and entraining was speedily carried out, and late the same day we arrived at Shorncliffe Station, detrained and marched to Caesar's Hill South, where we, together with the rest of the brigade, were to go into camp. Little, if any, preparation had been made for the reception and well being of the brigade; raw meat, without cooking facilities, and bread were available, but not in sufficient quantities. Some days elapsed before things properly settled down, and even then the catering arrangements were poor and were not satisfactory for the whole period of our stay in this camp.

The regiment remained three months in England, during which musketry training was carried out on the Hythe Ranges, and we managed to get in considerable training in bombing, Capt. W. W. Foster and Lieuts. A. H. Bell, M. V. McGuire and A. V. Evans proving invaluable and indefatigable instructors and laying a foundation which proved of greatest service later on, both in front of Messines and in the Ypres Salient. Other training was carried out, under regimental arrangements; whilst many inspections and ceremonial parades, generally in wet weather, were also held in various parts of the Shorncliffe Area, the most noteworthy of these being the inspection of the troops of the Second Division, early in September, by His Majesty the King and Field Marshal Lord Kitchener.

Our horses and saddlery having been taken away from us just prior to our departure from Canada, we were re-issued with other horses and new saddlery in England, but for some reason, unknown to us, when we had the horses we had no saddlery, and when we had the saddlery we had no horses.

While at Caesar's Camp a large number of extraordinary looking entrenching tools, said to have been invented by a stenographer employed in the Militia Department and manufactured in large quantities by order of the Minister of Militia, were issued to the brigade, with orders to give them a thorough test. The tool may be described briefly as a full-grown shovel with a hole in the middle of it, the handle on the other hand being very tiny and very collapsible, the idea being that the soldier, after digging in with the tool, could use the shovel as a sniper's plate, both for protection and to shoot through. The theory was fine, but after an exhaustive test by forty men, we found that, in half an hour's hard labour they had only succeeded in removing a small portion of sod at the expense of bruised and bleeding fingers and exhausted tempers, the handles collapsing at all times; further tests also showed that the tools were not bullet-proof. As the result of this and many other trials by various Canadian units, the tools were found to be utterly useless and were never sent to the front.

While at musketry it was discovered that the Ross rifles would not take, without jambing, a great deal of the S. A. A. issued. Our rifles were, therefore, turned in, in order that the chambers could be reamed out.

CHAPTER II

FRANCE AND THE TRENCHES

    Early in September we were officially informed that the brigade was part of the newly organized Second Division, commanded by Major-General Turner, V. C., who shortly after met the C. M. R. officers at the camp, told us what he desired and hoped to do, and in general made a very good im-
Sept., 1915   pression. Shortly after this visit, the division began moving to France, and our rifles being considered unsatisfactory, those of the Royal Canadian Regiment, recently arrived from Bermuda, were drawn in and issued to us in exchange for ours. All leave was stopped, and on the 20th the regimental transports were brigaded and entrained for Southampton. On the 20th orders were received to embark on the 22nd. The greater part of that day was spent in striking tents, cleaning up the camp and turning over the camp equipment to ordnance officers. Six p. m. saw the brigade, in heavy marching order, well on the way to the Folkestone docks, where, on arrival, hot and dusty, we were marched on to the boat and found relief in discarding our packs. Darkness was coming on when we started across under destroyer escort, reaching Boulogne without incident two hours later. Here, after the brigadier had gone through the necessary formalities with the M. L. O., we disembarked, formed up in front of the Hotel Louvre and marched up to a large camp situated near the Napoleon Monument.

    The morning of the 23rd of September was spent in adjusting equipment and resting; most of the officers spent a great deal of time in clipping each other's hair, and when they finally got through they were a queer looking lot, their heads being as close cropped as a billiard ball. After
Sept. 23, 1915   noon the brigade marched down to the Gare du Nord and entrained, the French carriages were extremely dirty and the only light available was from the candles we had taken the precaution to bring with us. In spite of this and the tediousness of the journey, everyone was in good spirits at the idea that we were at last actually on our way to take part in the great adventure.

    Bailleul was reached late at night, and the regiments detrained and formed up by the light of an oil flare, each, as soon as ready, marching off to the area allotted to it for billets. Our regiment was kept waiting for some considerable time in the Grande Place, but, after much delay and angry talk with the billetting officer, was finally placed in billets; the O. C. and part of the regimental

Zillibeke Bund

The Ramparts at Ypres

France and the Trenches

staff at last locating at 3 a. m. in the Hotel du Faucon, a queer old-fashioned hotel, without baths and entirely destitute of sanitary arrangements as we understand such in Canadian hotels, but this was more than made up for by the kindness of our hosts, who did all in their power to make us comfortable. Bailleul, at the time of our arrival a city with several thousand inhabitants and the scene of many happy times spent by the Canadians when out of the line, was occupied by the Huns for a few days in 1914 and later utterly destroyed during the German offensive of 1918.

The day after our arrival we received orders to get down to as light marching order as possible, and it was generally understood that we would take part in the Loos offensive, then, on the eve of opening, this, so far as we were concerned, did not materialize, but instead, on the 26th, we marched out to Oosterhove Farm and relieved a battalion of the Royal West Kents, the next day moving to Kortepyppe Huts. From here the different regiments of the brigade were sent into the front at Ploegsteerte for instruction by the Strathconas and the R. C. D.'s, who were then holding that section. About this time the 1st C. M. R. Brigade was transferred from the Second Division to the command of Brigadier General Seeley, one time Secretary of War for Great Britain, who at this period was in command of the Canadian Cavalry Brigade, the two brigades from this time on being known as Seeley's Special Forces.

On completion of this somewhat short training in trench warfare, we marched, by way of Mount Kemmel and the town of Dickiebusch, to the "O" and "M" trenches at Bois Carre. This march was particularly noteworthy for the round-about way which we were led, making it one of the longest and most tedious undertaken in three and a half years' service in France and Belgium.

Moving off from Kortepyppe Huts early on the 3rd of October, we marched steadily through rain and mud until Kemmel Dugouts were reached about 10 p. m. On arrival here, we found that there was shelter for but few, so the majority of the brigade bivouacked in the dark as best they could, no fires or lights of any kind being permitted. The day following at 2 p. m., as the brigade was forming up in close mass preparatory to moving off, a Bosche plane flying low circled slowly over us and returned to his own lines. As a result, luckily just as we had cleared the place, quite a heavy bombardment was directed on it.

Oct. 3, 1915

Although we left Mount Kemmel at 3 p. m., it was not until 4 a. m. the following morning that the relief of the West Ridings was completed, so circuitous was the route chosen; the roads, especially after passing Dickiebusch, were almost knee-deep in mud, and so weary were our men that, had the enemy chosen that particular time for an attack, he would probably have found things much to his liking. The sector we now found ourselves in was flat, with the water close to the surface. As a result, the defences were built chiefly above ground, with very shallow trenches dug down; the shelters also, such as they were, consisting generally of a sheet of corrugated iron and a layer of sandbags for head cover, being also on top, and these, though furnishing a certain amount of shelter from the weather, gave but little protection from even the lightest kind of shell fire. "A" and "B" Squadrons were in the front line, with "C" Squadron, commanded by Major Bapty, in support a short distance back in a very exposed position; consequently, the men had to lie dow during daylight or risk being shelled with whiz-bangs if they showed any signs of activity.

This being the first time in on our own, so to speak, many of the boys shortly after dawn, in spite of the fatigue of the previous night's march, instead of sleeping until their turn for sentry-go came, were up and looking for shots at the Bosches. German snipers were active and succeeded in wounding a couple of our men. On our side, Pat Joyce located a sniper in a tree and, bringing his Colt machine gun to bear, had the satisfaction of seeing the Hun's body crash head foremost to the ground. This sort of thing varied by bursts of artillery fire, practically all German, went on throughout the tour. On the 7th a direct hit on our support line killed two and mortally wounded one, and the same evening S. S. M. J. Marshall of "C" Squadron, walking up the P. & O. communication trench, was shot through the heart while passing up an enfiladed part of the trench. This tour, being our first in the front line, was remarkable for the rapidity with which all ranks fell into the routine of trench warfare; ration carrying and working parties were organized and carried on like old hands at the game, with the result that when, after four days, the regiment was relieved, quite a noticeable improvement had been made to the defence and the activity of the enemy's snipers considerably lessened by the watchfulness of our sharpshooters. Battalion headquarters, about three hundred yards behind the front line, in the Bois Carre, consisted of three small sandbag shelters, each about eight feet square inside and literally oozing moisture. One of these was occupied by the C. O., the adjutant and the signalling officer, Lieut. J. C. Agnew, while the other two were utilized as a signals office and shelters for runners and signallers. The remainder of our headquarters staff were located in similar shelters nearby. Although these headquarters were not shelled during our stay, all the surplus German bullets seemed to come our way, but, fortunately, without result, though the bullets often hit the shelters high up, and one or two of the signallers had narrow shaves. During this tour the 1st C. M. R.'s were in support and the 3rd C. M. R.'s were in brigade reserve, while all transport was brigaded in a field just out of Dickiebusch.

Oct. 7, 1915

On the 7th orders were received that the brigade would be relieved on the night of the 8th-9th, and on completion of relief 2nd C. M. R. would march to Aldershot Camp, situated about a mile from Neuve Eglise, a place named La Clyte being specified in the orders where lorries would be waiting to carry our packs to the camp.

The relief on the night of the 8th-9th of October, by the 20th Battalion,

France and the Trenches

commenced very late, as owing to their orders being changed, instead of entering the P. & O. and communication trenches at 8 p. m., it was after 10 p. m. when they began to arrive; consequently, by the time the last of our squadrons were clear and the regiment assembled, it was getting well on for dawn. As the different troops under their officers arrived at the assembly field, they rolled up in their blankets and groundsheets and obtained what rest they could while waiting for the last to be relieved. In the gray of the dawn the men were roused, fell in and, after the roll was called, moved off by troops on the long march to Aldershot Huts. Weary, unshaven and plastered with mud as they were, they looked a very different lot to what they appeared on the commencement of the march from Kortepyppe, but in those few days in the line, green troops as they were, they had found themselves and laid the foundation for the traditions and success in action which have made the reputation of the battalion second to none in the war.

Though this tour was a comparatively quiet one, it was notable for being the first time the regiment as a whole, under its own officers, held a part of the front line and came under artillery and rifle fire. The casualties were few, but were keenly felt, especially the death of S. S. M. Marshall, who was a fine soldier and keen sportsman, highly esteemed by all ranks.

While at Aldershot Huts we furnished several working parties on tramline and rear defences construction and were inspected by Lieut.-General Alderson, G. O. C., Canadian Corps, whose theme was the same he gave to all Canadian troops newly arrived, namely: "Finest body of men he had seen, etc., etc."

Soon after this, the brigade moved to billets on farms on the outskirts of Bailleul, battalion headquarters being established on a farm named Gibraltar. These barn billets, though somewhat drafty, were a great improvement on Aldershot Camp, which at that time was set in the midst of a sea of mud so deep that, if one had the misfortune to step off the narrow bath mat walks laid close to the huts, one had the greatest difficulty in extricating oneself. Gibraltar Farm, so named by the English troops, was a miserable place, with a boorish Flemish tenant who quite candidly said he would as soon have the Germans as the English in the country. Accommodation was extremely limited, so orderly room work had to be carried on in a corner of a barn filled with men. The weather from now on was dull, dreary and generally wet, with an occasional fine day, during one of which we had the pleasure for the first time of seeing a Bosche plane brought down by a Britisher. The German was circling round well behind the Canadian lines, evidently too interested in what was going on on earth to observe the Britisher emerge from the clouds above him; a burst of machine gun fire speedily made him turn and use every effort to get safely back to his own side; our man was too clever for him, however, and finally brought him down, the Hun crashing between the opposing lines. The men in the front line succeeded in bringing in the wounded German aviators and their machine gun, which, on examina-

Nov. 27, 1915

2nd Canadian Mounted Rifles

tion, proved to be a Colt, captured from the 14th Canadian Battalion during the Second Battle of Ypres. On the 27th of November at 2:30 p.m. the King, accompanied by the Prince of Wales and Lord French, inspected us in a field outside Locre. Everything went off well, the King going round the lines after the Royal Salute had been given; all the traffic was stopped on the roads while His Majesty came and went, and our planes circled overhead to keep any inquisitive Bosches from spotting the massed troops. The day following, while inspecting some English divisions, the King had a serious fall from his horse.

During this period, until the 28th of November, the regiment was continually out in all kinds of weather on working parties, sometimes digging trenches close up to the front line, sometimes constructing machine gun emplacements on rear defences, and again building trench tramways. Five men were wounded on these parties, but none very seriously.

Toward the end of November, Seeley's forces, now augmented by the 2nd C. M. R. Brigade, which had arrived in France during the latter part of October, relieved the 1st Canadian Division in the trenches opposite Messines, the Canadian Cavalry Brigade going in first. On the 28th of November,

Nov. 28, 1915 the 2nd C. M. R. took over the front line left of the Messines Road and astride the Petit Douve River, with the 3rd C. M. R. on our left and the 5th C. M. R. on our right, the Canadian Cavalry Brigade going into reserve. Owing to incessant rains, the trenches were in poor condition, the communication trenches being more than knee-deep in mud and water, and later becoming altogether impassable. Our battalion headquarters were in the ruins of Irish Farm, the best feature of which was a big cellar with about six feet of fallen brick for head cover, to which we retired during heavy shelling. About sixty of "C" Company were billeted in the remains of the stables, while in the barn on the other side of the yard was a large dump of engineer material. This was the centre of great activity during the night, working parties carrying away, and teams hauling in, material. All this occasioned a great deal of noise, and it was marvellous that the enemy did not shell the place heavily at night, but beyond very active machine gun fire at times, which did little harm, he took no notice. What few shelters there were in the front line were built in the parapet, with corrugated iron roofs covered with one, or at the most two, layers of sandbags, sufficient to stop a rifle grenade, but not much else. At this stage of the war the higher command considered it necessary that every bay in a trench should be manned and have sentries; under these conditions large numbers were always on duty, but even then many had to sleep on the fire steps owing to scarcity of shelters. No movement above ground was allowed round battalion headquarters during the day, runners, etc., coming and going by means of a very muddy communication trench. At 12:30 p.m. on the 30th the Hun, having evidently come to the conclusion that the farm was tenanted, turned his artillery loose on us, and for three hours the place was jumping with the explosions of everything from mere whiz-bangs to eight-inch shells. All hands took

A Canadian interested in Ypres Cathedral. In the foreground are the ruins of the Cloth Hall

The Cathedral and Cloth Hall at Ypres, at night

7

France and the Trenches

to the cellar, where owing to the confined space and the closeness of the bursting shells, the concussion was heavy. Telephone communication with brigade was cut by a shell bursting near the entrance to the cellar at the commencement; immediately after a message was put through asking for retaliation from our guns. During a lull the majority of the men were sent out to scatter along the communication trench, as the C. O. considered, and rightly, that to keep so many in one place was taking too many chances, for if a big shell penetrated the cellar, the slaughter would be appalling. On the following day, December 1st, at practically the same time, the Hun started the entertainment again; everybody this time took to the communication trench and no casualties were incurred. In the evening, however, he turned his attention to the front line, putting down a terrific barrage, mostly on the 3rd C. M. R. on our left and practically wiping out their Edmonton Squadron, which had all its officers killed or wounded and over seventy other casualties. Captain Oakes, one of the best officers in the regiment was killed while directing his men, and Major Fane, a big heavy man, commanding the Squadron, was blown out of the trench by a shell explosion. This very gallant officer, though suffering agony with a badly shattered leg and thigh, crawled back into the trench and continued to encourage his men, imbuing them with his spirit and refusing to leave until the terrible bombardment ceased and the other casualties evacuated.

Dec. 1, 1915

Our trenches were badly smashed, but our casualties were light, less than a dozen. As soon as the bombardment lightened, stretcher parties were organized to bring out the wounded and runners sent back for ambulances. Our orderly room in the farm was turned into an extra aid post, and our M. O., Captain McAskill, with his orderlies, worked indefatigably dressing the wounded and making them comfortable. One poor chap, a tunneller, who was brought in with his hand and scalp blown off, had his leave warrant in his pocket; he died shortly after.

Narrow escapes there were many: in one case a 5.9 fell in the communication trench between Cpl. Bill Board and S. S. M. Worrall, but didn't explode, though it nearly drowned both in mud and water. In another case a 5.9 came through the parapet, between the legs of Trooper Speechley, who was sitting on the firestep, and stopped against the parados; this also failed to explode. Speechley took it quite coolly, simply saying, "What do you know about that!" Lieutenant Moncrieff, who had just come round the corner and seen the occurrence, replied, "Why, made in Germany!" Such was the spirit of the troops.

Each day for the remainder of the tour, the Bosche laid down his "Hymn of Hate" on Irish Farm, but as he started and finished at the same time every day, we were able to avoid it quite comfortably by evacuating the farm for that period. The front line was shelled also at times, but never so heavily as on the 1st. We, on our part, suffering as we did in those days from a great scarcity of artillery and shells, did our

Dec. 3, 1915

best to strafe the Huns with rifle and machine gunfire, apparently with some result, as early on the morning of the 3rd a report came to battalion headquarters from Major Bardolph that there was a new barrier of sandbags on the Messines Road about 150 yards from our line, where previously had only been two trees cut down by shell fire and the remains of a house at the side of the road. These trees and ruins had evidently been used for a long period by the Bosche as either an outpost or a listening post, for on careful and patient observation through glasses, a communication trench from the German front line could be traced to the road and the ditch deepened along the road to the ruins. The sandbags were simply the natural result of our incessant harassing fire along the road at nights. The consternation raised at Canadian Headquarters by this barrier was tremendous, quite out of proportion to the cause, and in the light of after events would have been ludicrous had it not resulted for some time afterward in great ill-feeling and many fights between certain units of the 1st Division and the C. M. R.'s. Had we been allowed, as we were for raids in later days, to form our plans deliberately for the capture of the barrier, we would undoubtedly have done away with it before our relief was due. But this was not to be; at 11 p. m. the same night Brigadier-General Seeley's staff captain, Captain Docherty, came in with a peremptory order from the general to the effect that we must attack and capture the barrier before dawn. This gave us no chance to send out patrols to scout out the best way of approaching the objective; it didn't even give our bombers a chance to look at it over the parapet and so get some idea of what they would be up against. Under these circumstances, it was decided that the only thing to do was to make a frontal attack, by surprise if possible, along the road, the probability being that the flanks would be protected by wire entanglements. Lieut. N. Rant, scout officer, and Lieut. A. V. Evans, bombing officer, were chosen to lead two parties of bombers and bayonet men, another party being detailed to support the attack should it be successful. By dint of desperate effort, everything was arranged an hour before dawn and the attackers went over the top, Lieutenant Rant with his party leading, with Lieutenant Evans' party in close support. The Huns, however, were on the alert and commenced bombing before our men were in range; in spite of this, Rant and his men worked their way forward until stopped by wire obstacles and threw all their bombs into the barrier, but failed to get through the wire. Lieutenant Rant was blown into the ditch by the explosion of a Bosche bomb, and as soon as he got out was blown across the road and knocked silly by another bomb; Cpl. J. W. Potts was also wounded. As they were now out of bombs and the Bosche defence seemed to be growing stronger, the balance of the squad withdrew, carrying in their officer and the corporal. In the meantime, Evans' squad had been trying to work off the road to outflank the objective, but owing to unfamiliarity with the ground failed, and also withdrew after loosing off their grenades at the Hun. Nothing further could be attempted now, as day was breaking and the Hun was getting busy with his

France and the Trenches

artillery. We had, therefore, to report to brigade that the attack had been unsuccessful.

This lesson should have been sufficient, but was not. No regiment was allowed to formulate plans, but attack after attack was ordered by General Seeley with the same haste, and carried out with the same lack of success as ours, until the disastrous one in which the Strathconas had many casualties, losing one officer and two other ranks, badly wounded, taken prisoner by the Huns.

The barrier was finally dealt with quite easily after the First Division took over the line and sane military policy prevailed. Plenty of time was allowed to work out a scheme, with the result that a field gun, which was manhandled up to the front line, one night at a given time, when a barrage was laid on the German front line, opened direct fire on the barrier for five minutes, knocking it completely to pieces. A party of infantry then occupied the objective, finding little but ruins and dead bodies, and the gun was hauled back to safety almost before the Bosche could realize what was happening.

On the 8th the regiment moved back to support and from there to billets round Bailleul, on the return of the First Division to the line. From here working parties were sent forward continuously to repair and construct defences.

Dec. 8, 1915   These working parties were exceedingly hard on the men; long marches to and from work on muddy roads and through sodden fields, generally in pouring rain, were terribly trying to the hardiest constitutions, and it speaks well for both their physique and wonderful spirit that very few attended morning sick parades or were sent to hospital.

Christmas Day was spent very quietly; church parade was held and in the evening a good dinner in billets was provided for all ranks, and toasts to the King and our friends in Canada were drunk. On the 30th of December the

Dec. 25, 1915   officers of the brigade went to Meteren and were there informed by General Alderson that the 3rd Division had been formed, the 7th Brigade consisting of the P. P. C. L. I., who had come back to the Canadian Corps recently, together with the R. C. R., 42nd and 49th Battalions, all three of which battalions had come to France in October or November; the 8th Brigade would be composed of the two C. M. R. Brigades re-organized into infantry battalions, while the 9th Brigade would cross from England early in the coming year. Major-General Mercer was in command of

Dec. 30, 1915   the division, and Brigadier-General Victor Williams of the 8th Brigade. Orders were received the same day that all C. O.'s and adjutants of the C. M. R. Regiments were to attend a conference at General Williams' quarters in Bailleul the following day. At this meeting General Williams informed us that the 3rd C. M. R.'s would be broken up and absorbed by the 1st and 2nd, while the 6th C. M. R. would in like manner be absorbed by the 4th and 5th C. M. R.; that the brigade would be composed of the 1st, 2nd, 4th and 5th C. M. R. Battalions, and that the following day re-

17

2nd Canadian Mounted Rifles

organization and training of units as infantry would commence. Officers, especially those of the 3rd and 6th, who did not wish to serve in the infantry were given an opportunity to transfer to other branches of the service or return to Canada.

Up to the end of 1915, we received fifty-one reinforcements, principally base details and sick men who had been left in England, and were, as a cavalry regiment, practically at full strength, but now that we had been changed to infantry, a large reinforcement was necessary. On the 3rd of January, eight officers and one hundred and eighty-four N.C.O.'s and men were transferred from the 3rd C.M.R. to us and became our "D" Company, while a further six officers were taken on the strength on the same date, but did not actually join up until the following month. Major Doughty of the 31st Battalion, with a staff of infantry instructors, was attached to us, and by the end of the month we had become qualified gravel crushers, entitled to write P.B.I. after our names.

Jan. 3, 1916

During this period we, together with a French regiment, furnished a guard of honour in Bailleul for the presentation of French decorations to members of the two Canadian Divisions. The French guard was very smart and the French general very thorough, kissing each recipient on both cheeks after pinning on the decoration.

We were also inspected by Lieutenant-General Alderson and our new brigadier, General Victor Williams, in a field outside Meteren. General Alderson, after keeping us waiting long after the time set for the inspection, kindly told us we were not quite soldiers yet, but might hope to be some day, while General Williams caused a great deal of merriment through stopping in his remarks to take breath at the wrong time, thus: "You are a fine lot of men; I don't think"—pause for breath—"I ever saw a finer lot," etc.

On the 29th of January, I handed my appointment as adjutant over to Lieut. E. B. Irving and took command of "D" Company, late 3rd C.M.R., a splendid lot in every way, two of whom, W. Sharland and W. Mellor, were the first in the battalion to win Military Medals. The 3rd Division was now detailed by the corps commander to relieve the 1st Division for three weeks, and on the 2nd of February the battalion arrived at Red Lodge, going into support on the slope of Hill 63, in tents and huts, the whole brigade coming under command of the G.O.C., 1st Division, until his command was clear.

Jan. 29, 1916

During the morning of February 3rd, I had the honour of a visit from General Currie, one I did not at all appreciate, as he at once proceeded to reduce me to a nervous wreck by putting me through a whole catechism of questions as to where I was to go, and what I would do with my company in the event of the Huns breaking through the front line. At this point, when I was thoroughly uncomfortable,

Feb. 3, 1916

The taking of Vimy Ridge. As the Canadians advance, parties of Huns left their dug-outs only too glad to surrender

Canadians consolidating their position on Vimy Ridge

France and the Trenches

the Bosche commenced to shell the hill and some shrapnel, coming through the roof, wounded one of our batmen, Hawkins, broke a window and ended the interview, much to my relief. Ten minutes after the general left the shelling became more intense, and before it finished we had fourteen casualties.

While in support we did working parties, in which we had three more casualties.

Feb. 9, 1916

On the 9th the battalion moved into the front line trenches C1, C2, 142 in front of Wulverghem, astride the Messines-Wulverghem Road, a quiet sector, two companies being in the front line, one at Forbes Terrace dugouts and one in Rat Alley funk holes, while battalion headquarters were in very good shelters in MacBride Mansion dugouts. The Bosche had several barriers on this road, a fact which was noted during the relief of the 1st Division by ours. This tour was quiet and uneventful; on the left of the road our trenches were quite a long way from the enemy, while on the right they were fairly close, so to prevent any chance of the Bosche coming between we had patrols on the road all night as well as listening posts and a strong outpost well out on the left. These parties had some exciting times and narrow escapes when the Bosche swept the road with machine gun fire, but suffered no casualties.

Feb. 14, 1916

On the 14th our artillery put a half hour concentrated shoot on Ontario Farm, a German stronghold opposite us, but though the shooting was very good and all kinds of earth and timber, etc., were constantly in the air, yet within a quarter of an hour of the cessation of the shelling smoke could be seen coming from their dugouts, so they evidently had good deep shelters. In retaliation for this, we expected heavy shelling on the front line, but only a few came our way, doing little damage beyond destroying a couple of shelters and wounding two men. We heard afterward that the village of Nieppe received particular attention, a number of civilians and some soldiers being killed and wounded.

On the 14th the battalion was relieved and moved into reserve in Kortepyp Camp, which was subjected to long-range shelling by the Bosche on the following day, an ammunition column in the farm close by suffering several casualties in horses and men. After a few days here the 1st Division took over the area and the brigade moved back into its old billets around Bailleul.

CHAPTER III

THE SALIENT AND SANCTUARY WOOD

After three weeks of working parties, we marched to Camp F, near Ouderdom, behind the Ypres Salient, where we were to relieve the 24th Imperial Division, and on the 17th of March the 2nd C. M. R. relieved a battalion of the N. Staffords in support at Zillebeke Bund and Ypres, while it fell to the 1st C. M. R. to take over the front line at Hooge astride the Menin Road.

The Ypres Salient, forming as it did a semi-circle of trenches dug mostly on very low lying hills, with the Bosche holding the best and highest points of observation, was the scene of almost incessant activity on the part of both the Hun snipers and artillery. The defences were in a ruinous condition when our division took over, and our first work necessarily was the task of repairing and making it possible to walk round in a more or less upright position. This, of course, had to be done at night, any abnormal signs of life in daylight bringing shelling, while nine out of every ten who showed themselves were fired at by the Bosche snipers and killed, such was the speed and accuracy of their shooting. One German sniper in particular at Hooge was a most deadly shot; this man, who spoke very good English, used to call out remarks to the Canadians and once said that he was from New York, to which place he intended to return after the war. However, a shell called on him unexpectedly one day and he lost interest both in New York and the war.

On the 23rd of March we relieved the 1st C. M. R. in Hooge defences, "C" Company, under Major W. Bapty going in on the right of the Menin Road, and "D" Company going in on the left between the Menin Road and Y Wood in a series of posts established in ruined trenches, "A" and **March 23, 1916** "B" Companies going into support and reserve in Yeomanry Post and Zillebeke Bund, with battalion headquarters at Yeomanry Post, the battalion bombers, under Lieut. M. V. McGuire, going in close to the Menin Road and holding a series of trench posts terminating at the Hooge Stables, a heap of bricks, on the other side of which was the Bosche. This Stables post was the scene of constant bombing activity at nights, culminating on the night of the 24th in a determined bombing attack by the Huns which was successfully driven off by our bombers. In this affair, Pte. F. H. Vaughan performed a very brave act which, while it unfortunately resulted in his death, undoubtedly saved the lives of several comrades. In the height of the fight a German bomb landed right inside the post; Vaughan, shouting to the others to look out, at once seized it and had raised it above the trench to

The Salient and Sanctuary Wood

throw it out when it exploded, inflicting terrible injuries on him and wounding two or three others. Had it burst where it fell, it would undoubtedly have killed all in the post. Vaughan bore his wounds with heroic fortitude and died enquiring after his pals; he was recommended for the V.C., but it was not granted.

Several bombing attacks were also made on our other posts, but were easily driven off. On the 25th Major W. Bapty, while going his rounds, was hit and very severely wounded in the back by a sniper. Owing to the exceedingly bad condition in which the front line was at Hooge, it was necessary to relieve companies every three days, so on the night of the 25th "A" and "B" Companies took over from "C" and "D" Companies, being in their turn relieved three days later.

March 25, 1916

On the 26th the Bosche shelled our lines on the right of the Menin Road very heavily, destroying most of the new work and crumpling in the entrance to company headquarters, but, owing to one of those extraordinary streaks of luck which sometimes happened, hitting very few men.

On the night of April 4th the 49th Edmonton Battalion took over, and we moved back to Camp "D". The relief was completed without hitch, all companies marching into Ypres and entraining there. Battalion headquarters coming in later were caught by shell fire near the station and one shell killed Major R. J. Mutrie, second in command; Capt. A. Temple, adjutant, and Pte. J. M. Hatcher, and wounded Lieut. M. V. McGuire, R. S. M. T. Godfrey, Scout Sgt. W. S. Wilson and Ptes. W. Saling and W. E. Talbot. This was a most terrible blow to the battalion, losing as we did three of our most capable officers and several of our best scouts. Major Mutrie was a most capable officer of great promise, liked and respected by all. Had he lived he would undoubtedly have attained high rank. Captain Temple, one of the most lovable and unassuming of officers, was also one of the most reliable, always in the right place at the right time. Lieutenant McGuire's escape from death was miraculous, the shell exploding almost at his heels; over twenty pieces of shell were extracted from his body at the C.C.S.

April 4, 1916

During the night of April 23rd we relieved the 1st C. M. R. in the Sanctuary Wood trenches, "C" Company, now commanded by Lieut. F. B. Edwards, going into trenches 60 and 61, "D" Company going into trench 62 and the Loop, opposite which was the famous Birdcage, a German snipers' post of concrete and steel overlooking a good deal of our trenches, while "A" and "B" Companies went into close support trenches known as Charing Cross, Gourock Road and Cumberland Dugouts, battalion headquarters also being in Cumberland Dugouts. This was a much better sector, the trenches were much dryer and already, through the efforts of the 1st C. M. R., were high enough in most places to shut out the deadly observation of the snipers in the Birdcage. The lines at the north end of the Loop were less than forty yards apart, and here in the middle of No Man's Land was a small

April 23, 1916

2nd Canadian Mounted Rifles

crater which both sides used to bomb all night to prevent occupation by the other. The usual routine of trench warfare went on here, each side endeavouring to do as much damage as possible to the other by means of trench mortars and rifle grenades, etc., mostly at night, the Bosche probably doing most, owing to his superiority in trench mortars and artillery, for at this period, call as we might, we got mighty little response from our artillery, owing to lack of shells, and nine shells per diem was the limit for each Stokes gun, which weapon was just coming into use. At this period also, the Stokes gun had, when not actually in action, to be kept 1000 yards back from the front line.

April 30, 1916

We were relieved here on April 30th and went into support at Ypres, returning to the line at Hooge on May 11th. During this tour both our machine gun officer, Lieutenant Fennell, and our machine gun sergeant, J. P. Joyce, were killed by snipers. This trip, which lasted until the 19th, was uneventful as trench warfare goes, except for occasional bombing fights with the Hun. These fights, however, served to demonstrate the uselessness of the Ross rifle in the trenches, as it almost invariably jambed before five rounds rapid had been fired.

May 31, 1916

On the 31st of May we received a large batch of reinforcements. At this time we were in brigade reserve, "A", "B" and "C" Companies being with battalion headquarters in "D" Camp, near Ouderdom, while "D" Company was in Belgian Chateau Dugouts. The 1st and 4th C. M. R.'s were in Sanctuary Wood and Observatory Ridge, with the 5th C. M. R. in support in Maple Copse and Zillibeke Bund. Brigade headquarters were also in the Bund. The 7th Brigade was in the Hooge Sector, with the P. P. C. L. I. on the left of the 1st C. M. R.; the 2nd Brigade was on the right of the 4th C. M. R.

June 2, 1916

The morning of the 2nd of June dawned bright and sunny with nothing to warn us that our brigade was about to suffer the severest concentration of artillery fire yet put on by the Bosche. About 8 a. m., however, things began to get pretty lively back at Belgian Chateau, batteries near us opening up in reply to the German shelling, while all along the Kruistraat we could see the German 5.9's bursting, while the continuous roar in the direction of the front line warned us something very unusual was going on. At 11 a. m. orders came over the 'phone from the B. M., Major Stevens, that "D" Company was to move up at once to Zillibeke, reporting at brigade headquarters for orders. Before the message could be acknowledged the line went out. We immediately stacked our packs, leaving a guard over them of two batmen. In spite of the shells now falling between us and the chateau, too close to be pleasant, the company formed up as though on an ordinary parade and moved off in sections in single file at some few yards intervals straight across country, in this way avoiding the worst of the barrage which was coming down on every road and cross-road between us and the Bund, and arriving there with the loss of one man killed and one wounded. Round

The Salient and Sanctuary Wood

brigade headquarters we found every indication of a big show. Transport Farm, a short distance away, was receiving particular attention from the enemy's guns and caught fire, and a number of wounded were sitting or lying round. Major Stevens told me that both Major-General Mercer and Brigadier-General Williams had gone up the line early and that he could get no information about them; that all communication with the front line was cut; in short, that the Germans were on the offensive and that he had no means of knowing what was doing. We were to push on to an old disused trench, known as Zillibeke Switch, in front of the village of that name and hold on at all costs; also try and get in touch with the 5th C. M. R.'s in Maple Copse.

After each man had been issued with two Mills bombs and an extra bandolier of ammunition, we again moved, and arriving at the Switch, where I found Lieutenant Smith, T. M. officer of the 1st C. M. R., with about thirty survivors of the 1st and 4th C. M. R. mostly all wounded, extended out and commenced digging in, the old trench being so narrow and shallow that it afforded but little cover.

In the meantime, the Huns, having obliterated the front line system, as aeroplane photos taken later plainly showed, had come across and killed or captured those who had survived the bombardment. Survivors from the front line garrisoning S. P. 15 and the 5th C. M. R. in Maple Copse had, however, driven him off after hard fighting, and his artillery was now busy shelling those positions heavily. We hadn't been long in Zillibeke Switch before he spotted us and began to shell us also. Extending out still further to our right, we obtained touch with supports of the 2nd Brigade and our patrols got into touch with the 5th C. M. R. in Maple Copse. The liaison between the German infantry and artillery was very good in this battle; every time the infantry was going to attack they would shoot up a line of white flares, which immediately brought down their artillery barrage in the required direction.

At this period the Lahore Artillery was attached to our division, and though always good, they showed up particularly finely in this affair; one section of eighteen pounders was in the ruins of the village behind us, and though pounded heavily by the Hun artillery, one of the two guns being put out of action, they never ceased firing as long as they had shells. At times gunners would be unloading the shells and running to the guns with them before the limbers had halted.

During the afternoon we received some reinforcements with Lewis guns, and in the evening "A", "B" and "C" Companies of the 2nd C. M. R. reached Maple Copse, suffering many casualties as they came up. It was originally intended that they should counter-attack, but owing to congestion on the road near Ypres, they arrived too late, and Major Allen, who had gone ahead, decided to try and dig in a new line in the low ground between Maple Copse and Rudkin House. This also proved impracticable, the men immediately they deployed becoming subject to heavy shrapnel and machine gun fire, and no headway

2nd Canadian Mounted Rifles

was made. They were, therefore, withdrawn to the Copse. Later in the evening Capt. T. Le Duc made a daring reconnaisance of Rudkin House and found it unoccupied. During the night we threw out outposts and patrols, but the Bosche did not attempt any further advance, contenting himself with shelling us heavily most of the time, his infantry entrenching themselves in their newly won positions.

At 3 a. m. on the 3rd the 15th Battalion came up to our position, and working round to our right, eventually deployed in front of Valley Cottages, the 14th Battalion at the same time deploying in front of Maple Copse. The original intention had been to make a counter-attack with troops of the 1st Division at dawn, but owing to various causes, it was postponed until 8 a. m. It was a stirring sight to see these fine battalions forming up in open order with fixed bayonets under the enemy shell fire. We could see the officers marshalling their men as though on the training ground, then, in perfect order, they moved on up the slope and disappeared over the ridge. In the meantime, however, the Germans had got plenty of machine guns up and entrenched and were able to sweep the slopes up which the attack was developing with a deadly storm of bullets. In spite of this and their ensuing terrible losses, some of the men got to close quarters with the Huns, but being too few in number, had to retire, and for the rest of the day the wounded were coming back through our line. Our first aid men, by this time reduced to three, did wonderful work, Pte. Bernard Shipton in particular, regardless of danger, going wherever he could see any casualties, fixing them up and moving them into cover. He later received the M. M. for this.

June 3, 1916

By noon on the 3rd most of the officers of the 5th C. M. R. and a number of ours had become casualties—Lieutenant Berkinshaw, the adjutant, killed; Captain Redpath, Major Allen and Lieutenants Young, Strachan, Scott, Pue, Lewis and Latimer were wounded, while Captains Le Duc, Denison and Edwards and Lieutenant Cruickshanks were wounded but still on duty. At noon I received orders to take command of the C. M. R. line and found on going round that only four officers and about eighty men of the 5th were left, with seven officers and about three hundred men of the 2nd.

After the failure of the counter-attack the Germans shelled us more frequently than ever, while we on our part were expecting an infantry attack with every lull.

At midnight a runner got through from brigade bringing orders to me to evacuate the C. M. R. positions, as fresh troops were taking up a new line. Scarcely had I given the necessary instructions to the few surviving officers and N. C. O.'s when the Bosche laid down an extra heavy shelling on us which lasted until 1:45 a. m. and made it impossible for us to move. By 3 a. m., however, the last man was clear.

Our M. O., Captain McAskill, during this action established a dressing

The Salient and Sanctuary Wood

station in a cellar in Zillibeke and worked unceasingly throughout, doing superhuman work and only leaving when relieved by another M. O.

Late on the morning of the 4th before leaving Maple Copse, in company with Lieutenant Cruickshanks, I made a tour of the positions we lately held. For the time everything was quiet; the wrecked trenches held only the dead.

June 4, 1916 — The Copse itself, a beautiful grove of trees two days previously, was now nothing but a churned up tangle of shell holes and timber, shattered stumps and skeletons of trees sticking up through it, while the cemetery on its edge, with its white wooden crosses, was all but obliterated, only five splintered crosses remaining to mark its location. As we turned to leave, whiz-bangs bursting almost on our heels marked the re-opening of the Hun bombardment.

After a weary walk of some miles Camp B was reached and, thoroughly exhausted, we spent the rest of that day and night in resting up, having been without sleep under the heaviest and almost continuous shell fire for nearly forty-eight hours. Captain Wilkins, the heroic Padre of the 1st C. M. R., who was taken prisoner in this battle, was informed by a high German officer that their artillery fire in this engagement was the heaviest yet put on by them up to that time, not even excepting Verdun.

In the 2nd C. M. R. we had lost 50 per cent of our fighting strength, the 5th C. M. R. had lost more heavily, while the 1st and 4th C. M. R. had been pretty well wiped out. On the morning of the 5th of June the 8th Brigade paraded with a total strength of less than seven hundred, all ranks, for embusment to the Steinwoorde Area, where we were to re-organize. The total casualties in the brigade were 1786.

The 2nd C. M. R. were billeted in farms near Godewaersvelde and Abeele, and soon received strong reinforcements, making us numerically stronger than before the battle. N. C. O. instructors from the Coldstream and Grenadier Guards were sent to us, and before long the battalion was in splendid training again.

Lieutenant-Colonel Bott, being still acting brigadier, I remained in command until the first week in July, when he returned from leave and took over. In the meantime, we decided to start a battalion canteen, which we did, with 200 francs put up by the officers; a few days later Capt. G. O. Fallis,

July, 1916 — our chaplain, obtained a loan of 2000 francs for us from the chaplains' funds, which loan, by the way, we repaid in less than three months, and our canteen from then on was an assured success. A very moderate profit on cost of goods was charged, and the fund thereby established was used to buy extra food, such as oatmeal, vegetables, canned milk, etc., for the men.

A few days after we came to this area Lieutenant-General Sir Julian Byng visited us and watched the training going on, asking all sorts of questions about the Ross rifle. Shortly after we were re-armed with Lee Enfields.

2nd Canadian Mounted Rifles

Toward the middle of June, Lieut.-Col. J. Elmsley, D. S. O., commanding the Corps Cavalry, was promoted brigadier-general and given command of our brigade. He immediately began to make himself felt and, being a very capable and courteous officer, soon became respected and popular.

Brigadier-General L. J. Lipsett, C. M. G., was promoted major-general, in charge of the 3rd Division; a great many of us had known him in Canada and were delighted at the appointment.

The tremendous casualty list in the Canadian Corps resulting from the fourteen days fighting seemed to have thrown the Canadian reinforcing machinery in England badly out of gear, and in consequence, we received drafts representing nearly every province of Canada. Apparently an infantry pool had been formed and the men formed up in alphabetical order and told off according to the numbers allotted to each battalion requiring reinforcements. We were fortunate in getting a very good lot of men, keen, of good physique and eager to do their bit, and also received seventeen new officers, like the men, representing several provinces. In addition, R. S. M. Godfrey, C. S. M. J. L. Gray, C. S. M. J. E. Capstick, M. M., and Sergts. F. A. Heather, M. M., J. Foord and D. Morrison were recommended for and received commissions in the battalion before it returned to the trenches.

Training was confined to the mornings and consisted principally of parade ground work and musketry, the former under guards instructors, until the end of June, after which more extensive training, including bombing and trench manoeuvres by day and night, was undertaken, so that when the time came for us to take over the front line the new men, who were now in the majority, had a good practical knowledge of what would be required of them. Afternoons and evenings were devoted to games and recreation. Inter-company football and baseball matches and sports were organized with great success, culminating in one big sports day, on which, after hard competition, especially from Lieut. G. R. Pearkes and his bombers, "D" Company carried off the battalion challenge cup.

During the early part of July, Capt. W. W. Foster, who had been in charge of the 3rd Division bombing and trench mortar organization and had brought them to a high state of efficiency, returned to the battalion as junior major and took over command of "C" Company, and Capt. L. W. Miller was appointed adjutant to fill the vacancy caused by the death of Lieutenant Berkinshaw. A few days later Lieutenant-Colonel Bott, who had been on leave since Brigadier-General J. H. Elmsley, D. S. O., took over the brigade, returned to the battalion, and on the 17th of July we moved off, once more en route for the Ypres Salient.

On the 18th, Major Foster and I, together with several company officers and N. C. O.'s, many of whom had not yet been under fire, went up to the line in Sanctuary Wood as advance party to take over trench stores, etc., from the

In the foreground a smashed pill-box, Canadian pioneers carrying trench mats up to Passchendaele, and wounded and prisoners are seen in the background

A tank in a badly shelled mud area in Passchendaele, where the Canadians recently advanced—and it was through such ground as this that they advanced

The Salient and Sanctuary Wood

July 18, 1916
42nd Battalion before our people came in. At dusk, as we passed over the ground west of Maple Copse, everything was quiet except for a few bullets whispering over. Glow worms were plentiful, so it was only natural, when a green N. C. O., hearing a bullet pass close, asked what that noise was, for the wit of the party to promptly reply, "Glow worms, of course." Arriving at the 42nd Battalion's Headquarters at Dormy House, guides were furnished who took the advance party to the various company headquarters, and we began to make ourselves acquainted with the new defence system which had been commenced since the recapture of the position in June, the old one and most of the German system having been all but obliterated. The next night the battalion came in and relieved the Jocks, who went out for a well-earned rest.

Dormy House, our battalion headquarters, was a mere shell, but like most Flemish farm houses, had good cellars, and in these were installed our telephones, adjutant's office and so on, with a few bunks made out of poles and chicken wire. Above ground, one end was filled with engineer material and round trench mortar bombs generally called footballs or plum puddings, while the other end was sandbagged up and furnished a certain amount of sleeping accommodation in quiet times. A communication trench behind a hedge at the back of the building furnished hidden means of communication by day with the front line, and as the place was under full observation from the German line, every precaution was used to prevent movement across the open near it.

That part of the front now taken over by us had on the 2nd of June been the 4th C. M. R.'s line along Observatory Ridge, and during this tour we were kept busy digging out the new system, well started and advanced by our predecessors. The country had been so torn up that it was unrecognizable, the old trench system we had known was gone, the woods had been scarred and shattered until nothing was left but a desert of shell holes and splintered stumps, and everywhere was the smell of the dead. Special burial parties were still at work, and numbers of dead, now mostly Germans, were every night gathered and given Christian burial.

In this sector from the start we carried on an aggressive policy; by day our snipers gained and held control over the Huns, while at night our patrols haunted No Man's Land, confining the Bosche behind his wire entanglements.

July 24, 1916
The enemy had a large number of trench mortars opposite us, and these at times gave us quite a strafing, causing most of our casualties, while owing to their superiority in the air enabling the Hun planes to do as they pleased over the Salient, our artillery very often could not respond to our calls for retaliation, for fear of being spotted and shelled out. On the 24th of July, during one of these "Hymns of Hate," Lieutenant Quanbury, a promising young officer of "D" Company, received wounds which afterwards proved fatal.

On the 25th, Lieut. G. R. Pearkes and Bombing Sergt. C. K. Douglas located

2nd Canadian Mounted Rifles

July 25, 1916

a German listening post in a sap in No Man's Land opposite Trench 58. Coming back, they filled an ammunition box full of explosive extracted from Bosche bombs, then returned and dug it under the listening post; unfortunately, the fuse used was old and defective, so the explosion didn't come off. Nothing daunted, however, these two went and tore the listening post down; later, finding it had been strongly rebuilt and wired in, they again took the explosive out, this time with new fuse, dug it in without alarming the German sentries, and blew the whole thing out of existence. For this successful and audacious piece of work both were recommended for decorations, but none were granted.

In retaliation for this, the Germans put on a heavy trench mortar bombardment, landing especially heavily on "C" Company's sector. Our artillery, it being night, was quick to respond and silenced the Huns after half an hour's strafe. As luck would have it, a strong detachment of Pioneers was in the vicinity, and these Major Foster got to work on his damaged trenches with such good effect that they were in first-class condition before dawn, and it must have been very galling for Fritz, when looking across in the early morning to note the effect of his fire, to see our trenches in A1 shape, while his own looked what they were—ruined.

July 27, 1916

On the 27th we were relieved and went into support at Ypres, battalion headquarters being in the ramparts, with four companies stationed in the cavalry barracks and some headquarters' details at the convent. Ypres was still subject to daily shellings, and on the 28th a 5.9, landing in the yard of the convent, killed Lieut. P. J. Audy and Private Montgomery, besides wounding several others. At this time, while a good deal damaged, such buildings as the asylum, the cavalry barracks, the infantry barracks and St. Martin's Church were still very conspicuous among the ruins of Ypres and were favourite targets for enemy guns, especially during the night. The walls of the cavalry barracks in particular were thin and afforded no protection from shells to the troops billeted there. During this stay of our companies there the barracks were only shelled once; fortunately, the shelling commenced ten minutes after the men had left on the usual nightly working party. The first shell landed right in "D" Company's sleeping quarters, others landed in the Barracks Square, while still others hit the road but recently full of our men. The ramparts also were a favourite mark by day and night for the Huns' 5.9's, and time and again our lights were blown out by the concussion of the shells bursting on top and in front of our quarters, while it was a frequent occurrence, when returning from a visit to the companies during the day, to find ourselves cut off by numerous shells bursting in the vicinity of the Cloth Hall and Cathedral.

After six days here we moved back to reserve, whence we moved into the line opposite Hill 60 during the night of August 15th. These trenches were old and had not been affected by the June battle, but it was here that, since the

The Salient and Sanctuary Wood

Aug. 15, 1916 line stabilized in 1915, bitter underground warfare had been and was continuously waged. British and Bosche tunnellers, skilled in all the arts of mining, worked unceasingly to drive their workings under their enemy's defences, sometimes breaking through and fighting at grips in the narrow tunnels, at other times blowing the tunnels in and catching the workers like rats in a trap from which the only escape was death by suffocation or drowning. In this warfare, as in the air and above ground, our men proved themselves to be the better, in the end charging and exploding such huge mines at the Battle of Messines that Hill 60 was eliminated and the face of that part of the country changed entirely. During this tour our sentries reported sounds of tunnelling under our support trenches, and the tunnelling officer, confirming this by means of listening apparatus, at once commenced driving a counter gallery. We immediately took all possible precautions, detailing a counter-attack party and a consolidation party to rush and consolidate the crater should the enemy blow the mine. At nights, when the danger of explosion was greatest, the garrison of the front line took up positions in No Man's Land, while the supports formed to the flanks, leaving the threatened part vacant. In the day time, when the danger was not so pressing, necessary sentries only were stationed in the danger zone.

On the night of the 22nd of August the Bosche started to shell us rather severely. Supporting us was part of the 2nd Canadian Division Artillery, with Lieut. R. O. Bennett, at one time one of our officers, acting as liaison officer to us. They had plenty of shells and, like the rest of the **Aug. 22, 1916** Canucks, were expecting shortly to follow the 1st Division to the Somme, so when we called for retaliation and said about fifty rounds for a starter, they put over 500, and then some more for luck, completely silencing the Bosche in less than an hour and so effectually that on the following night our relief by Imperials was carried out with no interference from the Huns at all. We were particularly glad to be through with this tour, as, even at its best, trench warfare is trying and a strain on the nerves, but when you add to it the danger of hostile mining, knowing that at any moment you may be blown into space without any chance of hitting **Aug. 23, 1916** back, why, a man would be a hog who would want to stay in such a place any longer than necessary. Later on we heard that the mine had been blown without any loss to the British who relieved us or any gain to the Huns. On the night of the 23rd we were relieved by Imperials, and after putting them thoroughly in touch with the situation, moved out to billets at Abeele, where for the next ten days we put everything in order for a move to the Somme and carried on training.

CHAPTER IV

THE SOMME

On the 6th of September we marched to Caestre and entrained for the Somme, going by way of Calais and Doullens. Outside Calais the train stopped for some time and most of our officers went over to a refreshment canteen, run by some English ladies, to get a drink of tea, which when **Sept. 6, 1916** we got it was very hot. While we were waiting for it to cool our train started, and we had to run and run hard, much to the delight of the men. Late at night we arrived at Candas and detrained, marching by way of Montrelet to Surcamps, where we bivouacked in fields and orchards.

On the 10th we embussed on London motor omnibusses, arriving at the Brickfields, on the outskirts of Albert, in the early afternoon. At this stage of the Somme Battle, the Brickfields, quite a large, flat open tract of country, crowded with troops and transport, were within range of the Hun guns, but owing to the superiority of our air service over that of the Bosche, the enemy never got wise to the fact, and the Brickfields escaped anything but an odd shell or two.

On this day the balloting for the British Columbia Legislature was going on in a big marquee, but while the battalion was eating lunch the C. O., who had gone ahead with the brigadier-general, returned with orders for the battalion to move up to La Boiselle right away, preparatory to going into the line. As a result very few men or officers were able to record their votes.

The following day we moved up to the trenches at Pozieres, battalion headquarters being in dugouts in the cemetery, and on the night of the 10th "C" and "D" Companies relieved the 5th Battalion in front of Mouquet Farm. This was a holding tour only, but owing to the activity of the German artillery, we suffered a good many casualties both in the front line and Pozieres trenches.

On the night of the 13th of September one of our patrols, in No Man's Land, under Cpl. J. W. Stevenson, found and brought in three Australians who had been lying in a shell hole for eleven days. One was un- **Sept. 13, 1916** wounded but had stayed with his wounded pals, getting rations and water at night from the dead lying close by. None of them knew they were in No Man's Land, but thought they were behind the German lines.

On the night of the 13th the 1st C. M. R. took over the front line preparatory to raiding Mouquet Farm during the big show staged for the morning of the

Boche prisoners and wounded Canadians coming through the mud from Passchendaele

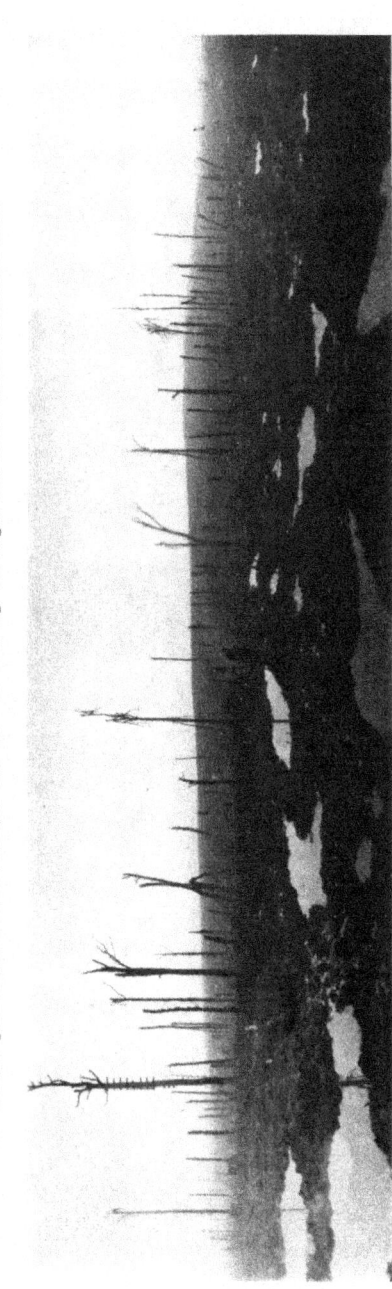

Passchendaele, now a field of mud. Note the trees on the left, which were used by the Boche as observation posts. The ground shows the mud through which the Canadians had to advance

The Somme

15th of September, and the battalion moved back to La Boiselle. In this place were some of the deepest dugouts we ever occupied, one in particular being over sixty feet deep.

At 3 a. m. on the 15th I reported to brigade headquarters in Sausage Valley as battalion liaison officer, and had a very good view of part of the artillery in action. The valley was quite narrow and the guns completely filled it, with just sufficient clearance for firing and movement of ammuni-

Sept. 15, 1916 tion limbers, while just off the edge of the La Boiselle-Contulmaison Road were the heavy howitzers. Dawn, the time for the infantry attack, was bright and clear; the air was filled with our aeroplanes and observation balloons, at one time I counted 42 aeroplanes and 34 observation balloons in sight, while the roar of the guns was so terrific that the Bosche shells which came our way were only noticeable by the dirt they threw up. Everything worked like a parade, a continual stream of motor lorries and ammunition limbers kept the guns supplied with shells, while further up motor and horse ambulances were loading the wounded who were beginning to arrive; soon, too, prisoners began to appear, first in small batches, then in larger bunches, generally escorted by walking wounded Canadians. The attack that day progressed well, ending with the capture of Courcellette by the 6th Brigade.

The raid of the 1st C. M. R. on Mouquet Farm was successful, but cost that regiment heavy casualties, with the result that, that night we returned to the front line with orders to take and consolidate the farm, which owing to its strength and commanding position made its possession essen-

Sept. 16, 1916 tial to the further advance of the corps. "C" and "D" Companies were put under Major W. W. Foster's command for the attack, the two other companies being held in readiness to support the enterprise which was staged for the night of the 16th. At the same time the 4th C. M. R., on our right, was to take the trenches in front of them. Immediately they arrived in line, Major Foster and Lieut. J. Foord led reconnaisance patrols out, and with great skill and daring succeeded, in spite of bright moonlight, in obtaining valuable information as to the approaches, which they later used to great advantage. In the meantime, parties of our men were busy sapping out from our line toward the German stronghold, the intention being to complete the system the following night. The attack was launched in brilliant moonlight, Major Foster leading the main attack, while Lieut. J. Foord led the attack on S.P.'s 34 and 41. Lieut. D. Morrison, who fell gallantly leading his men, was the only officer killed. Lieutenant Foord, though wounded in the face and chest by a German bomb thrown from a tunnel, refused to go out. So skilfully and quickly was the assault carried out, the Huns were speedily driven into the tunnels and, though summoned to surrender, only answered by firing up the entrances. Sentries were, therefore, posted on them, and under the direction of Lieut. G. R. Pearkes, stokes shells were brought up and thrown down every entrance, effectually

2nd Canadian Mounted Rifles

crumpling them in and dealing with the inmates. Working parties following up worked indefatigably, under heavy fire, at the consolidation, and before dawn a new front line was completed round Mouquet Farm and connected up with S. P.'s 34 and 41. Numbers of fugitives from our assault and that of the 4th C. M. R. apparently had to pass over the open about 150 yards in front of a platoon of "D" Company in our old front line, and Lewis gunners and riflemen at once got busy expending hundreds of rounds of ammunition, with the result that few Huns got away. One man afterward described it as like shooting rabbits at short range. No prisoners were taken. This success was due to the skilfully laid plans and leadership of Major Foster, backed by the determined bravery of the officers and men of the two companies engaged in the attack and consolidation. By it, a stronghold, which by reason of its strong position and system of underground communication, had until now defied the attacks of Imperials, became ours and was handed over with a completed new line of defence to a battalion of the Dorsets on the 18th, the 2nd C. M. R. moving out to Bouzincourt, by way of Albert, for a rest. Bouzincourt, like most of the villages in this district, was a collection of hovels inhabited now only by the old or very young and utterly devoid of sanitation, but affording a certain measure of shelter for the troops.

Sept. 24, 1916 On the 24th of September, I was ordered to take the battalion up to Courcellette on a working party, and we moved off in time to reach Pozieres at dusk, where engineers took charge of the companies and marched them up to work close behind Mouquet Farm and in and around Courcellette. Less than one hundred of all ranks were left in Bouzincourt, very fortunately as it happened, for that evening the Bosche shelled the village with H. V. long-range guns quite heavily, killing six and wounding fourteen of our men, while of the working party, only one was killed and four wounded.

Sept. 26, 1916 On the 26th of September we moved back to Albert and on the night of the 27th took over part of the Zollern and Hessian trench system, captured a day or two previously from the Huns by the 7th and 8th Battalions after very fierce fighting. The Zollern trench, which in particular had been very badly battered by our artillery and only afforded shelter from observation, was encumbered with dead Germans and a few wounded ones and our first problem was to get these out of the way; this was finally accomplished by putting the dead over the parados and sending the wounded out by the ration parties during the following night. In the meantime, the "B" Company men dug themselves in, as there were no dugouts to shelter in, there being only two half-finished ones, one of which had to be used for battalion headquarters and signallers, while the other was filled with wounded. "A" and "D" Companies, in the Hessian trench, were more fortunate, as it was still in good condition and had several dugouts. "C" Company and the Colt Guns were left at Picadilly Circus as reserves.

The Somme

Sept. 28, 1916

On the 28th of September the situation, shortly, was this: Our battalion was holding the left of the corps front, while on our left the Hessian trench, with only a bombing block between, was held by the Bosche for some hundreds of yards, beyond them again were the Imperials. Lieut.-Colonel Bott, Captain Miller, the adjutant, and battalion headquarters were established in "Toms Cut"; battle headquarters, occupied by myself and Capt. T. Godfrey, with some signallers and bombers, and "B" Company were in Zollern Trench; "A" Company, under Captain Irving, was in Hessian, next the Bosche, with "D" Company on the right. Orders had been received to drive the enemy out of the part of Hessian which he still held and to also take the important communication trench leading back to the Regina Trench. "A" and "B" Companies had been detailed by the C. O. to carry out the attack in conjunction with the 6th Yorks and Lancashires and were actually in position in No Man's Land when orders were received that the assault had been postponed until 5 p. m., 29th, so there was nothing for it but to bring them back into the trenches. Fortunately, this was done without incurring casualties.

The show came off at 5 p. m. the next day, and the Bosche put up a desperate resistance, the Yorks and Lancashires in particular suffering very heavily. Our boys soon cleared their part of the Hessian Trench, but ran into fierce hand-to-hand and bomb fighting in the communication trench; the possession of this remained in doubt for a long time, each party gaining or losing ground as they received or ran out of bomb supplies. At one time our men ran out of bombs and were being forced back when one man discovered a Bosche bomb store, and these restored the situation for a time; a Hun machine gun was also utilized until it jambed. Finally, just as the situation was becoming most desperate, Cpl. J. W. Stevenson arrived with a party carrying a fresh supply of Mills grenades. Sizing up the situation at a glance, the corporal, calling for others to follow, jumped out of the trench and running forward, followed by Pte. R. Joblin, until opposite the German bombers, proceeded to bomb them back at short range, the two continuing when their bombs were exhausted to shoot Germans with their revolvers, so demoralizing them that our men, coming up the trench, were enabled to drive them right back and establish a permanent block. In this action, Major Moncrieff was severely wounded and Lieut. C. Jefferson was killed; Lieut. A. Kennedy was wounded painfully in the arm while leading his company after Major Moncrieff fell, but carried on for some hours until ordered back by his C. O.; Captain Irving was also wounded, but carried on, leading his company in the assault, and afterward organized the captured positions with good judgment and skill. The work of the N. C. O.'s and men was splendid; in the face of heavy machine gun and rifle fire, without hesitation, they had dashed across the open and taken the trenches at the point of the bayonet, and despite heavy Hun reinforcements poured down the communication trench, had hung on, finally making good the captured positions. Our

2nd Canadian Mounted Rifles

casualties were numerous, but so many were the German dead, they had to be piled outside the trenches before consolidation could be carried on.

We had now some 600 yards more of front line to garrison, and as we could obtain no reinforcements from the other battalions in the brigade, owing to other operations pending, our resources were taxed to the utmost to keep our front even sparsely garrisoned. We managed, however, by pushing forward every available officer and man, leaving only as garrison for Zollern Trench one weak platoon of the 4th C. M. R., reduced by casualties to an officer and thirteen other ranks. Despite all this, we consolidated the new positions, and "D" Company, under Captain Edwards, dug an entirely new line of trench in No Man's Land opposite our right front, 100 yards nearer Regina Trench. Wonderful work was done by the battalion bombers, under Sergt. C. K. Douglas, night and day without rest during the whole tour they carried up water, bombs and rations over miles of country often swept by German machine gun and artillery fire. Sixty-three Prussians and Schleswig Holsteiners were captured in this show and were used to good advantage in getting out our wounded.

Two incidents, in addition to the main attack, distinguished this trip and showed how strong was the esprit-de-corps and fighting spirit in the battalion. At dawn on the 28th the Bosche made a determined bombing attack on our left post, garrisoned by eleven N. C. O.'s and men, with such effect that all but three, Corporal Strickland and Privates Booker and Hogland, were killed or wounded. These three, however, with rifle and bomb repeatedly drove the Huns back and hung on until reinforcements arrived. The other incident was on the 30th: During the fighting of the previous day the Yorks and Lancashires had so many casualties that they were unable to entirely clear their end of Hessian Trench and effect a junction with the S. Staffords. Their senior officer in the front line, Lieutenant Mason, therefore, asked for assistance from us, and Sergt. H. M. Gardiner, Lance-Cpl. A. C. Brown and Ptes. J. Edwards, J. Gittens and F. Scott, all skilful bombers, who were selected from the volunteers, went down and drove the remaining Hun posts out. The appreciation of this deed was expressed in a strongly worded letter of thanks sent by the 32nd Brigade to our brigadier.

On the 2nd of October we were relieved and moved back to Albert, where, on the following day, Lieut.-Colonel Bott handed over command of the battalion to me. The weather now had been unsettled and cold for some time

Oct. 2, 1916 and this, together with the unsanitary state of the country, rendered unavoidable by the unceasing artillery battle and almost incessant infantry fighting, which made it impossible to bury any but our own dead, had seriously affected the health of a number of the men, who were suffering from a form of dysentery aggravated by bad water. The next few days, therefore, were spent in resting up, baths, etc., with the Y. M. C. A. cinemas by way of amusement.

On the 8th of October we returned once more to the line, taking over Sudbury and Vancouver Trenches in front of Courcellette, astride the East and

The bridge across the St. Quentin Canal on the Arras-Cambrai Road, blown up by the enemy when he was driven from the town by the Canadians

The flooded station at Valenciennes; the enemy fired mines and destroyed the station, when they found they could not hold the town against the Canadians

The Somme

Oct. 8, 1916

West Miraumont Roads, from elements of the 9th Brigade. Battalion headquarters were in a small dugout on the edge of a sunken road near the ruined White Chateau, under which was a huge dressing station constructed by the Bosche. On arriving to take over, we found one entrance to the dugout had been blown in by Hun shell fire, and the dugout itself crowded with the staffs of three battalions of the 9th Brigade. Before going down we sent all our details into the dressing station, and it was fortunate that this was done, for half an hour later the Bosche got a direct hit on the entrance, killing two 60th Battalion runners and crumpling in the entrance so badly that it was nearly dawn before it was dug clear again.

Oct. 11, 1916

This tour was a peculiarly trying one to all ranks, coming as it did in wretched weather after nearly a month under almost continuous shellfire, combined with fierce fighting and working parties. With characteristic cheerfulness, however, both men and officers went to work to improve their positions and by the end of the tour had added materially to the strength of the position. We were not called on to go over the top, but suffered severely from hostile shell fire. On October 9th, Lieut. W. H. Pue, a very promising officer, was mortally wounded; the following day Lieut. C. G. Saunders was killed, while on the 11th of October, Capts. F. B. Edwards and R. Asser and Lieut. C. A. Krauss, battalion machine gun officer, were severely wounded. All these officers had done good work throughout the Somme operations, the last named in particular had brought his machine gun detachment up to a high standard of fighting efficiency. Our casualties in the ranks were equally heavy, over one hundred N. C. O.'s and men being killed or wounded.

Oct. 13, 1916

On the night of the 13th of October we were relieved by the 5th C. M. R. and turned our backs on the Somme Battle line for the last time, having done three strenuous tours, during two of which we had delivered successful assaults on the Hun system. The fighting had been hard, the Hun putting up stubborn and often treacherous resistance, while his artillery fire on the front trenches was persistent, heavy and accurate.

CHAPTER V

VIMY RIDGE

On October 20th the 8th Brigade said farewell to Albert and turned its face northward, whither the remainder of the 3rd Division Infantry were already headed. The weather now turned fine and we moved by march route, and train by way of Bouzincourt, Acheux and Aubigny to Etrun, taking over part of the front held by the 60th London Division on the 22nd of October, with battalion headquarters in the Chemin Creux, our sub-sector being opposite Thelus, south of the Lens-Arras Road, and so we came to rest at the foot of Vimy Ridge. This front during the Somme offensive had been very quiet; the 60th London Division, being only three months out from England and green at the game, had not attempted any aggressive work, while the Bosche, for his part, used this part of the line to rest up his battered, war-worn divisions from the Somme. The trenches were old, part of the famous French Labyrinth system, all right for dry weather, but never having been properly revetted, were due to cave in and become muddy and difficult to repair when the winter rains set in, which happened the ensuing week.

Oct. 22, 1916

Our tours of duty in this sub-sector consisted of six days in the front-line system, two companies being in front, with two in support, and relieving at the end of three days, followed by six days in support in Ecurie Defences, into the front line again for another six days, then back into divisional reserve at Etrun for six days, which just gave the battalion time for baths and a church parade, with a picture show or concert at the "Y" by way of entertainment. The billets mostly in barns, were leaky and cold, so that it was very hard to get clothes dried thoroughly. However, after a good deal of kicking from battalions to brigade and from brigade to division, we managed to get them fixed up fairly well. The officers of the four battalions bought the mess outfit of the Londoners for a thousand francs, the mess itself being situated in a large wooden hut, and this was the only time during our service in France that we had sufficient room for a battalion officers' mess.

Our first tours were uneventful, being devoted mainly to endeavours to maintain the trenches in a passable condition. At the end of the month we decided to raid the Hun lines, as headquarters required identification of the troops opposite the Canadian Corps. For this purpose, I selected Lieuts. C. K. Douglas and F. A. Heather, M.M., and a number of volunteers, mostly from the battalion bombers. During the first tour in November these officers and men went out on patrol

Nov. 20, 1916

Vimy Ridge

nightly, familiarizing themselves with No Man's Land, especially in the direction in which it was decided to raid. At this time we were covered by Imperial artillery, our own divisional artillery and heavy trench mortars being still at the Somme. I asked the officer in charge of the trench mortars to break up the German wire at two or three selected points; this he attempted to do, but having a very limited supply of ammunition, only succeeded in making a partial break in one place. While out in a sap observing and directing the fire, a Hun sniper spotted him and so irritated the officer that he used up his last "footballs" in sniping at the sniper, but with no success. We, therefore, had to think out some other way of getting into the Hun trenches and decided to use special wire mats for getting over the wire. Owing to the moon, the raid was not pulled off until the night of the 20th of November. On that night, guided by Scout Lance-Cpl. G. W. Graham, the raiders, with blackened faces and hands, stole across No Man's Land and, at a given signal, threw their mats on the wire, and led by their officers, rushed the German trench. The bombing squads, turning left and right, worked their way to the objectives set for them, overcoming a stubborn resistance as they went and bombing dugouts from which the Huns were firing. The party, led by Cpl. H. C. Manning, just as it reached its objective, was attacked by Hun bombers from a sap in the rear of the front line, and all but the corporal wounded. Bomber T. L. Armit's left arm was badly shattered by a bomb, but in spite of this, bracing himself against the trench, Armit covered Manning while he engaged and killed the Germans, afterward walking back to our line, where he collapsed. As a result of this raid, several dugouts with their occupants were destroyed, many Germans were killed in the trenches, one prisoner was taken and valuable identifications secured. This was the first of many successful raids put on by Canadians in the Vimy Ridge Sector, and the battalion received congratulatory messages from Lieutenant-General Sir Julian Byng, Major-General Lipsett and our brigade commander, Brigadier-General Elmsley. Later, General Lipsett came, personally thanked each of the raiders, and what was still more appreciated, obtained special leave to Blighty for them. Lieutenants Douglas and Heather were awarded the M. C.; Manning and Armit, the D. C. M., while Lance-Cpls. G. W. Graham and A. J. Castle, and Ptes. J. Edwards, G. S. Maxwell and A. O. Stevenson received M. M.'s.

From now on affairs livened up considerably, the German trench mortars and artillery fire getting at times quite heavy. It rained frequently, and in spite of all efforts, our trenches became steadily worse, mud being knee-deep in places, especially in Bidot communication trench. On Christmas Day it took me, with my runner, over four hours to get round the line. This Christmas any attempts by the Bosches to fraternize were nipped in the bud by the battalion snipers, who shot a few who showed themselves shortly after dawn, effectually discouraging any further efforts in that direction. New Year's Day was spent in Etrun in brigade reserve,

Xmas, 1916

2nd Canadian Mounted Rifles

Jan. 1, 1917   so the battalion had its Christmas and New Year's dinner combined. Our canteen sergeant had managed to purchase a quantity of beer, fresh pork, vegetables, flour, etc., out of which the company cooks evolved a really fine dinner; the sergeants' mess, of course, as is the habit of sergeants' messes, had rustled the best dinner of all, even down to champagne and Scotch whiskey; while the officers' mess had the time-honoured turkey, procured at great trouble and expense by our Q. M. from somewhere in France.

One event this year of some importance to us was the formation of the band. Anyone who has seen tired, trench-worn and battle-weary men met and played to camp by their band will realize the importance, almost necessity, of such an institution to a fighting battalion; as the music starts, men, who before were so tired that they could scarcely put one foot in front of the other, straighten up instinctively and march along, even cracking jokes with one another. In November, at a meeting of our officers, it was decided that it was up to us to purchase instruments and furnish necessary funds. As a result of this, while on leave I purchased the band instruments of the 62nd battalion from Lieut.-Colonel Hulme of Vancouver, while in the ranks we found some sixteen bandsmen, who made the nucleus of the band. Bombing Sergeant "Curley" Howells undertook to run the band practises until a bandmaster could be found; this he did, making up in enthusiasm what he lacked in knowledge, some of the bandsmen being unkind enough to say that he frequently conducted with his score upside down. Be that as it may, its numbers grew and it made such effective progress under Bandmaster S. C. Featherstone, who came to us from the 48th Battalion, and Band Sergeant Hayward that in a year's time it was reckoned one of the best bands in the division.

Major W. Bapty, who rejoined us in November, was appointed C. O. of the 8th Brigade Training Battalion at Villiers-au-Bois by our brigadier, and did invaluable work in this position until he left to rejoin the C. A. M. C. and became M. O. to the 102nd Battalion.

On the 4th of January we relieved the 4th C. M. R. in the front line, and owing to the impassable condition of the communication trenches, the relief had to be made overland after dusk. Hip gumboots were worn by everyone, but in spite of these, the men's feet were constantly soaked, so we estab-

Jan., 1917   lished a drying room at battalion headquarters and kept an extra supply of dry socks and clothes, so that changes could be provided for those in the front line. These efforts came under the direction of our M. O., Captain Armstrong, and were so successful that we did not have a single case of trench feet. By dint of hard work, we succeeded in keeping our sentry posts fairly well repaired and the water pumped out, but this was our limit, as with over three-quarters of a mile of front line trench and a similar length of support trenches, to say nothing of about two miles of communication trenches, by the time ration carrying and fatigue parties had been detailed and reliefs for the

Vimy Ridge

sentry groups told off out of a trench strength of six hundred, a very small number of men remained available for working parties, and the Pioneer Battalion never worked ahead of the support line.

Jan. 10, 1917   Moving back on the 10th to the Ecurie defences, the nights of the 12th, 13th and 14th were spent by the battalion in carrying up gas cylinders and fittings to the front line, where they were put in position by special R. E. men, or, as we called them, the Frightfulness Brigade. Our men carried up some four hundred altogether, and as each cylinder weighed about 160 pounds and had to be carried over land for half a mile through the mud, in the dark, considerable noise was made, but in spite of this, the job was completed without any casualties to us. As luck would have it, the wind veered round, and at the end of three weeks the cylinders were taken out by the division which relieved us without having been discharged.

Jan. 16, 1917   On January 16th the 10th Argyles relieved us in Ecurie, and we, in our turn, relieved the 5th C. M. R. in R2 Sub-sector, north of the Lille Road. That night and the following day light snow fell and the trenches, which were mostly in chalk here and quite good compared to our old ones, froze up. Near dawn of the 17th one of our Lewis gun patrols, in No Man's Land, under Lieut. C. J. Lewis, caught a big Bosche working party putting out wire in front of The Snout, and opened up on them at short range with very good effect. Many Huns fell and others were picked off while scrambling back into their trenches; daylight finally drove our patrol back to our line. Many of our posts here were in old craters, blown in the days when the French were there, and from these posts our snipers got excellent shooting, a day seldom passing without their getting at least two or three observed kills.

At 5:45 p.m. on the 21st, Fritz started to strafe us with every imaginable kind of trench mortar and rifle grenade, to which we responded by turning loose our 18-pounders, 4.5's and 6-inch guns, silencing Fritz in half an hour.

Jan. 21, 1917   During our stay in this sector our battalion section of scouts, observers and snipers were brought to a high state of efficiency, great credit being due to Lieut. "Paddy" Moran for this. All scouts and observers were thoroughly trained in map reading, with the result that on many occasions we were able to turn the 4.5 howitzers on to new earthworks and trench mortar emplacements with an accuracy which must have greatly worried the Bosche. Our snipers worked in pairs, in two-hour reliefs, from dawn to dusk, independently of companies, using telescopic Lee Enfields and Ross rifles with the woodwork trimmed down, the latter for long-range shooting. When a target was discovered one man fired while the other observed results with powerful field glasses, and no sniper was credited with a "kill" unless his partner reported seeing the body after deliberate observation. This was a very good check system, as each man did turn-about with rifle and glasses, and it is interesting to note that from the end of October until we left

2nd Canadian Mounted Rifles

this sector in February our snipers killed sixty-four Huns, in addition to nearly twice that number of suspected hits (bodies which could not be seen after falling,), while during the same period our casualties from all causes were seventeen killed and sixty-nine wounded.

The rest of our stay in this sector was uneventful, and on the 23rd we moved back to huts at Mt. St. Eloi. The weather was still very cold and so were the huts. Preparations were now commencing for an attack on a big scale and our battalion was out every day unloading and piling shells of all calibres. All along the St. Eloi Road ammunition was being piled on top of the ground in dumps divided into sections by walls of sand bags. Battalions of South African Negroes, fine, big, upstanding men, were employed on this work, and in addition battalions who, like ourselves, were out of line were called on. The Bosche, too, seemed to be uneasy about something, for his aeroplanes were constantly coming over, and he frequently shelled the village, on one occasion early in February wounding four of our men.

Jan. 23, 1917

On the 2nd of February, battalion headquarters and two companies moved up to support trenches at Ariane. On the 4th, I left to attend the 1st Army C. O.'s Conference at Condette, eight miles from Boulogne, arriving in Boulogne the following day, where we were instructed to put up at the Hotel du Nord. As, however, this hotel was beastly cold and the water frozen up, we moved to the Hotel du Londres and were made very comfortable. At this conference, which was presided over by Brigadier-Generals Studd and Hordern of the 1st Army Staff, were senior officers representing every corps in the army. We discussed many questions and submitted several recommendations, very few, if any, of which were acted upon. Thirteen Imperials and six Canadians were present; of the Canadians, Lt.-Col. R. P. Clark, 2nd Battalion; Lt.-Col. Prower, 8th Battalion, and myself were from British Columbia. At the end of the conference we inspected the 1st Army School, an institution to which we were continually sending officers and N. C. O.'s for courses of instruction. Leaving Boulogne on the 11th, I arrived at Hazebrouck the same night and found that the whole brigade was coming out for training.

Feb. 2, 1917

Feb. 11, 1917

The following day my faithful henchman, Darlington, and I started walking to Bruay, but, by good luck, got a lift in a motor most of the way. Here we met Lieutenant Rowberry, one of our billeting party, who told us the battalion was on the march and would arrive in Rimbert on the 14th. We, therefore, jumped a motor lorry going to Bubure and walked in from there. The billets in this town were very comfortable; the people, most of whom worked in the coal mines, when they found our boys knew how to behave themselves, made them heartily welcome, and in later days when the battalion was again billeted there the inhabitants turned out en masse to welcome us. While waiting for the battalion, I hunted for training grounds and had some difficulty in finding sufficient for company parades. However, we managed to get a rifle range

Vimy Ridge

against a big slag pile, and later on the army took over a large area of country for attack practise. At 2:30 p. m. on the 14th the battalion marched in, under Major Foster, D. S. O., and headed for the first time by its band.

            The following month was spent in continuous training, commencing with a new platoon formation in which were distinct Lewis gun, bomber, rifle grenadier and riflemen sections. The remainder of the month was spent in platoon and company training, a great deal of time being given to musketry,
Feb., 1917   bombing and Lewis gun practise on the move. In the meantime, the divisional engineers were laying out with flags and tapes on the country side a replica of that part of Vimy Ridge which our division was to assault. By way of variation and to develop individual initiative, we took each platoon in turn in bush fighting in a wood near by, and it was very pleasing to see the way they worked their way through the bush, stalking hidden machine guns and dummy snipers, while at the same time keeping touch with one another. Each platoon was also put through a practise attack using live bombs, rifle grenades and S. A. A., and the skill and dash which all ranks displayed augured ill for the Bosche when the big show came. The trenches we used for this training were on a gentle slope, at the foot of which was a very long and wide slag pile about sixty feet high, making a splendid protective screen to the village which lay beyond. All through our tours in the trenches, it had always been impressed upon me, and sometimes very unpleasantly, that the Huns considerably outranged us with their rifle grenades, the extreme distance for our Mills 23 being eighty yards, in comparison to one hundred and fifty to two hundred yards attained by the Huns with their grenades, and an idea had long stuck in my head that on the first opportunity I would try out
Feb. 17, 1917   a sawn-off Lee Enfield, so on the 17th of February I got Armourer Sergeant Stallport to saw eleven inches off the barrel of a Lee Enfield rifle and found, after a thorough test, that we could get up to one hundred and eighty yards accurately with an ordinary blank cartridge, while with a blank stopped with soap we attained a range of two hundred and ten yards. The following day we demonstrated the rifle to Brigadier-General Elmsley and Major-General Lipsett, both of whom were greatly taken with it, and the latter gave us permission to cut down a limited number of rifles. A week later, Lieutenant-General Sir Julian Byng watched us at work with it and expressed approval. After this quite a number of battalions in the division adopted and used it until the eleven-inch rod for the Mills 23 was brought out a few months later, giving similar range with the ordinary rifle and doing away with the necessity of shortening the barrel. We also found that the sawn-off rifle shot quite accurately up to two hundred yards, while, with bayonet fixed, it made an exceptionally good weapon for trench fighting.

    At the beginning of March we commenced practising over the taped trenches, sometimes by companies led by N. C. O.'s only, sometimes as a battalion led by junior officers, always inculcating the doctrine that, however many leaders

2nd Canadian Mounted Rifles

March, 1917

fell, others must be ready to step in and lead on to final success. On various occasions British and sometimes French staff officers came and watched us. Finally on the 15th of March the corps and division commanders, with their staffs, watched our brigade practise the attack in accordance with the barrage table; the two generals in particular studying every phase of the advance and finally at the close putting the battalion commanders through a very close questioning as to our reasons for the various formations we had used.

The following Sunday we bade farewell to our good French hosts and friends and marched to Maisnil-la-Ruitz, where we found fairly good billets and remained until Tuesday, March 20th.

The past five weeks in Rimbert had been of great benefit to the battalion, for while all ranks worked hard during the day, the nights were free from interruption and the billets were good. Wednesday and Saturday afternoons were given over to football and baseball matches between companies or with other battalions, and Sundays, with the exception of an hour on church parade, were free. Our invaluable and indefatigable quartermaster, Capt. T. C. Pennie, had managed to practically re-clothe the battalion—best of all, we had, after much strafing with Q. branch at division, managed to get all the boys refitted with underclothes. Good hot baths were available here, and this we found always to be the case in any coal mining area we happened to be in. Reinforcements received had brought us pretty well up to strength, so that altogether we were in good shape to take a tumble out of Fritz.

On Tuesday morning battalion headquarters, with "A" and "C" Companies, leaving "B" and "D" Companies in Maisnil-la-Ruitz, marched to Villers-au-Bois, now a scene of stirring activity. Enormous dumps of ammunition dotted along the side of the roads were still being added to, huge piles of engineer material were being assembled, light railways and water pipe lines were being laid, many batteries were already dug in and others were daily coming up and waiting under cover of the woods round Mt. St. Eloi for nightfall ere moving forward to their allotted positions, while enormous howitzers, up to 15-inch calibre, were being dragged along by powerful caterpillar tractors to positions in the woods and among the ruins, whence presently they would pound away at the steel and concrete strong points of the Bosche on the slopes of the "Ridge."

March 21, 1917

During the night of March 21st we took over our battle position in front of Chassery and the Twin Craters, some 500 yards in width, "A" Company, under Captain Gray, taking over the front line, with "C" Company, under Major Godfrey, in support; "B" and "D" Companies, under Major Cameron and Lieutenant Heinekey, moving up to Villers-au-Bois. This tour in the line was for the purpose of giving every one an opportunity of observing the country we were to attack over, and getting our jumping off trenches dug. In order to keep the men as fresh as

A view of Domart, on the Canadian Front, where they are driving the Germans back

Canadians advancing. French troops, who have dug themselves in are seen in the foreground. (Most likely 2nd C.M.R., as they were next to the French)

Vimy Ridge

possible, the front-line company was relieved every two days by the support company and went back to Villers-au-Bois, one company moving up from there into support.

During the morning of March 22nd the Huns made a very daring raid on one of our outposts at Chassery Crater, killing three and taking two prisoners. When the firing broke out Major Foster and I, having just been round the outposts, were standing on the firestep in a communication trench talking to Captain Gray and watching the batteries shelling toward Arras. Jumping up on top, we were just in time to see some Germans disappear into the crater and our Lewis gunners firing at them. Realizing that an attack had been made and not knowing to what extent it might develop, I sent Gray to bring up supports, while Foster and I went forward after arming ourselves with bombs; nothing further occurred, however. These craters were held on one lip by us, on the other by the Bosche, saps being run out from the front line to them and groups of five to eight men holding each post. Apparently a few Germans, covered by concealed riflemen, had successfully stalked and captured the two sentries, the covering party shooting down the remaining men when they attempted to go to their comrades' rescue. The episode, on the eve of a great battle as it was, was very serious and annoying, for in spite of all cautioning and instruction, one could never tell how much information the Huns could get out of the men by either direct or indirect methods. We found out afterward, however, from captured documents, that these two men, Burgess and Hastings, had told a mass of lies, which apparently annoyed the Bosche, for at the end of the paper they were put down as of a low type of intelligence.

March 22, 1917

To wipe out this affront, and also to obtain identification, we decided to raid the Bosche lines, and on March 31st our raiders, led by Lieut. Fernley Smith, after blowing up the wire with a bangalore torpedo, broke into the German trenches behind Chassery Crater and killed the garrison. Cpl. John Morton, with his Lewis gun crew, while covering the raiders' withdrawal, also distinguished themselves by taking up a position on high ground, in the face of enemy rifle fire, and wiping out a strong German party which attempted to counter-attack. No prisoners were taken, but a great many of the enemy were killed and valuable identifications and papers were obtained. This tour, but for these two events, passed without incident, our jumping off trenches were dug, by night, without interference by the enemy, and the battalion was withdrawn at the end of the month for a rest prior to the "big show," which was now definitely set for the 9th of April.

March 31, 1917

Our batteries for the past week had been shelling the German positions steadily, and now and again, as a sort of preliminary training for the Huns, putting on a creeping barrage which at first brought down his curtain fire, but which later he disregarded when he found no infantry attack developed. Our

2nd Canadian Mounted Rifles

artillery strength was tremendous, there being in the actual attack itself a gun firing on every fourteen yards frontage, but at no time prior to the battle was the artillery allowed to develop more than 40 per cent. of its actual strength. The indifference of the enemy to all these preparations was as extraordinary as it was inexplicable; in observation his superiority was marked both on land and in the air, at least on our front, for at this period we frequently had Bosche planes over our back areas, and in one week alone I saw three of our slower flying planes shot down by speedy Hun airmen. Owing to the flatness of the country, many of our batteries had to take positions practically in the open, their principal cover being slight depressions in the ground and camouflage; yet in spite of all this, his guns, which should have kept busy shooting up ours and making their positions untenable, did comparatively little beyond slightly increasing their counter battery activity and taking an occasional burst of hate at Mt. St. Eloi or the infantry positions and billets.

On the night of the 5th of April we commenced taking up our battle positions, "B" Company going to the front line and "D" Company moved into Cenot Cave, while battalion headquarters moved into battle headquarters in Boyau Poquet in the front-line system. At dusk on Saturday, the 8th,
April 5, 1917   "A" company came up to Cenot Cave and "C" into the Pylones
April 8, 1917   support line, and as our recently prepared jumping off trenches had been destroyed almost entirely by the combined action of the weather and the enemies guns, we had to set to and re-dig them that night.

Sunday, the day before the "big show," was fine, with only an occasional light shower, all the company commanders came up to battle headquarters in the afternoon and we went over, very carefully, for the last time, every detail of the assault. The men were in excellent spirits, and keen; the battalion dumps were well filled not only with grenades and ammunition, but with extra water and rations. Toward evening the weather again changed and soon became stormy and wet. The guns on both sides had almost ceased firing, only breaking out fitfully now and again. For the past two days our medium and heavy trench mortars had been pounding the Bosche wire until practically nothing was left of it, and now we pushed out parties of men who, under the protection of covering parties, cut many paths through our own entanglements. The stormy night was a great help to us in this, and the work was accomplished without incident.

At 2:30 a.m. on the 9th all hands had breakfast, and at 3 a.m., after the rum ration had been served out, the companies began moving to their assembly positions, a difficult and tedious movement, owing to the stormy blackness of
April 9, 1917   the night, which, however, very effectively covered the troops, now everywhere taking up positions along the whole battle front. In the order of battle for the Canadian Corps, the 1st Division was on the right, opposite Thelus, the sector we had held during the winter; north of them came the 2nd Division, flanked by the 3rd Division, with

Vimy Ridge

the 4th Division on the left. The 8th Brigade held the right of the 3rd Division, with the 7th Brigade on the left, the 9th Brigade being in divisional reserve. Our brigade objectives on the north included the Ecole Commune, at the crest, allotted to the 4th C. M. R., with the Lens Arras Road, on the south, cutting deep through the Ridge, for the 1st C. M. R., while La Folie Farm, in the centre, was for the 2nd C. M. R., the 5th C. M. R. being in brigade support, all three battalions having to push beyond these to the reverse slope and establish outpost lines; a total depth of nearly a mile, with an approximate width of five hundred yards to each battalion.

The 2nd C. M. R. attack was to develop as follows: "B" Company, under Major Cameron, was to lead and capture the German front line, including part of the famous Arnolf Graben tunnel, a tunnel dug deep under ground for a long distance and capable of sheltering large numbers of troops from the heaviest bombardment, mop up thoroughly, after which, leaving one platoon as garrison, they were to reform, follow up and reinforce "C" Company in Swischen Stellung. In the meantime, "C" Company, under Major Godfrey, followed by "D" and "A", was to go through and take the Swischen Stellung, part of a strong second-line system of defence half way up the Ridge, and consolidate it; "D" Company was to carry on and take La Folie Farm, while "A" went through and established the outpost line.

The question of assembly positions had been one of the most serious and trying problems, one method being to form companies fairly close up behind one another, at some fifty yards intervals between each; the other to form up with intervals of one hundred and fifty to two hundred yards between companies. In the former case, the companies would all move off at zero and close up to the barrage, allowing the intervals to increase after passing No Man's Land, and standing a sporting chance of escaping the German protective barrage which sooner or later was bound to come down; while the latter three companies would have to pass through the Huns' protective barrage and were almost certain to suffer many casualties while doing so. Again, against the first method was the fact that, if the Huns suspected anything and put their barrage on before zero and after the men had assembled, we were bound to suffer very severely indeed. Taking everything into consideration, including the element of surprise, after talking it over thoroughly with the officers, I decided on the first method, with the result that when the Bosche barrage, swift as it was, came down, it came down on almost empty trenches, and fully justified my decision.

Company commanders had been instructed to fire three white verey flares in quick succession immediately they captured their objectives, and so obviate any delay caused by the despatch runners' slow progress through the mud, and an observation post had been built whence the progress of the attack could be observed.

At 4:30 p. m. word came in that the companies were in position, and also a section of Vickers guns, the officer in charge of which had been instructed to work them up in his own time and establish them in the outpost line. The hour

2nd Canadian Mounted Rifles

before zero was terribly trying. Did the Bosche suspect anything? Would his barrage come down on those masses of men waiting so quietly and patiently? Standing on top there, watching and praying as the time passed slowly by, so quiet was it, except for the wind and rain and an occasional gun firing, one could hardly believe that in a few brief moments from now one of the greatest and most vital battles of the war was about to commence. Five minutes to zero came, and still all was quiet, the darkness being only occasionally lit by the usual flares from the Hun lines. Thirty seconds before zero two Wombat mines, near Chassery Crater, were blown up by our sappers, and almost immediately the air was full of brilliant signals of different colours put up by the alarmed Bosche sentries, but zero had come, and with one great shattering roar, every gun behind our lines came to life. Looking back, everywhere were great flashes of red and white flame from the leaping guns, while looking forward, the fires of hell seemed to be raining on the doomed German lines; near by, our shrapnel barrage showed as a line of red hot fragments in the still dark morning, moving forward at the rate of one hundred yards every three minutes; further up, thermite and H. E. bursting on the German defences looked like miniature spouting volcanoes; best of all, one could see by the light of the bursting shrapnel our men moving steadily forward. Thirty seconds after zero the enemy's protective barrage came down, fortunately mostly behind our assembly positions, now nearly empty; while our battle headquarters became the centre of attention, and the trenches all round were soon pretty well crumped in. Soon after dawn the rain squalls changed to snow, with a high wind blowing.

April 10, 1917

All our objectives and a number of prisoners were taken on time, and new battalion headquarters were established by 10 a.m. in a large German dugout in the Swischen Stellung. At 9 a.m. the Bosche was shelling both his and our old front lines very heavily, but by watching where the shells burst for a while all battalion headquarters got through.

The slopes of the Ridge furnished an unusual sight as we plodded our way forward; here and there groups of men, quite regardless of the shells which the Bosche seemed to be scattering around on the chance of hitting something, were in some cases swapping smokes as they moved forward, while in others they were stopping to eat; again, we would pass a few dead Huns or parties of live ones bringing our wounded down the hill.

At Swischen Stellung, which had been badly wrecked by our fire, we found "C" Company digging in. After examining part of the dugout which had been selected for headquarters, Dick Spinks, the battalion scout officer, and I went forward to La Folie Farm, nothing more than a heap of ruins set in a grove of trees, also badly knocked about by shell fire. While here a Bosche plane came over, flying just above the tree tops, and fired some smoke signals, which resulted half an hour later in our new positions being shelled severely by 5.9's at intervals for the remainder of the day. Proceeding on to the outpost line, we found the two companies, "D" and "A", under Lieutenant Heinekey and Captain Gray,

Capt. J. MacGregor, V.C., D.S.O., M.C.

A view of Bourlon Village

Vimy Ridge

respectively, busy digging in, well over the crest of the Ridge, after posting outposts in the bush near the bottom of the hill.

The weather had cleared somewhat and we had a great view of the Douai Plain: in front of us and only a short distance from the Ridge were Vimy and Petit Vimy, and the Lens-Arras Railway, with the mine, Fosse of La Chaudiere, while in the distance were Lens, Avion and Mericourt, with all their fosses as yet untouched, almost a view of the promised land, but the infantry had already gone to the extreme range of our field guns, and until they were brought forward no further advance could be reasonably undertaken.

During the actual assault our losses were not severe, but as is often the case after an attack, our casualties were greatly increased while consolidating and holding the captured positions. Lieut. J. E. H. Christie was killed very early in the day; Lieut. A. G. Pimm, battalion signals officer, while directing the laying of a telephone line, was mortally wounded and died a few hours later, and Lieut. Fred Heather, M. C., M. M., was killed instantly by shell fire while directing his men in the consolidation of the outpost line. Lieuts. R. Lees, R. J. Darcus and J Mavor were wounded during the assault, while in the evening Capt. J. L. Gray, M. C., was gassed by gas shells. Forty-four other ranks were killed and one hundred and forty-nine wounded during the day; many of these casualties were the result of the shelling directed on our new position by the Bosche plane which had chaperoned our advance earlier in the day.

By dusk our outpost line was pretty well consolidated, with Vickers guns and the two Colt guns still left to the battalion dug in behind for covering fire. "B" and "C" Companies were still busy digging in on the Swischen Stellung system, while a company of the 5th C. M. R., sent up by the brigadier general in support, were digging in close behind. The day had been a most successful one, as, though part of the 4th Canadian Division to the north had been held up, yet by nightfall practically the whole of the famous Ridge, which the Bosche considered impregnable, was completely in our hands. The attack, long anticipated by the enemy, as shown by captured documents, was delivered so swiftly and suddenly that it literally caught the Huns with their boots off, for Lieuts. H. M. Gardiner and J. M. Mackenzie, with their men, on entering the Arnolf Graben tunnel actually captured Germans half dressed. The dash with which both officers and men, in darkness, snow and mud, took their objectives one after the other, speedily overcoming all opposition, was wonderful. Cpl. John MacGregor of "C" Company successfully rushed a German machine gun and disposed of the crew; Lance-Corporal Mackenzie, a big Lewis gunner of the same company, single handed, took five Bosche officers prisoner in a dugout. Corporal Zuehlke was treacherously shot in the arm by another Bosche officer who had offered to surrender in another dugout. So keen were some of "D" Company's men that they went through our own barrage to get to La Folie Farm, instead of waiting for it to lift, while some of "A" Company's snipers penetrated to the edge of the scrub at the foot of the slope and picked off a number of the disorganized and fleeing Huns. During the balance of the day many Germans

2nd Canadian Mounted Rifles

were found hiding in tunnels and dugouts and sent to the rear; after I left my new headquarters for the outpost line, fifteen came out from an obscure part of it and surrendered.

The following day the hostile shelling was not so severe, probably due to the enemy pulling his guns back; the morning was fine and bright, and we could see parties of the enemy moving in the distance. In the afternoon, which was stormy with frequent snow squalls, we received orders to **April 11, 1917** push out battle patrols and get touch with the enemy, with a view to testing his strength. Each battalion sent out two strong battle patrols, ours being under Lieuts. G. P. Heinekey and H. M. Gardiner, two officers who had done splendid work the previous day. They found Petit Vimy strongly held, and coming under heavy machine gun and rifle fire, suffered severely, Lieutenant Heinekey being severely wounded, and Lieut. R. Spinks killed, Sergeant Jacobs and forty-two other ranks killed and wounded. Having done their work and driven in the enemy outpost, the patrols withdrew, bringing in their casualties.

The next day was again stormy with frequent snow squalls. In the morning there was great excitement in the outpost line, as some German infantry and transport came in range in the open; Lieutenant Rowberry's Colt guns at once opened up, knocking over a team, then everyone with a rifle **April 12, 1917** started firing, resulting in a general stampede on the part of the target, quite a number of casualties being inflicted on them. This was the last time our Colts came into action, as shortly after they were turned in and replaced by Lewis guns.

At 10:30 p. m. we were relieved by the 60th and the 52nd Battalions of the 9th Brigade and started out for Villers-au-Bois. The march out was terrible, through sticky mud a foot deep with fresh snow on top, and the men soaking wet and tired out with three days' fighting and digging. It took hours to traverse the few miles back to Villers-au-Bois.

The next few days were spent in cleaning up, baths, renewing kit and so on, no regular course of training being undertaken. On the Friday following the battle, General Lipsett came round and thanked the men for the splendid manner in which they had stormed the Ridge.

On the same day the 9th Brigade carried on the advance and reached the outskirts of Avion on the 14th, the Bosche having withdrawn to a new line in that vicinity.

On April 18th the battalion moved up to the Swischen Stellung, now a divisional support area, and on the 25th moved back into reserve at Suburban Camp in Villers-au-Bois. Vimy Ridge at this time was a most interesting sight. Where, before the battle, only parties of men not exceeding **April 18, 1917** two together were allowed to cross the open in daylight, there was now a scene of stirring activity; thousands of men were constructing roads, laying down light railways and building camps of wooden

Vimy Ridge

huts; infantry and artillery transport lines were dotted everywhere, and the standard gauge railway was being extended through Arras to the foot of the Ridge.

From now on until the 7th of May we furnished working parties for building roads over the Ridge, and reinforcements of six officers and 218 other ranks arrived during this period. On May 6th and 7th we took over the new outpost line in front of Avion, astride the Lens-Arras Railroad, from the 43rd Battalion, headquarters being established in La Chaudiere.

May, 1917

On the night of the 8th, "A" Company's visiting patrol shot up a patrol of eight Huns who attempted to cut them off, killed one and wounded and captured one, who proved to belong to the 93rd R. I. R.

The previous night the Germans counter-attacked and retook Fresnoy, which had been captured on the 3rd of May by the 1st Canadian Division and handed over to the 5th Imperial Division two or three days later. Fresnoy was some miles south of our line, but the enemy's preparatory bombardment extended north of us, and from 10 at night until 3 a. m. of the 8th he treated us to thousands of gas shells, tapering off toward morning with 5.9's and 8-inch. His shooting was excellent, for three out of four 4.5 howitzers which were dug in close behind battalion headquarters were blown clean out of their placements by direct hits. Fortunately for us, the Bosche didn't know the exact location of our positions and most of the shells fell well out in the open, so our casualties were light. Except for spasmodic shelling by the Huns, the rest of the tour was uneventful, and on the night of the 11th we were relieved by the 49th Edmonton Battalion and moved back to Toronto Area, near Machine Gun Fort, on the old Pylones support line, going from there on the following day to Villers-au-Bois.

The following week was spent in cleaning up and training, afternoons being given over to sports. On the 20th we moved back to the Ridge and were set to work digging new defences and putting up wire entanglements. At times our work parties, who were under observation from Lens and Mericourt, were shelled. As a result Lieutenant Steer was killed on the afternoon of the 22nd. The same day, Lieutenant Darcus, with three of his men, who were putting in screw stakes, unknowingly stirred up a buried bomb and were all wounded. Night bombing, by the air forces on both sides, was now becoming very fashionable, and the Huns bombed our back lines nearly every night; our transport was lucky, but a labour battalion near by had over forty casualties in one night.

May 20, 1917

On the night of the 27th we relieved the 43rd Battalion in front of Avion, battalion headquarters going into an elaborate German dugout in a sunken road, renamed Nanaimo Road. During this tour we were pounded quite often and heavily by the enemy artillery, but our guns being now well up, in good positions and plentifully supplied with shells, had no difficulty in taking them on and silencing them after duals of varying length.

May 27, 1917

2nd Canadian Mounted Rifles

During this period both sides were busy digging new trench systems to take the place of the outpost lines, and one Wednesday night, when one of our battle patrols tried to take a German outpost by surprise, they found the garrison gone and had to retire as the Bosche artillery commenced shelling them. The following night a strong party of Huns, in turn, attacked one of our outposts, but were driven off and followed up by our battle patrol, which, however, again had to retire on being strafed with gas shells.

The 5th C. M. R. relieved us in the front line on the night of June 1st, and we moved back into support, with headquarters in La Chaudiere, where we were still subjected to the attention of Fritz' artillery, and from the manner in which he was paying particular attention to batteries, communication,
June 1, 1917   trenches and support trenches, we concluded that he was contemplating an attack, and this came off on the night of June 4th, but never succeeded in reaching our front line, at this time held by the 1st and 5th C. M. R. The German infantry, in addition to being caught by our infantry and machine gun fire, was also caught by our artillery barrage and suffered severely before they got back to their own lines. For our own side, not even our local support came into action.

On the 8th of June we moved back into brigade reserve at Vancouver camp, where we received 200 reinforcements and furnished working parties on the Ridge for the next four days, moving back into division reserve at Villers-au-Bois on the evening of June 12th, whence, after three days'
June 8, 1917   training and sports, we moved back into the line, taking over from the 58th Battalion on the night of the 17th. Nothing unusual happened during this tour, and on the night of the 21st we moved into support, after being relieved by the 5th C. M. R. On the 22nd we extended our support system, "A" Company moving into Scotia trench, west of the Lens-Arras Railroad, and two platoons of "D" Company up to Halifax trench. While in support we carried on improving the trenches and building S. P.'s at night.

On the night of the 25th we were relieved by the 43rd and 58th Battalions and marched back to Villers-au-Bois, with a halt at the Quarry line for breakfast.

The 2nd Army, under General Sir H. Plumer, had on the 7th of June fought one of the most successful battles of the war, capturing the Messines Ridge, blowing up the famous Hill 60, wiping out the Ypres Salient and taking many guns and thousands of prisoners, and to help the offensive movement thus commenced, the other armies were expected to worry the Bosche as much as possible to keep him from withdrawing troops to send against the 2nd Army. For the Canadian Corps, the 4th Division so far had made several attacks on the outskirts of Lens, nipping off various sections of trenches, while our artillery all along the system held by the corps, by putting down barrages on the Bosche front line system, worried him greatly and made him expect another assault. At the end of June, the 3rd Division was to go back to a "rest" area, but on June 29th the relief of the division was cancelled, it having been decided to

Section of the R.A.F. passing the saluting base, in Mons Square, on the occasion of the entry into the town of the First Army Commander. The Canadians captured this town on the day that the armistice was signed.

Vimy Ridge

continue the push toward Lens, and the 3rd Division was ordered to take over the 4th Division front on the 1st of July. Therefore, the 2nd C. M. R. moved up to Souchez and relieved the 87th Battalion in the support area instead of going out.

This tour was uneventful, our brigade taking its turn in divisional reserve, and Avion being occupied with little further resistance from the Huns, though afterward they made it a very disagreeable residence at times.

On July 25th the division was relieved and the battalion marched to Rimbert, where the usual programme of cleaning up and training and sports was carried on.

On August 3rd, Major W. W. Foster, D. S. O., left for Camblain L'Abbe to take command of the 52nd Battalion, and Major L. W. Miller succeeded him as 2nd in command of the battalion.

Aug., 1917
August 15th again saw us on the march from Rimbert, this time to Gouy Servins. Next day we received orders to take part in two days manoeuvres extending over the Loretto Ridge, Ablain St. Nazaire, the Carency Valley and surrounding country. The manoeuvres started well, but in the evening the brigade was ordered to return to Gouy Servins in readiness to proceed north and relieve the 1st Division, which, together with the 2nd, had been heavily engaged in the capture of Hill 70, near Loos. At 5:20 p. m. on Sunday we marched off for LesBrebis, a mining town, a few miles from Loos, with the mines still working, despite the fact that the Bosche shelled the place quite often. That night the Huns shelled the town, but miraculously no casualties resulted. At 9 p. m. the next day we moved into the reserve supports area in the cellars of Loos, a most undesirable residence, for the Bosche frequently shelled and gassed it. Loos, the theatre of the gallant attack in 1915 by the Scottish and British Territorials, and now nothing but ruins, lies at the foot of Hill 70, a miniature Vimy Ridge, possession of which gave to the armies holding it observation for miles to almost every point of the compass and which now, thanks to the gallantry of our 1st and 2nd divisions, enabled our gunners to dominate with their fire all avenues of approach to Lens, and made its possession to them of no further value except as a very dangerous link in their line of defence.

The next day, August 21st, the Huns shelled Loos all day, and that evening we relieved the 4th Battalion in close support, taking over from the 1st C. M. R.

Aug. 21, 1917
on the 24th in the front line. At this time the Hill presented every aspect of a fierce and sanguinary battle; most of the German trenches had been crumpled in by our shell fire, while everywhere one went were dead Huns and, in some cases, Canadians. These last we gathered together and our Padre gave them Christian burial; afterward we did the same for the Germans.

During this tour the Hun was in a very nasty temper and shelled us frequently, inflicting many casualties. On Saturday, while some of our stretcher-bearers were carrying out two severely wounded men from "D" Company, a

2nd Canadian Mounted Rifles

Bosche plane, a big yellow fellow, flying low, opened fire on them, fortunately without results. His unsportsmanlike action, however, brought almost immediate retribution, for one of our Lewis gunners, looking out to see what was happening, saw him, and loosing off a pan at him, by a lucky chance, hit him, sending him, smoking, back toward his own line, where, our observers reported, he fell in flames at Cite St. Auguste.

"A" Company, under Major Foord, was during this tour posted in a deep gravel pit, or cutting, at the foot of the Hill, the open end of which was in full view of the Hun lines. Rifle pits had been hastily dug on the outer edge, while on the inner side were some large dugouts, well furnished and shell-proof, which had evidently been a German headquarters of sorts; these furnished ample shelter for those not on duty in the rifle pits. "D" Company, on the other hand, had only some half-dug trenches which could only be deepened during the night, while to get to either company during daylight one had to dodge along communication trenches which, owing to shell fire, were now only about three feet deep. The two companies were separated from each other by some three or four hundred yards of open, which, though under observation by day, had to be constantly patrolled by night. The first night I went round the outposts in company with Major Miller and Lieutenant Blake we drifted out of our way while crossing this space, and on approaching "A" Company's flank were greeted by the sentry with two shots, which luckily missed us; our language probably stopped him firing again. On questioning him, he said his orders were to fire first and challenge afterward anyone coming from No Man's Land, and on taking our bearings, we found he was quite right, so complimenting him on his shooting, we moved on, reaching the gravel pit just as the Bosche put down one of his "Hymns of Hate," which lasted about fifteen minutes.

Aug. 28, 1917 The next night we were relieved by the 18th Imperial Brigade and moved back to Les Brebis, whence, after a twelve-hour rest, we marched to Marqueffles Farm, arriving there at 4:15 p. m. The following day we were fortunate enough to get baths for the whole battalion, and on Tuesday, 28th, we were attached to the 9th Brigade and relieved the 52nd Battalion in Cite St. Pierre in brigade reserve. This mining village, which had been captured by the 2nd Division in the battle of Hill 70, was one of the most strongly fortified places I ever saw in France. The houses were all in ruins, but the greater number of cellars had been loopholed for defence and roofed with from four to six feet of reinforced concrete, on top of which again were three to six feet of loose bricks and tiles from the walls and roofs of the houses. These were our shelters now and were still intact, so it speaks well for the officers and men of our 2nd Division that they stormed and took such a position from the picked troops of Germany. We were here four days and worked on burying cable, bringing up munitions, and so on.

During the night of Saturday, September 1st, we were relieved by the 52nd Battalion and moved back to Marqueffles Farm, whence we marched the fol-

Vimy Ridge

Sept. 1, 1917   lowing afternoon to Mt. St. Eloi, arriving there at 5 p. m. After a stay of twenty-four hours we moved off, and crossing Vimy Ridge after dusk, relieved the 15th West Yorks in local support, and on the following night relieved the 18th W. Yorks in the front line opposite Mericourt.

The line we now held was to be our jumping off sector in a proposed offensive by the corps in which it was intended to capture Mericourt and the Sallaumines Ridge, and penetrate to the Haute Deule Canal west of Lens, in this way rendering the city untenable by the Huns and throwing it
Sept. 17, 1917   into our hands without the tremendous cost which would be entailed by a frontal attack. After two days in the front line we were relieved by the 43rd Battalion and moved back to Vimy and the foot of the Ridge, being employed until September 17th in digging communication trenches and shelters in our battle area.

CHAPTER VI

Paschendaele

On Sept. 17th after relief by the 49th Battalion we marched over the crest of the ridge to Zivy Dump and travelled from there by light railway to Fraser Camp Bois D'Allou, arriving at midnight. Leaving the next day at 1 p.m. we marched by way of Cambligneul to the farming village of Caucourt, where we were given fairly good billets. Here for the next two weeks we practised musketry, wire cutting, street fighting and over taped trenches indefatigably, just as we had for Vimy Ridge, but on October 4th the brigadier-general told me it was doubtful that the show would come off, owing to the slow progress of the battle up north. This was most disappointing after all our hard work of the past month, besides which everybody now knew his job and all were keen. We carried on with the training, however, until the 11th of October, when General Horn, commanding the 1st Army, inspected the brigade, and in a farewell speech told us how sorry he was to lose the corps, but that we were needed by the 2nd Army up north; he hoped, however, that afterward we would return to the 1st Army. We knew then that we were destined for Paschendaele. Our four weeks at Caucourt, however, were not wasted; the battalion had had a good rest, for though worked hard while on parade, the men had plenty of time for games and sports, with band concerts, etc., in the way of amusement; clothing and boots had been renovated and renewed, while baths and the Foden Lorry had reduced the cootie question, always an urgent one, to a minimum; so, when at 2:30 a.m. on the 15th the battalion marched out of Caucourt en route to Savy to entrain, it was in top-notch fighting condition. The train journey was, as usual, deadly slow but uneventful. However, we finally arrived at Caestre at 12:30 p.m., and detraining, marched to Hondeghem, just outside of Hazebrouck, where we were billeted in farmsteads.

Sept. 17, 1917

On the 17th I in company with the other battalion commanders, travelled by bus to Wiltje, from where we walked to the Anzac front line on Abraham Heights and had a good look at the country that, sooner or later, we were to attack. We could see Paschendaele village, a very commanding position, still a long way off, while further to the north Westroosebeke seemed to us just as dominant a feature as Paschendaele. This being our first visit to Ypres since August, 1916, it seemed strange to see traffic moving freely by day through streets and along roads which in the old days one travelled, even at night, in constant expectation of shell fire.

Oct. 17, 1917

On our way up we had a fine view of a fight between a British and a Bosche

Paschendaele

plane, which ended by the Bosche crumpling up and crashing a few hundred yards from where we were, while the Britisher, after following him down nearly to earth, flew off, stunting as he went.

During the next three days parties of officers went up to look over the line

At 2:40 a. m. on October 22nd we marched off from Hondeghem in the rain, en route to Caestre, where the "Y" provided every man with a mess tin full of hot tea. At 6:30 the battalion entrained and two hours later, detraining near

Oct. 22, 1917
Ypres Asylum, marched through the north end of Ypres to X Camp, a very wet camp of tents between St. Jean and Wieltje.

That night between eight and ten Hun planes bombed the camp; fortunately, beyond two horses killed and two wounded, we had no casualties. Other units, however, were not so fortunate, all suffering to a more or less degree. On October 24th the Huns came over and again bombed the camp, this time in the middle of the day. We were again fortunate, no one being hit, though one bomb dropped very close to battalion headquarters.

Later we relieved a New Zealand battalion in intermediate reserve in what was called Capricorn Keep, a hopeless mess of crumped in fragments of muddy trenches and partly submerged ruined pillboxes, right among our medium and heavy batteries; consequently, we came in for shelling at all times and had several casualties. Battalion headquarters was in a small, very wet pillbox, which, from the looks of things, had been used as a refuse dump, tins of bully, chunks of bad meat, sodden sacks of mouldy bread and bloodstained clothing being among the articles we shovelled out in an endeavour to make the place habitable, and always, in spite of all our endeavours, there was about six inches of foul smelling water on the floor. The companies were partly in funk holes, partly in pill boxes; the funk holes, fortunately, were in a comparatively dry area, but, of course, were scant protection against shell fire. Practically the whole country was mud and shell holes full of stinking water, a most dismal and desolate desert with here and there skeletons of trees, shattered pillboxes or derelict tanks to vary the landscape. Each brigade had a single duck walk, laid by the engineers, up which all troops moved; off it, no progress could be made owing to the mud. The one used by us ran from Wieltje to the front line and was six miles long. The guns in a great many cases had to be put on plank platforms, and mostly the only shelter the gunners had from the enemy's shelling was a slight sandbag wall hastily thrown up. Conditions under which the field artillery laboured could hardly have been worse; with battery positions exposed constantly to destructive and harassing fire, soaked night and day with mud and water, suffering heavy casualties all the time, the men stuck it, working their guns to the limit. Their supply of shells had all to be packed for miles through the mud and the mortality among the mules and horses was terrible; they were to be seen lying dead everywhere, smashed by high explosive or dead from exhaustion. The infantry went nearly the limit in endurance at Paschendaele, but the gunners, I think, had a worse time, for they were kept in longer under fire, without the relief of going over the top, and many batteries

2nd Canadian Mounted Rifles

did twice as long in the battle area as any infantry brigade, and with it all, they never failed to respond, and respond effectively, when called on.

On the evening of October 25th the battalion moved up to Cluster Cottages, so called from a number of Bosche pillboxes grouped on a slight slope and connected up by very muddy trenches in which funk holes were dug. These pillboxes, built of reinforced concrete, had been smashed and **Oct. 25, 1917** twisted by our heavy shells, but still furnished shelter. The one occupied by myself, Major Miller and Captain Douglas, our adjutant, was just six feet square inside, not much room, but fairly dry, which latter fact enabled us to write despatches decently. The next one, occupied by our signallers and runner, considerably bigger and more smashed about, had an interesting ornament in the shape of a huge 12-inch dud shell lodged between the twisted iron rods and concrete of the roof. With our usual luck, we were about two hundred yards in front of a number of 18-pounder batteries, with the result that, when the Bosche started straffing them, which he did frequently and fiercely, it became intensely interesting and warm for us, as we received the benefit of all shorts. However, the first attack by our corps **Oct. 26, 1917** came off at 5:40 a.m. on the 26th, when, to put it briefly, our division, holding the left of the 2nd Army, was to push across the swampy ground and gain footing on the dryer slopes beyond. The 4th C.M.R., later reinforced by the 1st C.M.R. and supported by three companies, "A", "B" and "C", of the 2nd C.M.R., kicking off on time, succeeded, in the face of stubborn resistance and in spite of mud sometimes knee-deep, in advancing 400 yards through Wolf Copse and capturing Wolf Farm and three very strongly defended pillboxes. The 9th Brigade on our right was still more successful, gaining a firm footing on the famous Bellevue Spur, while on our left the Naval Division, holding the right of Gough's 5th Army, managed to gain about 200 yards, so the line was now echeloned from a small gain on the left to the deepest advance where the 2nd Division had advanced on comparatively dry ground.

The following night we took over the 4th C.M.R. line and commenced consolidation, completing it sufficiently for the next attack, and incidentally, our men shot quite a number of overbold Huns. During this, the battalion lost one of its most promising officers in Major Foord, M.C., an **Oct. 27, 1917** "original" who had won promotion from the ranks. Two minutes after Major Miller and I, who were going the rounds, had left his shelter in the trench, a shell struck it, wounding him fatally in the head, and he died a few minutes later, never regaining consciousness.

During the attack by the 4th C.M.R. and for the two following days a party of seventy-five of our men, led by Lieut. Bernard Shipton, M.M., and our Padre, Capt. T. C. Colwell, worked unceasingly, carrying out the wounded, regardless of the shell fire, which was heavy. Several were wounded, but the remainder carried on until every wounded man had been carried back to the dressing stations.

Paschendaele

The 5th C. M. R. relieved us on the night of October 28th, and "B" and "D" Companies, commanded respectively by Major Cameron and Lieutenant Wilson, were attached to them for the next operation. The following day the brigadier instructed me to move up to Kronpriz Farm, battle headquarters of the 5th C. M. R., and co-operate with Lieut.-Colonel Draper in the coming attack. We knew well that an extremely hard task was ahead of the brigade, a thousand yards of swamp had to be crossed under heavy artillery and machine gun fire before we could gain a footing on the rising ground beyond, while if for any reason the troops on our flanks failed to get ahead, we would be subject to enfilade fire from a number of German pillboxes.

Oct. 28, 1917

During the night the battalion moved up into close support, and at 5:50 a. m. on the 30th of October, the 5th C. M. R. kicked off for our brigade and, led by Major Pearkes, M. C., made a gain of over 1200 yards, gaining a foothold in three fortified farms beyond the swamp. Their casualties, however, were very heavy, and it was decided that to hold our gain two companies, "A" and "B", of the 2nd C. M. R., must at once be sent to reinforce them. In the meantime, however, the British brigade on our left had been almost annihilated by artillery fire and had made no gains, and the German barrage playing fiercely along our assembly trenches made the situation still more critical. The companies, however, deployed successfully, but came almost immediately under heavy enfilade fire from the left, in addition to the storm of shrapnel and high explosives. Undeterred, they pushed forward, floundering through mud and water, in many cases pulling one another out of the mire. On the right, Major Cameron fell, and the remaining officers of "B" became casualties, but the N. C. O.'s carried on and, leading the thinning platoons, arrived in time to assist in repelling the first counter-attack. On the left, "A" Company, more heavily engaged by the machine guns in the pillboxes, pushed on in groups; Lieutenant Lyle with seven men being the first to arrive, reinforced a three-man post of the 5th C. M. R. with three more and, pushing on, established another post with his remaining four. Lieutenant Mavor, with a badly smashed hand, got through next with another group, further strengthening this flank, and more groups, gradually getting through, thickened the defence sufficiently to hold on until night. Many counter attacks were broken up, the supply of ammunition being maintained by collecting it off the casualties, and all through the remainder of that day this precarious position, twelve hundred yards in advance of the troops on our immediate left, was resolutely and successfuly held by thirty-seven officers and men of the 5th C. M. R. and eighty-five officers and men of the 2nd C. M. R.

Oct. 30, 1917

At dusk "C" and "D" Companies, sadly thinned by the unceasing shelling by the Bosche of our positions, moved up and, reinforcing the line, relieved the 5th C. M. R., who in their turn moved back to Cluster Cottages. All through the night we pushed up water, rations and ammunition, while three companies of the Shropshire Light Infantry, which were attached to us, dug in a line of

2nd Canadian Mounted Rifles

rifle pits connecting our left flank with the right flank of the 5th Army.

The following day the Hun strafed us heavily with gas and high explosive, but in spite of this, we succeeded in clearing our wounded. All that day, too, Hun planes hovered over trying to spot our new line, and our boys had to lie doggo in their shell hole defenses, but as soon as night came consolidation was again feverishly carried on and more water, rations and ammunition pushed up, with such good results that when on the night of November 1st we were relieved by the 1st C. M. R., we handed over a very fair line of defense well stocked with water and ammunition. After the relief, on the way out, we came under a heavy and persistent gas shell barrage, and Lieutenant Shipton, who had worked so heroically and indefatigably throughout the battle, was hit by a gas shell while tending two of his wounded men and died next day from the effects.

Oct. 31, 1917

In this battle the 5th C. M. R. had over 400 casualties and the 2nd C. M. R. nearly 300.

On the 2nd of November we moved back to "S" Camp at St. Jean, and on the 4th we entrained at Ypres for Abeele, where we went into billets which we had occupied in 1916. The next few days were spent mostly in refitting and cleaning up. On the 5th, Major-General Lipsett congratulated the battalion on its splendid work, and on the 8th, the corps commander inspected and thanked the brigade.

Nov. 2, 1917

Group of 2nd C.M.R. Officers, 1915

CHAPTER VII

THE FINAL GERMAN OFFENSIVE

On the 12th of November we moved up to Ypres again in busses and marched up to California Trench and "A" Camp, near Wiltje. The men were still feeling the effects of the previous tour and were very tired by the time we reached the camp. The following day most of the battalion was on a working party, pulling 18-pounder guns, which had been blown into the mud, out of it, and that night the Bosche, after shelling the 9th very heavily counter-attacked, but with no success. We, however, stood to from 8 p.m. until 11 p.m., ready to move forward. The following two days we had working parties, while on the 15th, by way of diversion, the Gothas came over three times and bombed the camps. On the 16th the battalion left Paschendaele for good and went into billets for rest, training and reinforcements at Estrie Blanche. For its share in the Battle of Paschendaele, the 3rd Division was twice specially thanked by Sir Douglas Haig.

Nov. 12, 1917
Nov. 16, 1917

During this period of refitting and training I had the good fortune to be sent to Bertangles, a few miles out of Amiens, on a course of instruction in liaison between the infantry and the air service. Arriving there on the 8th of December, I found several brigadiers and colonels who, like myself, were detailed for instruction. Officers of No. 16 Squadron, R. F. C., were our instructors, and the late Brigadier-General Shepherd, D. S. O., M. C., R. F. C., was in charge of the school. On the 9th we motored over to Candas and were shown through the shops there where 3000 R. F. C. mechanics were employed assembling machines and stripping salvaged machines, etc. The next morning we went up with the pilots, who demonstrated observation from various heights. That afternoon we flew over various parts of the Somme battlefields and back areas. The following morning I went up in D. H.-4, having arranged with the pilot for a trip over Lens after a visit to Bapaume and the famous Butte de Warlencourt, but, unfortunately, as we were passing over the latter place the machine developed engine trouble and we had to return to the aerodrome. That afternoon we were given a practical demonstration of contact patrol work from the airman's point of view, and the following day had more contact patrol work, ending up with a sham battle between two flights of planes, which was very exciting, one being too engrossed in getting after the other plane to notice the various stunts performed by the pilot. The 13th was a dud day, and on the 14th, much to our regret, our week's course came to an end, and we motored

2nd Canadian Mounted Rifles

back to our various headquarters, having had a most interesting and instructive time.

On Monday, December 17th, orders to move down to Hill 70 came in; on Tuesday we marched to Busnettes via Lillers; on Wednesday to Houchin via Chocques, Annezin and Bethune, and on Thursday to Mazingarbe, relieving the 6th Yorks and Lancashires, commanded by Lieut.-Colonel La Vie, in the support area at Loos the following night.

The weather now turned cold and frosty with flurries of snow. On December 24th two American officers were attached to us for three days; they were quiet, nice chaps, not a bit anxious to impress on us the fact that the United States was winning the war, but on the other hand,

Dec. 25, 1917 much impressed with the terrible devastation of Loos, Hill 70 and the near by villages, this being their first visit to a devastated zone. Christmas Day was cold and fine and quiet, and passed much as other days in the line, working parties going on as usual.

On the 27th we relieved the 4th C. M. R. in the front line and at once began to prepare to raid the Huns, our patrols, clothed in white smocks I had made, being invisible at a very short distance at night in the snow, which now lay in No Man's Land, were enabled to work close up to the

Dec. 27, 1917 enemy wire and find the weak spots. The year closed with the enemy registering some of our communication trenches with trench mortars and artillery. Lieut. W. J. Wilson, out with a patrol on New Year's Eve, was mortally wounded by a chance bullet in No Man's Land, his gallant soul passing with the Old Year. In his death, we lost both a gallant officer and a loved comrade, an officer popular with all ranks both for his unceasing cheeriness under all conditions and his solicitude for the well being of his men.

The year 1918, which was to see such downs and ups for the Allied Armies, was ushered in for us by an attempted raid by the Huns. At 7:40 p. m. on January 1st the enemy shelled us very heavily, and Lieutenants Apps and Bowen were mortally wounded. At 7:50 p. m. he put a box barrage

Jan. 1, 1918 around our front line and attacked in two places, but was driven off by our rifle and Lewis gun fire without getting into our trenches. Our losses in this affair, considering the severe artillery fire we were subjected to, were extremely light; besides Apps and Bowen, both of whom died the following day at No. 7 C. C. S., one N. C. O. died of wounds and three men were wounded.

The next day we were relieved by the 4th C. M. R. and moved back to Mazingarbe, where on the 3rd and 4th the companies had combined Christmas and New Year's dinners.

While out this time, raiding parties were selected from "B" and "C" Companies and practised over taped trenches. On the 9th we went back into the line, and on the way in I called at brigade headquarters at Previte Castle dug-

The Final German Offensive

outs and completed arrangements for the raids with the brigadier and the artillery colonel. Our plans were to enter the Bosche line at two points, one on our left, where the trenches were only fifty yards apart, and the other opposite our centre, where they were five hundred yards apart. Lieut. J. MacGregor, D. C. M., of "C" Company, with a picked party, was to take the left, while Lieut. H. D. Williams, of "B", with his party, was to enter at the centre an old trench called "Heaven Sap" crossing No Man's Land, giving the latter party a certain amount of cover. At a given time the artillery were to box barrage certain sections of the German line and at the same time the raiders were to enter the trenches, get what prisoners they could, at least one or two, kill the rest of the garrison, destroy the dugouts and return to our line. Both parties were provided with special light bath mats for crossing wire.

On the 10th of January the Huns again registered all our communication trenches, so on the 11th, the snow being all gone and all arrangements completed, I decided to pull the raids off at 2:10 a.m. the following morning. Lieutenant Williams, with his party, on account of the distance,

Jan. 10, 1918 started from our lines before midnight and reached the enemy wire without incident. Lieutenant MacGregor, with his lot, were not so fortunate, however, as a vigilant Bosche, spotting movement, opened fire twenty-five minutes before zero, luckily hitting no one. MacGregor, however, proved equal to the occasion, gradually working round his men and telling them when zero came to follow him to a new way over the wire. At zero "B" raiders, again fortunate in finding the wire no obstacle, led by Williams, cleared their objective, killing fourteen Germans and taking a prisoner, who, however, made a break to get away in No Man's Land and so was bayonetted. "C" raiders, for their part, following MacGregor in spite of bombs and fierce machine gun fire from the German trenches, laid their bath mats over the wire and stormed in to the position, which was heavily held; parties working to plan in different directions, killed with bomb and bayonet many Huns and dropped quantities of bombs into three dugouts crowded with Germans who refused to come out when called upon. MacGregor himself captured one prisoner and chased a machine gunner, who, however, proved too agile and escaped. Two prisoners in all were captured in this raid and valuable information obtained, the battalion receiving the thanks and congratulations of the divisional and corps commanders.

The remainder of this tour was quiet and uneventful, and on the 14th we went back into support in Loos and Hartz and Harrison craters, where we put in most of our time fixing trenches which were becoming very bad owing to soft weather and rain.

We were relieved in this section on the 20th by the 8th Battalion and marched to Mazingarbe, whence we marched the following day, by way of Petit-Sains, Hersin-Coupigny, Barlin and Houdain to Divion, where we remained in billets until February 18th and went through the usual routine of refitting and training.

2nd Canadian Mounted Rifles

On the 18th of February we bade farewell to our good friends at Divion and marched off to Villers-au-Bois, the next day relieving the 21st Battalion in our old stamping ground in front of Vimy Ridge. The following month was spent in front of the Ridge in the regular monotonous round of trench warfare, the enemy, beyond an occasional burst of shelling, being exceptionally quiet.

On the 20th of March the 116th Battalion relieved us and we moved back to Suburban Camp at Villers-au-Bois, arriving there at 1:30 a. m. on the following morning, imbued with the idea of rest and baths for all hands, but Fate had other than baths in store for us, for the Hun offensive **March 20, 1918** started the same morning on the 5th and 3rd Army fronts, and the next day saw us again on the march, this time to Roclincourt, and from Roclincourt on the 23rd we moved up into the front line at Arleux Loop and relieved the 2-7 West Yorks. We now knew the seriousness of the situation down south, so, as there was a scarcity of S. A. A. and rifle grenades, etc., in the Loop, got busy and, by the following day, had plenty of everything up and the position thoroughly reorganized for defense. At this period General Currie was down south with the 1st and 2nd Divisions, and the 3rd and 4th Division were attached to the 13th Corps, whose **March 27, 1918** staff work struck us, to say the least, as pretty ragged. On Wednesday, the 27th, the 1st C. M. R. were to relieve us, but later the unfortunate 1-13 Londons (Kensington Regiment), who had been and were still in the line opposite Gavrelle, were taken out and, dog-tired, marched round to relieve us. This happened on the night of the 27th-28th of March, when the Hun offensive at Arras was launched, and while our sector was immune from infantry attack, it was subjected to a heavy high explosive and gas barrage from 3 a. m. until 8 a. m., during which time the relief was going on, and as a result, the tired Londoners suffered many casualties. The relief was finally completed at 5:55 a.-m., and Captain Douglas and I, with our headquarter signallers and runners, struck out for Neuville St. Vaast, where the battalion was to assemble, and much to our delight, we found on arriving there that the companies had all come through with hardly a casualty.

At 8:30 p. m. we marched off again, this time to Ecurie. On the 29th we stood to all day, finally receiving orders at 5 p. m. to march back to Neuville St. Vaast, and here we heard, much to our indignation, that the G. O. C., 13th Corps, had evacuated our front line in front of Vimy Ridge **March 29, 1918** without so much as an attempt at a raid by the Bosche, and pulled the infantry half way back to the foot of the Ridge. Even the Huns didn't expect such an easy gift as this, for it was the next day before their patrols entered the evacuated trenches. So peremptory was the order and so short the notice to the Kensingtons that, not only did all trench munitions fall into the enemy's hand, but also an 18-pounder gun behind Arleux Loop and a 9.2 heavy trench mortar. From March 30th to **April 4, 1918** April 4th the whole battalion was set to digging rear defences; in fact, from the look of the countryside, it seemed as though

"Decorations" 2nd C.M.R., January, 1919

The Final German Offensive

every last man had been set to digging, and indeed, for the next two or three months hundreds of miles of trenches were dug for many miles back of where any trenches ever existed before.

On April 5th we moved up to reserve line behind Farbus and relieved the 5th C. M. R. in the front line before Acheville on the night of April 10th. The 75th Canadians relieved us the following night and we marched back to Neuville St. Vaast, where we entrained for Loos and relieved the 5th Lincolns in our old stamping ground on Hill 70, our brigade remaining in this sector until the 2nd of May.

On the night of April 25th our 4-inch Stokes fired a thousand gas shells into the Bosche lines round Lens, while simultaneously 1500 drums of gas were also projected over, and as each of these drums contained thirty-six pounds of compressed chlorine and phosgene gas, the Huns must have had a pretty thin time.

April 27, 1918 On the night of the 27th a picked body of raiders from "D" Company, under Lieut. F. A. Sprague, entered the German trenches and, meeting with fierce resistance, had to kill the entire garrison. Seventeen bodies were searched, and it was found that, beyond buttons and shoulder straps, all usual identifications such as discs, papers, etc., had been left behind. It is, therefore, most probable that these men were assembling to raid us when the assault by our men was delivered. The buttons and shoulder straps, however, proved valuable, as they showed the 1st Bavarian Division had relieved the 220 R. I. R. in front of us.

The following night we went into support on relief by the 4th C. M. R., and during the night of May 1st the 9th Royal Sussex relieved us and we moved back to Les Brebis. During this stay at Hill 70 the German offensive against the Portuguese, a few miles north of us, took place, leaving us in a very decided salient and subject to long-range enfilade artillery fire, which caught us one morning in Les Brebis, knocked the houses about our ears and caused several casualties.

May 5, 1918 On leaving Les Brebis the brigade moved by bus to Ourton, and from Ourton, on the 5th, we marched to Ham-en-Artois by way of Divion, Burbure, Rimbert and Lillers. On the 9th we marched from Ham-en-Artois to Busnes and bivouacked in a farmyard on the outskirts. This part of the country had been evacuated by the natives during the Bosche offensive, and our division was now distributed, by brigades, in support to British divisions which had been thrown in to hold the new line. We remained here for twelve days familiarizing ourselves with the country from the outpost line back and practising open warfare. The weather was fine and hot, so the afternoons were spent by the men mostly in bathing in La Bassee Canal or the streams which abound in that flat country.

On the 21st we struck camp and marched back to Fontes for musketry. General Elmslie, our brigadier, left us on May 25th, owing to ill health, and in him we lost one of the best officers and soundest brigadiers in France. Lieut.-

2nd Canadian Mounted Rifles

May 21, 1918 — Col. D. C. Draper of the 5th C. M. R. was given command of the brigade. May 28th found us on the move again, this time to Guarbecque, where we again practised offensive warfare. On the 31st of May the 9th Brigade took over, and we marched to Estree Blanche by way of Molinghem and Mazinghem.

Up to this time we had been in army reserve; we were now in general headquarters reserve and liable to be sent to any point on the British front. For the next three weeks we put in long and strenuous days on the Bomy training area, practising offensive warfare in conjunction with tanks and artillery. On June 23rd the 3rd Divisional sports were held at Linghem and were a great success, the Midway features being better than many of those seen at big Canadian fairs in peace times.

June 23, 1918

On June 25th the battalion marched to Aire and entrained for Savy, detrained at 7:30 p. m. and marched to billets at Villers St. Simon and Givenchy-le-Noble, arriving at 11 p. m. thoroughly tired.

On the 29th we marched to Wailly and the following night relieved the 24th Battalion in front of Neuville Vitasse. The brigade remained in this sector for the next three weeks, but so well and thoroughly had the 2nd Division gone after the Huns that, though we scoured No Man's Land with battle patrols varying from five to forty in number, we could never get to hand grips with the Bosche.

On Sunday, July 14th, we received word that a German offensive would start on the French front at Rheims the following morning; it did, but this time, owing to the French preparedness, came to a standstill very shortly and was more than counteracted by a French offensive at Soissons on the 19th, which resulted in the capture on the first day of 8000 prisoners and 100 guns.

At this time we were in support at Bretencourt, and on Sunday, luckily, marched to Dainville to see a musketry demonstration with tracer bullets. During our absence the Germans shelled the village, killed two of our men who had been left behind and wounded three others, and Lieutenant Rugg, incidentally dropping a 5.9 into battalion headquarters mess, utterly wrecking it. When I suggested to Madame that perhaps now she would move to a safer town, she merely remarked: "Oh, no! That is the ninth shell to hit the house, but the others were small ones, and the two ends of the house are still good. C'est la guerre, Monsieur, C'est la guerre."

July 23rd found us on the march north again, this time to Anzin, by way of Dainville and Louez, where we did musketry and working parties. On the 29th we received word that the brigade would move to Ypres, and that afternoon the 4th C. M. R., with advance parties from the other battalions, entrained for the north. The following day, however, instead of following our advance parties north, we marched south, destination unknown, by way of Dainville, Warlus, Simencourt, Fosseux and Barly to Sombrin-en-Lucheux, arriving after an eight-hour march. The next morning at 4:45 we marched to Mondicourt, through Humbercourt, where we entrained, detraining that afternoon at Prouzel, eight miles south of Amiens, and finding billets alongside a French army corps.

July 23, 1918

CHAPTER VIII

THE LAST HUNDRED DAYS

     We now knew that an offensive was planned, but had no idea where we would attack. August 1st was spent in the usual inspections before battle, iron rations, S. A. A., and so forth, being checked up. August 2nd was wet; in spite of this, we had a practise with tanks in the morning and at 9 p. m.

Aug., 1918   marched off on the first of a series of night marches which eventually ended in the Battle of Amiens. Our destination that night was Hebecourt, only a few miles, but the traffic was so great that we only reached our billets in the small hours of the morning.

     The following day the brigadier took me, with Colonel Rhodes of the 5th C. M. R. and Major Maxfield of the 1st C. M. R., up to Bois-de-Boves, whence we walked up to the trenches held by the 4th Australian Division in front of Hangard-en-Santerre and looked over the country we now knew

Aug. 3, 1918   we were to assault. It was a pretty, rolling countryside, dotted with woods and battered villages—a country offering great possibilities for defence to a determined garrison, but figuring on the element of surprise, we did not see why we should not be successful. The going promised to be good, shell holes were very scattered, and the trenches had been hastily dug, in many cases through fields of wheat, still standing and now almost ripe, while through our glasses we could see that the Germans had practically dug no trenches behind their front line, evidently figuring eventually on a further advance on Amiens.

     We returned to Hebecourt in time to march off with our battalions at 10:30 p. m. for Bois-de-Boves. This night the traffic was thicker than ever; for miles the roads were packed with three lines of slowly moving transport of all kinds, through which the battalion had to work its way slowly until at 3:30 a. m. it arrived at the Bois-de-Boves and bivouacked among the trees.

     While this trek of the corps was on all movement ceased at dawn, every man, horse and vehicle being hidden away in woods and villages until the fall of night again gave the signal for the march to recommence. During this period of preparation thousands of tons of ammunition, bombs, petrol, engineer material and so forth were being brought up and stored in Boves Wood. Nothing short of disaster could have befallen had the Bosche suspected anything and shelled the vicinity, but fortunately, General Currie's brilliant device of sending Canadian battalions to Ypres so deceived the Intelligence Department of the enemy that he actually published a summary shortly before the 8th of August stating

2nd Canadian Mounted Rifles

the Canadian Corps was in the north, and his first knowledge of our presence in the south was when we handed it to him personally.

On Sunday, August 4th, our Padre held a voluntary church parade, and we again moved forward at 10:30 p. m. into some French support trenches south of the Roye Road; on Monday night we moved back a few miles into trenches north of the Roye Road, giving the other trenches up to the 9th Brigade, which was to attack on our right. Tuesday and Wednesday were spent by officers and N. C. O.'s going up in very small parties to the front line to study the enemy position and in serving out extra rations and munitions to all ranks. All traffic ceased by Wednesday morning; guns of all calibres were to be found behind every hedgerow and farm building, covered with camouflaged netting, while the shells were hidden in the hedges and buildings.

Aug. 4, 1918

On the night of the 7th, while the infantry was assembling, the artillerymen and machine gunners got their guns into position and the tanks began to work up toward their jumping off positions. The weather up to now had been cloudy by day and inclined to rain at night, all in our favour, and this night a heavy ground fog came on. At midnight we started for our assembly positions and so thick was the fog that it was difficult to distinguish the men until they came within a few feet of one. The battalion was in position at 3:15 a. m. close up behind the 1st C. M. R., who were to take Hangard, our job being to go through them and take Demuin, about a mile further on. Everything was quiet. The Australians, who had held the line until we commenced to assemble, were clear. Half an hour before zero we could distinctly hear the rumble of the tanks moving forward and could only hope and pray that the Bosche would not get wise and drench us with artillery fire before the start came. Four-twenty a. m., zero—two seconds before the time a couple of our machine guns began to chatter and then came the heavy crash of thousands of big guns, mingled with the incessant rat-tat-tat of thousands of machine guns. Ten minutes to give the 1st C. M. R. a start and away we go, but not before the Bosche barrage had caught our right flank. Owing to the fog, nothing could be seen of the gun flashes or bursting shells, we had to trust to luck for direction. Our tanks got lost in the fog and didn't catch up until late in the morning. Passing through the 1st C. M. R., busily engaged in rooting out machine gun nests in Hangard, our companies pushed on and by 6:20 a. m. had captured Demuin, with a large number of Germans, and established outposts beyond the village. On our left, the 16th Canadian Scottish were well up, while on our right, the 9th Brigade had its objective, and so far as we could learn, an unqualified success had been won. Shortly after, other troops carried on exploiting the victory; regiment after regiment of cavalry, with a number of Mark 5 and Whippet tanks and batteries of artillery, went through us that morning. The sun came out brilliantly, and for the rest of the campaign the weather man decided to stay in our favour. The remainder of that day we rested by our piled arms, ready to move, but at 5 o'clock we were ordered to

Aug. 7, 1918

2nd C.M.R. Originals, 1919

The Last Hundred Days

bivouac in a field near Demuin. Our transport came up with our field kitchens, and we now felt that we were at last into moving warfare, with a chance of getting our own back at Fritz.

For this day our casualties were light; unfortunately, Lieutenant Griffiths and thirteen rank and file were killed by shell fire, while Captain Rowberry, Lieutenant Campbell and sixty-two rank and file were wounded.

The following morning we marched off, with our band playing "Marseillaise," moving forward in support three and four miles at a time, frequently under fire from the German heavies, but, as they were firing blindly and without observation, we had no difficulty in avoiding the shelled areas. That afternoon the 4th and 5th C. M. R. pushed forward and captured La Folies and Bouchoir villages, some thirteen miles from our start of the previous day.

Aug. 9, 1918

At 6 p. m. the brigadier sent for me, and telling me it was necessary to capture Le Quesnoy-en-Santerre, a fortified village about one and a half miles from Bouchoir, in order to insure the following day's advance, gave orders that the 2nd C. M. R. was to take it before dark. At that time the battalion was some eight kilometres from Bouchoir, and I pointed out to the brigadier that it was impossible to issue necessary orders, march eight kilometres, attack over two more and capture a strong position in less than three hours of daylight still remaining, more especially as we had had no opportunity of observing the country to be captured, but that we would endeavour to complete the programme by dawn, and this he agreed to. At this period our right flank was on the north of the Roye Road, with the left flank of the French resting on the south of the Roye Road somewhat behind our line. As we were to make an attack unsupported at the start on either flank, two batteries of Vickers guns were attached to the battalion to cover and prevent any Bosche attack getting in behind us, and in addition, a section of field artillery and three tanks were attached to us, but unfortunately, the tanks broke down before they got to the jumping off place, and the artillery officer, though definitely told by me the hour of the start and where I would start from, never turned up with his guns. Brigadier-General Brutinel of the Corps Motor Machine Guns very kindly furnished us with fifteen motor lorries, with which "A", "B" and "C" Companies were moved up to Bouchoir, where they debussed under cover of a screen of motor cyclist machine gunners. "D" Company, in support, marched.

Aug. 10, 1918

At 3 a. m. on the 10th we commenced the advance, the intention being to push as close up to the village as possible by dawn and take it with the bayonet. However, when we got half way we encountered the German outpost, heavily garrisoned, who put up a fierce resistance, and from then on opposition was met with all the way. "B" and "C" Companies, on the left, suffered severely, but were not to be denied and, clearing three lines of trenches with the bayonet, gained a footing in the north end of the village by 6 a. m. "A" Company, on the right, also suffered very heavily from machine gun nests south of the Roye Road, but fought its way forward stubbornly until most of its

2nd Canadian Mounted Rifles

officers were casualties. Fortunately, about this time, a tank, which had been sent up by the general on hearing the three had broken down, arrived, and on its attention being attracted in that direction, crawled over and pounded the nests out of existence with its Hotchkiss guns. By 7 a. m. the village was completely in our hands, with several machine guns and over two hundred prisoners, and we were entrenching on the far side. Our casualties were heavy; Captain Whitlow and Lieutenant Hanna were killed, and Lieutenants Harris, Palmer, Trees and Williams were wounded, while 45 N. C. O.'s and men were killed and about a hundred and ten wounded. On the other hand, our success enabled the French to come up on our right with practically no opposition, and the same occurred on our left. We had taken over two hundred prisoners, and when we came to count the piles of dead Germans found over two hundred of them also.

The following day the 32nd British Division passed through, and the battalion moved back to a small wood in the rear of Bouchoir, where we stayed resting up and conducting salvage operations until the 16th, when we moved back to Le Quesnel Wood, on relief by the 2nd Canadians.

While at Bouchoir and Le Quesnel we received several drafts of reinforcements, as a result of which we left numerically stronger than when we came in.

At 8 p. m. on the 20th we embussed at Maison Blanche on the Roye Road, debussed at 2:30 a. m. on the 21st and marched to Coulamont, where we rested until 8:30 p. m., when we marched to Sambrin. At 8:30 p. m. on the 22nd we marched to Beaufort, and the following day while the battalion was marching and bussing to St. Sauveur, east of Arras, General Lipsett took the brigadier and our battalion commanders up to the line held by the 51st Scottish Division, north of the Scarpe, where we spent the day studying the German positions held on Orange Hill and Monchy.

The following two days were spent in refitting the battalion with bombs, S. A. A., etc., and elaborating plans for the attack. The capture of Orange Hill, the key to Monchy and necessary to enable our artillery to come up, was allotted to the 2nd C. M. R.; the 4th C. M. R. were to take the low ground on the left, and the 1st and 5th C. M. R. were to take Monchy. Zero hour, originally set for 5 a. m., was changed almost at the last minute to 3 a. m., the corps commander having decided on a moonlight attack. Unfortunately, the night was squally and rainy. No Man's Land on our particular front was nearly a mile wide, and we assembled in it as far forward as the line set for the commencement of the barrage would permit. Our plans were to move up along the lower north slope of Orange Hill two companies abreast, each in column of sections in file; each company as it came to its allotted objective would swing right, taking the enemy on his flank and rear. This plan, if successful, would do away with a certain amount of confusion always attendant on leapfrogging companies in an attack and would also avoid the machine gun fire bound to sweep the front slopes of Orange Hill. Here again the principal factor of success would be the element of surprise. This morning at zero there was no fog, now and again the moon would break through the rain and clouds, giving a little light. The same

The Last Hundred Days

old roar of guns and bursting shells, but this time we were tight up to our barrage and the sight was wonderful. The flash of the shell bursts showed the men moving steadily forward with fixed bayonets, many of them smoking and joking. Our plans worked perfectly; as we moved up the flank of the hill we could see the flashes from the German machine guns firing to their front down the slope until stopped by the bombs or bayonets of our men taking them in the flank. One sacrifice 7:7 field gun was also taken in this way, the gunners dying at their gun, which was afterward swung round and used against its previous masters. By 5 a. m. the Hill was ours, and the 1st and 5th C. M. R.'s passed through to Monchy. Later the 7th Brigade passed through, and we moved up in support of the 5th C. M. R.

On the 27th we were attached to the 7th Brigade and supported the 42nd Battalion, but the day passed without incident to us, although we suffered somewhat from shell fire.

On the 28th we were attached to the 9th Brigade and moved in support of the 43rd Battalion and part of the 5th C. M. R., finally digging in on Seventy Ridge, near Remy. In this skirmish our casualties were very light. At 2 a. m. on the 29th of August we were relieved by the 1st Warwicks and moved back into trenches outside of Arras, later in the day moving into Arras.

The following day we marched to billets in Habarq for a rest, which, however, only lasted a couple of days, as on the 2nd of September we received orders to march back to Arras again, and arrived at 4:30 p. m.

On the 5th we marched up to the support area just south of Vis-en-Artois, taking over from the 42nd Battalion, battalion headquarters moving into some wooden huts on the crest of the ridge. The Bosche, however, did not encourage us to stay there, shelling us occasionally, so on the 7th, after he had damaged our hut, we decided we had better move down the slope. At this period the advance north of the Scarpe had not been pushed, so the Canadian left flank rested on the river several miles ahead and stretched back at right angles, with the result that the whole support area round Vis-en-Artois was within artillery range of the German batteries grouped near Vitry-en-Artois, and as at this time the countryside was covered with artillery and infantry horse lines and bivouacs, the Huns had great opportunities for effective area shoots and took full advantage of them, accounting for many horses and men. Added to this, the Gothas bombing at night made things lively and kept us from oversleeping ourselves, so that when we received orders to relieve the 116th Battalion in the outpost line at Ecourt-St. Quentin no one was sorry. At this part of the outpost line, west of the Canal du Nord, wide stretches of water divided us from the enemy, and with the exception of a certain amount of shelling and a few patrol encounters, the tour was quiet.

Sept. 5, 1918

On the 18th the battalion came out of the line, later moving south to positions behind the 4th Division, which was moving up to storm the Canal du Nord and Bourlon Wood. At this time the colonels in the brigade were all on leave,

2nd Canadian Mounted Rifles

Sept. 18, 1918

having been ordered off by General Draper, and Major L. W. Miller, D. S. O., was in command of the 2nd C. M. R. After the 4th and 1st Divisions had most successfully and gallantly stormed the Canal and taken Bourlon Wood, the advance on the 28th of September was continued by the 3rd Division, and the 2nd and 1st C. M. R.'s, on the left and right, respectively, were ordered to pass through the 7th Brigade and push through to the Cambrai Canal on the morning of the 29th. The information given to our brigadier by the G. O. C., 7th Brigade, was to the effect that his outpost line was well past St. Olle, on the Cambrai Road; this was afterward found to be incorrect, with the result that our barrage came down well beyond the village, which was filled with German machine guns; consequently, before the two battalions reached the allotted assembly area and were properly deployed, they came under heavy machine gun fire from St. Olle Church and houses and suffered severely. Realizing the position, Major Miller swung the companies across the road, attacking the positions in the open, the 1st C. M. R. taking care of St. Olle. Pushing forward steadily under heavy fire, the railroad was reached, and our attack swung toward Neuville-St. Remy, on the Canal. By this time most of the officers and many N. C. O.'s and men had become casualties, and the situation became critical when a German machine gun nest firing across 300 yards of open brought the advance to a halt. Capt. J. MacGregor, grasping the situation at a glance, picking up a rifle, immediately dashed forward in spite of the fire, reached the guns, bayonetted several of the gunners, took the rest prisoners and put the guns out of action. Returning to the men, he led them forward successfully until finally St. Remy was cleared of the enemy and our outpost line firmly established on the Canal. For his gallantry in this action, Captain MacGregor was awarded the Victoria Cross. This was the most desperately fought engagement of the war for our battalion, possibly the most desperate for the whole corps, but the results were far-reaching, for when some days later, after much fighting the Germans finally gave way and retreated, the picked troops of the German Empire had been almost annihilated, and from then on until Armistice, for us at least, it was a matter of advance guard actions.

The capture of Valenciennes by the 4th Division on the 2nd of November was the only other show of any size after Cambrai. Our casualties were very heavy, fourteen officers and two hundred and sixty-three other ranks being killed and wounded.

I arrived back from leave on September 30th, but together with Lieut.-Colonel Laws of the 1st C. M. R. was retained at brigade headquarters until October 4th, going round the different positions with the G. O. C.

The battalion was now in support in the Marcoing line in fairly good dugouts, the 4th and 5th C. M. R. having taken over the outpost line. At 5 a. m. on the 9th of October the 4th and 5th C. M. R. crossed the Canal into Cambrai

The Last Hundred Days

Oct. 9, 1918
on the tail of the retreating Huns, taking a few prisoners and several guns without opposition and establishing an outpost line on the eastern outskirts. The following day the brigade was relieved by Imperial troops and marched back to the Hindenburg line at Inchy-en-Artois, where we remained until the 20th. While here the brigade was visited by the Prince of Wales and inspected by the corps commander.

On the 19th we were informed that the division was to move north and go through the 1st Division, which was at that time following up the retreating enemy. On the 20th the battalion moved by bus to Bruille-lez-Merchiennes; progress was somewhat slow, as mine craters had been blown at crossroads to hinder the advance. We were now among the French civilian population which had felt the iron rule of the Bosche, and a terrible time they had had. The old fellow on whom I was billeted informed me that they had been forced to grow garden truck and cultivate it; when it was fit for use, they had to obtain a permit to gather it and had to pay the Huns for it. If they took any without permission, they were sentenced to not less than fifteen days in solitary confinement. They were also forced to work in the mines, were fed on beets and water and received no pay whatever, and everything, including stock, of any value, had been taken from them.

The 7th and 9th Brigades were now in touch with the enemy and forming the advance guard, with our brigade in support. On the 22nd the battalion moved up to Erre and the next day to Grand Bray. Here again were more signs of Bosche frightfulness, many of the finer houses having been polluted by the filthy Huns.

On the 25th we moved to Hasnon and on the 27th took over the outpost line on the Conde Canal, south of L'Escaut Fleure, along the railway through the north part of Fresnes, from the 42nd Battalion. The inhabitants of Fresnes

Oct. 25, 1918
had been evacuated by the Huns, who here had systematically gone through the most of the houses, smashed up the ornaments and furniture and ripped up the mattresses, evidently searching for money. Wide stretches of water separated us from the enemy, who had blown up all bridges and cut the banks of the canal in several places.

On the 1st of November the 4th Canadian Division commenced their attack on Valenciennes and completed the capture early on the 2nd of November. On the same day the 2nd West Yorks took over our line, and we moved into billets in Raismes prior to taking our share in the advance once more.

On November 4th the 4th and 5th C. M. R. formed the divisional advance guards, and on November 5th we marched through Valenciennes to Onnaing, and going through the right half of the 5th C. M. R. at 4 p.m. continued

Nov. 4, 1918
advancing and pushing in the Bosche rear guard until darkness called a halt. Continuing the advance the following morning along the Mons Road, we attacked and took Quievrechain-Quievrain, on the Franco-Belgium border, with a hundred and seventy-seven

2nd Canadian Mounted Rifles

prisoners and several machine guns, and established a bridge head. A very fine piece of work was here done by Lieut. J. K. Potter and his platoon: pushing rapidly along the road regardless of everything, they reached the crossings of La Honnelle River and, before the enemy knew they were anywhere near, cut the leads to the mines under the bridges and so secured a crossing over which our transport and artillery were later enabled to deploy without delay. In the meantime, while the platoon held the bridge, Potter followed the lead wires another 300 yards and, walking into a house, captured four officers and men who were leisurely preparing to connect the batteries. "A" Company, on our left, was not so fortunate. The 5th C. M. R., in their advance, had run into an impassable morass, leaving the flank of "A" exposed to a galling enfilade fire from machine guns and trench mortars. Captain Lyle and Lieutenant Hereron were killed while leading their men; Lieutenants Blake and Hart kept the situation well in hand, however, and eventually a position along the river was seized and held.

The following day we continued the advance into Belgium and captured the villages of Hensies, La Coix and Montroeuil. In the former village men of "B" Company found the bodies of three young Belgian women who had been murdered by the Huns. During the day's advance Lieutenant McDermid and C. S. M. MacKenzie were mortally wounded and Lieutenant White severely wounded.

On the 8th we made preparations to cross the Mons-Conde Canal, and that night the 5th C. M. R. put over strong patrols, while one patrol of ours crossed in a boat, the Huns having shortly before blown up the bridges and withdrawn. The 7th Brigade now came up and went through on the 9th of November.

On the 10th we marched to Boussu and found the populace greatly excited; crowds met us as, headed by our band playing "Marsellaise," we entered the town, and girls gave us flowers and favours made of Belgian colours. We had very good billets here; the people seemingly could not do enough for us, and we heard the usual stories of Bosche brutality and tyranny.

CHAPTER IX

Armistice and Home

On the 11th the Armistice was signed, but I cannot say that there was any great rejoicing over it among the fighting troops. I think we realized even then that, while we had beaten the enemy to the point of surrender, another two or three months of, for us, comparatively easy warfare would have completely broken him up beyond repair as a fighting machine.

Nov. 11, 1918

On the 12th we marched through crowds of people by way of Jemappe to Mons, where the whole division stayed for the next month, giving and being given receptions and dances, and making many good friends.

On the 11th of December we left Mons with great regret and marched by Hain St. Pierre, Pont-a-Celles and Patard to Ceroux-Mousty, near the Field of Waterloo, where we stayed until December 28th, when we marched by way of Rhode St. Genesse and Lennick St. Quentin to Dottignies, whence in February we moved by train to Havre, from Havre to England and from England to Canada, arriving back in Victoria on a brilliantly sunny April day to meet with a wonderful reception from the townspeople and our comrades who had returned before us.

Dec. 11, 1918
April, 1919

On April 3rd the Battalion ceased to exist, and the members, once more civilians, scattered to their homes.

DECORATIONS

APPENDIX I

Decorations

VICTORIA CROSS
Capt. John MacGregor, M. C., D. C. M., Cambrai, Sept. 29th, 1918.
Major George Randolph Pearkes, while with 5th C.M.R.'s at Passchendaele.

D. S. O.
Major Merril Vincent Allen.
Major William Wasborough Foster.
Lieut.-Col. George Chalmers Johnston.
Major Laurence Walter Miller.
Lieut.-Col. George Randolph Pearkes, while commanding 116th Battalion.

BAR TO D. S. O.
Lieut.-Col. George Chalmers Johnston.
Lieut.-Col. William Wasborough Foster, while in command 52nd Battalion.

2ND BAR TO D. S. O.
Lieut.-Col. William Wasborough Foster, while in command 52nd Battalion.

MILITARY CROSS
Capt. Arthur Chester Armstrong, Battalion Medical Officer, for Vimy Ridge, April 9th, 1917.
Lieut. Graham Cruickshank, Ypres and Somme.
Hon. Capt. Thomas Collins Colwell, Chaplain, Passchendaele, Oct. 30th, 1917.
Lieut. Charles Frederick Hugh Keith Douglas, raid, Nov. 20th and 21st, 1916.
Lieut. James Foord, Mouquet Farm, Sept. 16th and 17th, 1916.
Capt. John Logan Gray, Somme, Sept. 29th, 1916.
Capt. Thomas Godfrey, Vimy Ridge, April 9th, 1917.
Lieut. Frederick Ambler Heather, M. M., raid, Nov. 20th and 21st, 1916.
B. S. M. Howe Hewlett, W. O., Class 1, Passchendaele and Hill 70.
Capt. George Chalmers Johnston, Sanctuary Wood, June 2nd, 1916.
Lieut. Lewis Alexander Kennedy, Somme, Sept. 29th, 1916.
Lieut. John Mavor, Passchendaele, October 24th, 1917.
Lieut. John MacGregor, raid, January 12th, 1918.
Capt. Percy Guy Routh, Brigade Transport Officer, January 1st, 1917.
Lieut. Fernley Smith, raid, March 30th and 31st, 1917.
Lieut. Bernard Shipton, Passchendaele, October 30th, 1917.
Lieut. Frederick Alexander Sprague, raid, April 27th, 1918.
Lieut. Humphrey David Williams, raid, January 12th, 1918.
Lieut. Govan Blake, Quievrechain, November 6th, 1918.

Appendix I—Decorations

Lieut. Richard John Darcus, Cambrai, September 29th, 1918.
Lieut. David Charles Gough, Arras, August 26th, 1918.
Lieut. Lawrence Alfred Goodship, Cambrai, September 29th, 1918.
Lieut. Claude Leighton Hart, Cambrai, September 29th, 1918.
Lieut. John Cunningham Hogg, Cambrai, September 29th, 1918.
Lieut. George Duncan McDermid, Arras, August 26th, 1918.
107425 Cpl. Hugh Christie Manning, raid, November 20th and 21st, 1916.
Capt. George Randolph Pearkes, while with 5th C. M. R.
Lieut. Frederick Pye, Arras, August 26th, 1918.
Lieut. John Keith Potter, Quievrain, November 6th, 1918.
Capt. Gordon Trevor Rant, D. C. M., Le Quesnoy-en-Santerre, August 10, 1918.
Capt. Wesley McConnell Robb, Battalion Medical Officer, Amiens, August 8th to 11th, 1918.
Capt. Alfred Hubert Rowberry, Amiens, 1918.
Lieut. Louis Montague Robbins, Cambrai, September 29th, 1918.
Lieut. Henry Alvin Whitmore, Le Quesnoy-en-Santerre, August 19, 1918.

BAR TO MILITARY CROSS

Capt. John Logan Gray, M. C., Vimy Ridge, April 9th, 1917.
Lieut. Claude Leighton Hart, M. C., Quievrain, November 6th, 1918.
Capt. John MacGregor, V. C., M. C., D. C. M., Quievrain, November 6th, 1918.
Lieut. Frederick Pye, M. C., Quievrain, November 6th, 1918.

DISTINGUISHED CONDUCT MEDAL

107065	Pte. Thomas Napier Armit, raid, November 23rd, 1916.	
107296	L/Cpl. William Hayward, Somme, 1916.	
108311	Pte. Richard Joblin, Somme, September 29th, 1916.	
107425	Cpl. Hugh Christie Manning, raid, November 20th and 21st, 1916.	
116031	Sgt. John MacGregor, Vimy Ridge, April 9th, 1917.	
107409	Battalion Scout Sgt. John Leslie MacCoubrey, Vimy Ridge, April 9th to 11th, 1917.	
180701	Cpl. H. Patterson, Passchendaele, October 30th, 1917.	
107521	Sgt. Gordon Trevor Rant, Mouquet Farm, September 16th and 17th, 1916.	
117515	Signal Sgt. Phillip Rogers, Passchendaele, October 30th, 1917.	
117553	Cpl. John Walter Stevenson, Somme, September 29th, 1916.	
117548	L/Cpl. A. J. Stark, Passchendaele, October 30th, 1917.	
116045	Cpl. Alfred Oscar Swanby, raid, January 12th, 1918.	
107623	Sgt. Henry Alvin Whitmore, Ypres and Somme.	
135342	C. S. M. Alexander Angus, Cambrai, September 29th, 1918.	
135250	Pte. Harold Brooks, Le Quesnoy-en-Santerre, August 10th, 1918.	
108190	C. S. M. William Clarence Dick, Demuin, August 8th, 1918.	
118088	C. S. M. Kenneth McRae, M. M., Le Quesnoy-en-Santerre, August 10th, 1918.	
423374	C. S. M. David McKenzie, M. S. M., Le Quesnoy-en-Santerre, August 10th, 1918.	
107437	Transport Sgt. Robert Stanley Marston, Cambrai and Arras.	
441406	Sgt. William Pilkington, Cambrai, September 29th, 1918.	
161126	L/Cpl. Harry Thomlinson, Arras and Cambrai, 1918.	
107607	Sgt. William Craik Wilson, Arras and Cambrai, 1918.	

BAR TO D. C. M.

116045 Sgt. Alfred Oscar Swanby, D. C. M., Les Quesnoy-en-Santerre, August 10th, 1918.

2nd Canadian Mounted Rifles

MILITARY MEDAL

115006	Cpl. James Todd Armstrong.
107054	Driver Louis Marius Anderson.
50484	Med. L/Sgt. Arthur William Board.
443418	Pte. Thomas Booker.
107076	Sgt. Ralph Berwick.
135428	Pte. Arthur Barrett.
107081	Sgt. William Baverstock.
706693	Pte, James Brown.
108128	C. S. M. John Edward Capstick.
107144	Pte. Arthur Coles.
2056	L/Cpl. Alfred John Castle.
447362	Pte. A. C. Carmichael.
108190	Sgt. J. C. Dick.
464535	Pte. W. Elder.
435524	Pte. James Edwards.
525308	Pte. Horace Wilfred Galbraith.
781964	Cpl. Wesley Garrod.
107254	Sgt. Edwin Martin Gardiner.
107256	L/Cpl. George William Graham.
463641	Sgt. L. A. Goodship.
107276	Sgt. Frederick Ambler Heather.
117303	Cpl. Edward Hives.
107292	Sig. Sgt. William Hayward.
107280	Pte. C. E. Huntley.
687407	Sgt. C. Hereron.
161097	L/Cpl. John Richard Jones.
107356	Cpl. B. Kildahl.
428307	Pte. W. J. Lowe.
108377	Sgt. Wilfred Mellor.
118088	Cpl. Kenneth McRae.
107423	Cpl. P. K. Mowat.
107428	Pte. George S. Maxwell.
116028	Cpl. John Morton.
160945	Cpl. Gustave Marcy.
107478	Sgt. E. Palmer.
441474	Pte. James Pilkington.
687751	Pte. Amelio Pizzolato.
931793	Cpl. Edgar Patrick Rock.
116037	C. S. M. Robert Richman.
107513	Cpl. William John Riley.
441573	Pte. David Rustige.
116091	Pte. Alexander Reid.
107573	Pte. Bernard Shipton.
107532	C. S. M. William Smith.
108527	Pte. William Sharland.
117563	Cpl. Frederick Clarence Strickland.
126363	Pte. Adam Olliver Stevenson.
687616	Pte. F. Spooner.
436599	Pte. E. W. Standing.
135565	L/Cpl. A. Shearer.
463829	Pte. H. Stant.
707191	Cpl. Henry Sivertz.
117646	Sgt. Frederick Garfield Sladen.

Appendix I

135069	L/Cpl.	Louis Tanner.
107642	Pte.	Henry Westlake.
117612	Pte.	C. L. Weaver.
781371	Sgt.	W. O. Wand.
827072	L/Cpl.	A. D. White.
135596	Pte.	George Watson.
435737	L/Cpl.	William Thomas Bennett.
117157	Cpl.	Norman Daniel Bontillier.
116153	Pte.	William Bridgeman.
781021	Pte.	Ernest Belleghem.
2025177	Sgt.	John Brass.
781592	Pte.	John Beattie.
542089	Pte.	William Belmont Batten.
118059	Cpl.	William Daniel Connors.
687090	Sgt.	Frederick Carr.
227681	Cpl.	William John Campbell.
826530	Pte.	James Cumberland.
3313	Pte.	Thomas Miller Dalgleish.
2020211	Pte.	Frederick George Dobie.
707116	L/Cpl.	Claude Deane Freeman.
2025210	L/Cpl.	Wallace Keith Dorman.
116411	Pte.	Charles Stephen Ellis.
931438	Pte.	Thomas Rideout Furneaux.
3032997	Pte.	Jack Feldman.
437405	Pte.	Leslie Forman.
116407	Pte.	Roy Graham.
916241	Cpl.	Frank Gordon Gray.
107306	Sgt.	William Henry Hallmark.
107273	Pte.	Arthur Hayhurst.
781481	Pte.	J. A. Hall.
916035	Pte.	George Francis Johnston.
1027688	Pte.	Albert Warren Jennings.
931818	Pte.	Frederick Kenney.
2142319	Pte.	William McKinley King.
117363	Cpl.	Douglas Lowe.
931819	Pte.	David Lavigeur.
3032965	Pte.	William Luxford.
100569	Sgt.	John Walter Ross McCormick.
2142350	Pte.	Frederick Allen Martin.
116809	Cpl.	Duncan Lothian McGibbon.
443361	Pte.	Peter McDonald.
227651	L/Cpl.	Arthur Mallett.
826560	Pte.	William Maloney.
161007	Sgt.	Alexander McDonald.
931697	Pte.	Duncan Morgan.
116022	Med. Sgt.	John Frank Mahoney.
160087	L/Cpl.	John McKenzie.
931461	L/Cpl.	Alexander Marnoch.
436914	Pte.	John Marshall.
826568	Pte.	Thomas Maley.
931388	Pte.	Sexton James Nicholls.
826019	Cpl.	Stephen O'Connor.
440861	Sgt.	David McHardy Oram.
441367	Pte.	Edwin Pack.

2nd Canadian Mounted Rifles

441896 Sgt. Lawrence James Pybus.
441785 Pte. Maurice Edwin Parsons.
687991 Cpl. Alfred Franklin Paine.
180113 Pte. Robert Palmer.
441466 Sgt. John Edward Ross.
706489 Pte. William George Stewart Riley.
2142329 Pte. Edward Steven Richards.
916644 Pte. Percy Rollins.
916437 Pte. Albert William Reid.
435402 Pte. William Charles Frederick Rhodes.
107506 Pte. Henry Arthur Rogers.
136512 Pte. John James Simpson.
116572 Sgt. John William Shipley.
107539 Sgt. Hartley William Simpson.
116040 Pte. Harold Scott.
464438 Pte. Albert Joseph Soles.
135025 Pte. Norman James Spence.
629443 Pte. Rudolph Simard.
782471 L/Cpl. Bruce Schamahorn.
135231 L/Cpl. James Taylor.
707135 Pte. William Robinson Whitley.
931362 Cpl. Isaac Miller Watson.
447611 Sgt. Benjamin Franklin York.

BAR TO MILITARY MEDAL
118088 Sgt. Kenneth McRae, M. M.
3032997 Pte. Jack Feldman, M. M.
687751 Pte. Amelio Pizzolato, M. M.
916644 Pte. Percy Rollins, M. M.
707191 Cpl. Henry George Sivertz, M. M.

2ND BAR TO MILITARY MEDAL
707191 L/Sgt. Henry George Sivertz, M. M.

MERITORIOUS SERVICE MEDAL
423374 C. S. M. David McKenzie.
107469 S/Sgt. E. C. Partington.

FRENCH CROIX-DE-GUERRE
Capt. Arthur Chester Armstrong, Battalion Medical Officer.
Lieut.-Col. George Chalmers Johnston, Battle of Amiens.
Lieut.-Col. William Wasborough Foster, while in command 52nd Battalion, Battle of Amiens.
Lieut.-Col. George Randolph Pearkes, while in command 116th Battalion. Battle of Amiens.
707254 Pte. Joseph Arundel, battle of Amiens.
916700 Pte. Albert Edward Harwood, battle of Amiens.
687447 Pte. George Francis Elmer Manery, battle of Amiens.
441058 Sig. L/Cpl. Walter Paddle, battle of Amiens.
Lieut. James Rutherford Robertson, battle of Amiens.

BELGIAN CROIX-DE-GUERRE
425517 Pte. E. A. Youngman.
Lieut.-Col. William Wasborough Foster, while in command of 52nd Battalion.
916757 Pte. Norman James Ryan.
107606 C. S. M. D. S. Wright, C. M. G. C.

Appendix I—Decorations

CROSS OF ST. GEORGE, 4TH CLASS (RUSSIAN)

707209 Pte. V. Boskovitch.
107248 Sgt. A. Gillespie.
Capt. F. B. Edwards.

MENTION IN DESPATCHES

Major M. V. Allen, January 2nd, 1916.
108184 C. S. M. William Davidson, April 9th, 1917.
Capt. F. B. Edwards, January 2nd, 1917.
Capt. D. S. Evans, February 21st, 1918.
107234 B. S. M. Thomas Godfrey, June 15th, 1916.
107263 Sgt. D. C. Gough, January 2nd, 1917.
Lieut. G. P. Heinekey, November 7th, 1917.
Lieut.-Col. George Chalmers Johnston, April 9th, 1917, November 7th, 1917, January 2nd, 1917.
687961 L/Cpl. William Lockyer, April 7th, 1918. (Recommended for Posthumous V. C., November 6th, 1917, Passchendaele).
Capt. Lawrence Walter Miller, January 2nd, 1917.
Major Lawrence Walter Miller, January 5th, 1918.
107425 Cpl. Hugh Christie Manning, January 2nd, 1917.
Lieut. P. J. Moran, June 1st, 1917.
107437 Transport Sgt. Robert Stanley Marston, November 7th, 1917.
Lieut. John Impey Monteith, November 7th, 1917.
Capt. Thomas Cameron Penny, November 7th, 1917.
107484 C. S. M. Francis Arthur Pearce, April 7th, 1918.
Lieut. Alfred Hubert Rowberry, April 7th, 1918.
107603 Med. L/Cpl. Ernest Owen White, January 2nd, 1917.
107607 Sgt. James Craik Wilson, April 9th, 1917.
107636 B. S. M. Thomas Crawford Wasson, April 9th, 1917.

APPENDIX II

Honour Roll of Officers, Warrant Officers, N.C.O'S and Men Killed in Action or Died of Wounds

Rank	Name	Killed or Died of Wounds	Place	Date
Capt.	Bell, A. H.	D/W	Meteren	Mar. 16, 1916
Major	Mutrie, R. J.	K	Ypres	Apr. 5, 1916
Capt.	Temple, A.	K	Ypres	Apr. 5, 1916
Lieut.	Fennell, T. H.	K	Hooge	May 17, 1916
Lieut.	Berkinshaw, E. L.	K	Santuary Wood	June 3, 1916
Lieut.	Audy, P. J. T.	K	Ypres	July 28, 1916
Lieut.	Quanbury, J. H.	D/W	Santuary Wood	Aug. 14, 1916
Lieut.	Morrison, D.	K	Mouquet Farm	Sept. 16, 1916
Lieut.	Jefferson, C.	K	Hessian Trench	Sept. 30, 1916
Lieut.	Temple, C. C.	K		
Lieut.	Dunk, S.	K	Hessian Trench	Oct. 1, 1916
Lieut.	Saunders, C. G.	K	Hessian Trench	Oct. 11, 1916
Lieut.	Pue, W. H.	D/W	Sudbury Trench	Oct. 15, 1916
Major	Moncrieff, N. H.	D/W	Sudbury Trench	Nov. 18, 1916
Lieut.	Brichta, G. J. O.	K	(Attacher R.F.C.)	Mar. 6, 1917
Lieut.	Christie, J. H. H.	K	Vimy Ridge (Attack)	Apl. 9, 1917
Lieut.	Heather, F. A., M.C. M.M.	K	Vimy Ridge (Attack)	Apl. 9, 1917
Lieut.	Pimm, A. G.	D/W	Vimy Ridge (Attack)	Apl. 9, 1917
Lieut.	Spinks, R. C.	K	Vimy Ridge (Attack)	Apl. 10, 1917
Lieut.	Steer, C. P.	K	Vimy Ridge	May 22, 1917
Major	Foord, J., M.C.	K	Passchendaele	Oct. 28, 1917
Major	Cameron, D. U.	K	Passchendaele	Oct. 30, 1917
Lieut.	Martin, J. J.	K	Passchendaele	Oct. 30, 1917
Lieut.	Shipton, B., M.C., M.M.	D/W	Passchendaele	Nov. 2, 1917
Lieut.	Wilson, W. J.	D/W	N. E. of Loos	Dec. 31, 1917
Lieut.	Apps, C.	D/W	N. E. of Loos	Jan. 2, 1918
Lieut.	Bowen, H. T.	D/W	N. E. of Loos	Jan. 2, 1918
Lieut.	Griffiths, G. H.	K	Demuin	Aug. 8, 1918
Capt.	Whitlow, F. M.	K	Le Quesnoy	Aug. 10, 1918
Lieut.	Hanna, D. B.	K	Le Quesnoy	Aug. 10, 1918
Lieut.	Palmer, B. M.	D/W	Le Quesnoy	Aug. 10, 1918
Major	Van Kleeck, S. B.	K	Cambrai	Sept. 29, 1918
Lieut.	Trees, C. F.	K	Cambrai	Sept. 29, 1918
Lieut.	Langhorne, F. H.	K	Cambrai	Sept. 29, 1918
Lieut.	Harris, F. W.	K	Cambrai	Sept. 29, 1918
Lieut.	Cook, J.	K	Cambrai	Sept. 29, 1918
Lieut.	Francis, A.	K	Cambrai	Sept. 29, 1918
Capt.	Lyle, H. S., M.C.	K	Quievrain	Nov. 6, 1918
Lieut.	Hereron, C., M.M.	K	Quievrain	Nov. 6, 1918
Lieut.	McDermid, G. D., M.C.	D/W	Quievrain	Nov. 7, 1918

Appendix II—Killed or Died of Wounds

No.	Rank	Name	Killed or Died of Wounds	Place	Date
					1915
107436	C.S.M.	Marshall, J. T.	K	Dickiebusch	Oct. 7
107450	Pte.	Marshall, B. R.	D/W	Dickiebusch	Oct. 8
107645	Pte.	Woodward, W. H.	D/W	Dickiebusch	Oct. 8
116021	Pte.	Leather, H. J. O.	K	Irish Farm	Dec. 1
					1916
108623	Pte.	White, W. P.	K	Red Lodge	Feb. 3
108488	Pte.	Rivett, J.	K	Red Lodge	Feb. 4
108084	Pte.	Bartlett, J.	D/W	Red Lodge	Feb. 5
107102	Cpl.	Bayntun, A.	K	Hooge	Mar. 24
423076	Pte.	McAuslan, J. T.	K	Hooge	Mar. 24
107632	Pte.	Wright, C. H.	D/W	Hooge	Mar. 24
107595	Pte.	Vaughan, F. H.	D/W	Hooge	Mar. 25
108497	Pte.	Robinson, J.	D/W	Hooge	Mar. 25
107546	Pte.	Speeden, R.	D/W	Hooge	Mar. 25
442933	Pte.	Bard, H. A.	K	Hooge	Mar. 26
107172	Pte.	Coleman, C.	D/W	Hooge	Mar. 26
442939	Pte.	Bere, R.	D/W	Hooge	Mar. 27
107537	Pte.	Sharp, W. A.	K	Hooge	Mar. 27
107629	Pte.	Wood, E. F.	K	Hooge	Apr. 4
107290	Pte.	Hatcher, J. M.	D/W	Sanctuary Wood	Apr. 5
7761	Pte.	French, C.	K	Sanctuary Wood	Apr. 23
435484	Pte.	Beaton, A.	D/W	Sanctuary Wood	Apr. 23
117547	Pte.	Stanton, A. S.	K	Sanctuary Wood	Apr. 25
117144	Pte.	Adkins, W. J.	K	Sanctuary Wood	Apr. 26
116007	Pte.	Dunlop, E.	D/W	Sanctuary Wood	Apr. 26
107556	Pte.	Silsby, C. J.	K	Sanctuary Wood	Apr. 26
107474	Pte.	Pangbourne, G.	D/W	Sanctuary Wood	Apr. 26
107635	C.S.M.	Worrall, J.	K	Sanctuary Wood	Apr. 26
117243	Pte.	Farquhar, D. B.	K	Sanctuary Wood	Apr. 26
117342	Pte.	Knott, A. R.	K	Sanctuary Wood	Apr. 26
107617	Cpl.	Wright, W.	D/W	Sanctuary Wood	Apr. 29
117380	Pte.	McDermot, J. G.	K	Ypres	May 5
107340	Sgt.	Joyce, J. P.	K	Hooge	May 6
117399	Pte.	McQuinn, N.	K	Hooge	May 16
117444	Pte.	Nethercott, H. A.	K	Hooge	May 16
117534	L/Cpl.	Sinnott, E. E.	K	Hooge	May 17
107577	Pte.	Somerset, B.	K	Hooge	May 17
442356	Pte.	Crook, W.	K	Hooge	May 17
117233	Pte.	Duke, C. W.	K	Hooge	May 19
107447	Pte.	Moir, D. N.	K	Hooge	May 20
117146	Pte.	Black, W. B.	D/W	Hooge	May 22
443686	Pte.	Barnes, F. V.	D/W	Sanctuary Wood	June 2
117250	Pte.	Frankish, J. G.	K	Maple Copse	June 3
117609	Pte.	Watson, J.	K	Sanctuary Wood	June 3
463201	Pte.	Ward, A.	K	Sanctuary Wood	June 3
108225	Pte.	Fleming, W.	K	Sanctuary Wood	June 3
117418	Pte.	Massender, R.	K	Sanctuary Wood	June 3
423872	Pte.	Bjerke, K. O.	K	Sanctuary Wood	June 3
117121	Pte.	Bailey, P. M.	K	Sanctuary Wood	June 3
117139	Pte.	Berry, L.	K	Sanctuary Wood	June 3
108103	Pte.	Bland, W. G.	K	Sanctuary Wood	June 3

2nd Canadian Mounted Rifles

No.	Rank	Name	Killed or Died of Wounds	Place	Date
					1916
117313	Pte.	Horne, F. J.	K	Sanctuary Wood	June 2
107144	Pte.	Coles, A.	D/W	Sanctuary Wood	June 3
117212	Pte.	Crees, R.	K	Sanctuary Wood	June 3
107175	Pte.	Crerar, R.	K	Sanctuary Wood	June 3
435023	Pte.	Foster, E.	K	Sanctuary Wood	June 3
117252	Pte.	Froment, W. J.	K	Sanctuary Wood	June 3
117254	Pte.	Garvin, F.	D/W	Sanctuary Wood	June 3
115026	Cpl.	Hamilton, A.	K	Sanctuary Wood	June 3
107313	Pte.	Hindle, C. S.	D/W	Sanctuary Wood	June 3
107298	Sgt.	Holland, J. J.	K	Sanctuary Wood (Bde. M. G.)	June 3
436834	Pte.	Miller, D.	K	Sanctuary Wood	June 3
117432	Pte.	Moore, L.	K	Sanctuary Wood	June 3
108394	Pte.	Monkman, T. N.	D/W	Sanctuary Wood	June 8
447456	Pte.	McFarlane, J. W.	K	Sanctuary Wood	June 3
117384	Pte.	McFayden, R. S.	K	Sanctuary Wood	June 3
117385	Pte.	McGarrity, D. P.	K	Sanctuary Wood	June 3
117386	Pte.	McGlashan, H. D.	K	Sanctuary Wood	June 3
117394	Pte.	McLennan, J. D.	K	Sanctuary Wood	June 3
463148	Pte.	Newnham, J.	D/W	Sanctuary Wood	June 6
108455	Pte.	Patterson, A. C.	K	Sanctuary Wood	June 3
117468	Cpl.	Patterson, L.	K	Sanctuary Wood	June 3
117491	Pte.	Quantz, D.	K	Sanctuary Wood	June 3
425280	Pte.	Russell, L. C.	K	Sanctuary Wood	June 3
107522	Pte.	Ritchie, D. V.	K	Sanctuary Wood	June 3
463172	Pte.	Redfern, A.	K	Sanctuary Wood	June 3
463578	Pte.	Stronach, A.	K	Sanctuary Wood	June 3
422909	Pte.	Sturgeon, J. H.	D/W	Sanctuary Wood	June 3
463901	Pte.	Thomas, G. A.	K	Sanctuary Wood	June 3
107615	L/Cpl.	Ward, A. E.	K	Sanctuary Wood	June 3
425507	Pte.	Wren, R. E.	K	Sanctuary Wood	June 3
107243	Pte.	Gynne, W.	D/W	Sanctuary Wood	June 4
117340	Pte.	Knight, C. H.	D/W	Sanctuary Wood, Maple Copse	June 4
107615	L/Cpl.	Wilson, D. J.	D/W	Sanctuary Wood	June 5
107083	Pte.	Bessett, C. J.	D/W	Sanctuary Wood	June 7
107533	L/Sgt.	Stillingfleet, H.	D/W	Sanctuary Wood	June 8
107644	Pte.	Wheatley, S.	D/W	Sanctuary Wood	June 8
117150	Pte.	Blake, J. A. T.	D/W	Sanctuary Wood	June 16
117606	Pte.	Warren, D. S.	D/W	Sanctuary-Wood	June 19
107312	Sgt.	Hilliard, G. E.	K	Sanctuary Wood	June 27
107080	Cpl.	Barr, P. S.	K	Sanctuary Wood	July 9
442677	Pte.	Gregory, J. P.	K	Sanctuary Wood	July 25
442902	Pte.	Lee, E. J.	K	Sanctuary Wood	July 27
441820	Pte.	Patterson, J.	K	Sanctuary Wood	July 27
116024	Pte.	Montgomery, W. T.	K	Sanctuary Wood	July 28
117638	Pte.	Davies, A. C. W.	D/W	Sanctuary Wood	July 29
464407	Pte.	Andrew, J.	D/W	Sanctuary Wood	Aug. 1
135584	Pte.	Tanner, J.	K	The Bluff	Aug. 2
117350	Pte.	Leckie, W.	K	The Bluff	Aug. 12
135884	Pte.	Tomlinson, J.	K	The Bluff	Aug. 12

Appendix II—Killed or Died of Wounds

No.	Rank	Name	Killed or Died of Wounds	Place	Date
					1916
117506	Pte.	Roberts, G.	D/W	The Bluff	Aug. 14
135859	Cpl.	Sutton, A. N.	K	The Bluff	Aug. 16
434229	Pte.	Cooke, A.	K	The Bluff	Aug. 18
117635	Pte.	Wormald, J. W.	D/W	The Bluff	Aug. 19
117106	Pte.	Allan, J.	D/W	The Bluff	Aug. 20
441304	Pte.	Noakes, H. N.	K	The Bluff	Aug. 22
425305	Pte.	Sexsmith, W.	K	The Bluff	Aug. 22
135958	Sgt.	Brown, H. J.	K	Pozieres T., Mouquet Fm.	Sept. 12
463960	Sgt.	Campbell, R.	K	Pozieres T., Mouquet Fm.	Sept. 12
118074	Pte.	Killip, R. H.	D/W	Pozieres T., Mouquet Fm.	Sept. 12
117398	Pte.	McNamara, H. L.	K	Pozieres T., Mouquet Fm.	Sept. 12
117565	Pte.	Strachan, D.	K	Pozieres T., Mouquet Fm.	Sept. 13
117253	Pte.	Gaffney, W. H.	D/W	Pozieres T., Mouquet Fm.	Sept. 14
117290	Pte.	Hawkes, S. T.	D/W	Pozieres T., Mouquet Fm.	Sept. 14
135106	Cpl.	Brackett, C. A.	D/W	Pozieres T., Mouquet Fm.	Sept. 15
107171	Pte.	Chapman, F.	K	Pozieres T., Mouquet Fm.	Sept. 16
107164	L/Cpl.	Cross, C. H.	K	Pozieres T., Mouquet Fm.	Sept. 16
435809	Pte.	Edwards, W. B.	K	Pozieres T., Mouquet Fm.	Sept. 16
117335	Pte.	Kerstens, A. B.	K	Pozieres T., Mouquet Fm.	Sept. 16
112255	Pte.	Matthews, H. C.	K	Pozieres T., Mouquet Fm.	Sept. 16
116023	L/Cpl.	Meaney, J.	K	Pozieres T., Mouquet Fm.	Sept. 16
117392	Cpl.	McKay, P. A.	K	Pozieres T., Mouquet Fm.	Sept. 16
442541	Pte.	McIntosh, W.	K	Pozieres T., Mouquet Fm.	Sept. 16
107401	Cpl.	McEwan, A.	K	Pozieres T., Mouquet Fm.	Sept. 16
425198	Pte.	Pegg, Geo.	K	Pozieres T., Mouquet Fm.	Sept. 16
441748	Pte.	Palmer, E.	K	Pozieres T., Mouquet Fm.	Sept. 16
425261	Pte.	Robertson, J. M.	K	Pozieres T., Mouquet Fm.	Sept. 16
135883	Pte.	Trotter, E.	K	Pozieres T., Mouquet Fm.	Sept. 16
135886	Pte.	Twaddle, J.	K	Pozieres T., Mouquet Fm.	Sept. 16
464547	L/Sgt.	Boult, E. G.	D/W	Pozieres T., Mouquet Fm.	Sept. 17
117584	Cpl.	Thompson, J. R.	D/W	Pozieres T., Mouquet Fm.	Sept. 17
107069	Pte.	Anson, R. N.	D/W	Pozieres T., Mouquet Fm.	Sept. 18
135651	Pte.	Bell, H. D.	K	Bouzincourt (wk. party)	Sept. 24
127324	Pte.	Bridge, A. S.	D/W	Bouzincourt	Sept. 24
435819	Pte.	Fraser, A. L.	K	Bouzincourt	Sept. 24
136585	L/Cpl.	Spearing, E. J.	D/W	Bouzincourt	Sept. 24
107593	Pte.	Thompson, H. G.	D/W	Bouzincourt	Sept. 24
126209	Pte.	Black, J. A.	D/W	Bouzincourt	Sept. 25
115029	Pte.	Harper, H. J.	D/W	Bouzincourt	Sept. 25
117604	Pte.	Stephens, W.	D/W	Bouzincourt (wk. party)	Sept. 25
434634	Pte.	Treloar, P. G.	K	Hessian Trench	Sept. 29
136243	Pte.	Unthank, R. D.	K	Hessian Trench	Sept. 29
135598	Pte.	Watt, W.	K	Hessian Trench	Sept. 29
107608	Pte.	Waite, W.	K	Hessian Trench	Sept. 29
422813	Pte.	Tessier, A.	K	Hessian Trench	Sept. 30
136609	Pte.	Tory, J. F.	K	Hessian Trench	Sept. 30
446401	Pte.	Trigg, C.	D/W	Hessian Trench	Sept. 30
127029	L/Cpl.	Toms, W. G.	K	Hessian Trench	Sept. 30
135591	Pte.	Veater, L.	K	Hessian Trench	Sept. 30
435728	Pte.	Woods, P.	K	Hessian Trench	Oct. 1
117145	Pte.	Atkinson, G. S.	K	Courcellette	Oct. 9

2nd Canadian Mounted Rifles

No.	Rank	Name	Killed or Died of Wounds	Place	Date
					1916
425293	Pte.	Scott, J. R.	D/W	Hessian Tr. and Somme	Sept. 16
442558	Pte.	Cavallero, E.	K	Hessian Trench	Sept. 28
136200	Pte.	Brown, H. J.	K	Hessian Trench	Sept. 28
464025	Pte.	Axon, C.	K	Hessian Trench	Sept. 28
446450	A.L./Sgt.	Ebden, T. J.	K	Hessian Trench	Sept. 28
117292	A/Cpl.	Heatley, T.	K	Hessian Trench	Sept. 28
107426	Pte.	Mason, P. S.	K	Hessian Trench	Sept. 28
117420	Pte.	Mitchie, A.	K	Hessian Trench	Sept. 28
107432	Pte.	Montgomery, D.	K	Hessian Trench	Sept. 28
117310	A/Sgt.	Hood, T.	K	Hessian Trench	Sept. 29
117123	Pte.	Baker, F.	K	Hessian Trench	Sept. 29
136275	Pte.	Barnes, W. E.	K	Hessian Trench	Sept. 29
117133	Pte.	Beckett, G.	K	Hessian Trench	Sept. 29
15115	L/Cpl.	Doyle, G.	K	Hessian Trench	Sept. 29
108323	Pte.	Keynes, R.	K	Hessian Trench	Sept. 29
161157	Pte.	McDonald, J.	K	Hessian Trench	Sept. 29
118085	Pte.	McEwan, A.	K	Hessian Trench	Sept. 29
464146	L/Cpl.	McKay, J. S.	K	Hessian Trench	Sept. 29
117442	Pte.	Nelson, J.	K	Hessian Trench	Sept. 29
464677	Pte.	Norris, L. H.	K	Hessian Trench	Sept. 29
58125	Pte.	Ouimet, P. A.	K	Hessian Trench	Sept. 29
464232	Pte.	Riley, J.	K	Hessian Trench	Sept. 29
425279	Pte.	Russell, J. E.	K	Hessian Trench	Sept. 29
159599	Pte.	Sokoloski, V.	D/W	Hessian Trench	Sept. 29
180609	Pte.	Doman, P.	K	Hessian Trench	Sept. 30
135415	Pte.	Agnew, R.	K	Hessian Trench	Sept. 30
135639	Sgt.	Armitage, S.	K	Hessian Trench	Sept. 30
135092	Pte.	Armstrong, G.	K	Hessian Trench	Sept. 30
135635	Pte.	Atkinson, T. S.	K	Hessian Trench	Sept. 30
117128	Pte.	Barss, H. E.	K	Hessian Trench	Sept. 30
463954	Pte.	Brown, R. R.	K	Hessian Trench	Sept. 30
464557	L/Cpl.	Joussiffe, E.	K	Hessian Trench	Sept. 30
117330	Pte.	Keating, B. T.	D/W	Hessian Trench	Sept. 30
107349	Pte.	Kermode, W. H.	K	Hessian Trench	Sept. 30
108377	C.S.M.	Mellor, W.	K	Hessian Trench	Sept. 30
160963	Pte.	Murray, J.	K	Hessian Trench	Sept. 30
117523	Pte.	Scott, J.	D/W	Hessian Trench	Sept. 30
107565	Pte.	Shiers, J.	D/W	Hessian Trench	Oct. 1
107163	Pte.	Crooks, W. D.	K	Hessian Trench	Oct. 2
117624	A/Sgt.	Whittle, E.	K	Hessian Trench	Oct. 2
160635	Pte.	Haggett, R. R.	K	Hessian Trench	Oct. 2
57550	L/Cpl.	Harris, H. E.	K	Hessian Trench	Oct. 2
447590	Pte.	Martin, W. A.	K	Hessian Trench	Oct. 2
441311	L/Cpl.	Pateman, E.	K	Hessian Trench	Oct. 2
126882	Pte.	Shaw, J.	K	Hessian Trench	Oct. 2
136642	Pte.	Shedlock, C.	K	Hessian Trench	Oct. 2
126552	Pte.	Sheehan, J. W.	K	Hessian Trench	Oct. 2
700092	Pte.	Dahlbury, O.	D/W	Hessian Trench	Oct. 4
425314	Pte.	Silcox, C.	K	Somme	Oct. 9
434310	Pte.	Foster, J.	K	Somme	Oct. 9
446023	Pte.	Slipp, L. L.	K	Somme	Oct. 12

Appendix II—Killed or Died of Wounds

No.	Rank	Name	Killed or Died of Wounds	Place	Date
					1916
180661	Pte.	Parker, S.	K	Somme	Oct. 9
107558	Sgt.	Smith, A. S.	D/W	Hessian Tr. and Somme	Oct. 12
446421	Pte.	Tabbener, A. J.	K	Hessian Tr. and Somme	Oct. 12
463194	Pte.	Urquhart, J. W.	K	Hessian Tr. and Somme	Oct. 13
447434	Pte.	Stain, M.	K	Somme	Oct. 10
135098	Pte.	Barlow, C.	K	Somme	Oct. 10
447543	Pte.	Stevens, J. P.	K	Hession Tr. and Somme	Oct. 10
441053	Pte.	Pickard, A.	D/W	Somme	Oct. 10
161152	Pte.	Reid, J. S.	K	Somme	Oct. 10
440149	Sgt.	Robinson, A. J.	D/W	Somme	Oct. 10
117577	Pte.	Stewart, A.	K	Somme	Oct. 11
434470	Pte.	Hill, W.	K	Somme	Oct. 11
107180	A/Cpl.	Duncan, J.	D/W	Somme	Oct. 12
442705	Pte.	Kennedy, P. N.	D/W	Somme	Oct. 12
701224	Pte.	McAdam, R.	K	Somme	Oct. 12
135442	Pte.	Brown, A.	K	Somme	Oct. 13
161226	Pte.	Nicholls, E. S.	K	Somme	Oct. 13
441570	Pte.	Rodgers, J. J.	K	Somme	Oct. 13
441065	Pte.	Read, E. C.	D/W	Somme	Oct. 13
107383	Sgt.	McCarvell, J. J.	D/W	Somme	Oct. 22
422801	Pte.	Edwards, A. W.	K	Roclincourt	Oct. 22
135858	Pte.	Setford, A.	K	Roclincourt	Nov. 4
113017	Pte.	Gervin, W.	D/W	Roclincourt	Dec. 18
117405	C.S.M.	Mainwaring, J.	K	Roclincourt	Nov. 19
136438	L/Cpl.	Enright, W. J.	K	Roclincourt	Nov. 19
440191	Pte.	Pritchard, R. S.	D/W	Roclincourt	Nov. 21
443270	L/Cpl.	Knox, F. V.	K	Roclincourt	Nov. 21
425326	Pte.	Slater, W. P.	D/W	Roclincourt	Nov. 25
464571	Pte.	Dollamore, A. R.	K	Roclincourt	Dec. 1
117460	Pte.	Parker, G.	K	Roclincourt	Dec. 5
180106	Pte.	Moar, W.	D/W	Roclincourt	Dec. 13
117226	Pte.	Dickens, J. W.	D/W	Roclincourt	Dec. 18
135581	Cpl.	Sutherland, J. C.	K	Roclincourt	Dec. 15
781435	Pte.	Robertson, L. S.	K	Roclincourt	Dec. 24
435524	Pte.	Edwards, J.	D/W	Roclincourt	Dec. 25
					1917
117583	L/Cpl.	Harker-Thomas, B. B.	K	Roclincourt	Jan. 1
136639	Pte.	Barnaby, F.	D/W	Mt. St. Eloy	Feb. 1
227712	A.L/Cpl.	Cavanagh, T.	K	Vimy Ridge	Mar. 22
781099	Pte.	Garroch, P.	K	Vimy Ridge	Mar. 22
707096	Pte.	Arden, J. A. P.	K	Vimy Ridge	Mar. 22
781038	Pte.	Burchmore, W. F.	K	Vimy Ridge	Mar. 27
116639	Pte.	Groves, R. E.	K	Vimy Ridge	Mar. 27
782354	Pte.	Holt, J. E.	K	Vimy Ridge	Mar. 27
422749	Pte.	McKay, R. M.	K	Vimy Ridge (raid)	Mar. 31
117109	Sgt.	Allen, F.	K	Vimy Ridge	Mar. 31
781992	Pte.	Huff, P.	K	Vimy Ridge	Mar. 31
781808	Pte.	Hopkins, W.	K	Vimy Ridge	Mar. 31
782330	Pte.	Poole, A.	K	Vimy Ridge	Mar. 31
782220	Pte.	Deeprose, J. A.	K	Vimy Ridge	Mar. 31

2nd Canadian Mounted Rifles

No.	Rank	Name	Killed or Died of Wounds	Place	Date
					1917
687786	Pte.	Wain, A. L.	K	Vimy Ridge	Mar. 31
706523	Pte.	Allard, F.	K	Vimy Ridge (attack)	Apr. 9
227750	Pte.	Adams, C. E.	K	Vimy Ridge (attack)	Apr. 9
687245	Pte.	Adams, L. V.	K	Vimy Ridge (attack)	Apr. 9
136274	Pte.	Anthony, J. F.	K	Vimy Ridge (attack)	Apr. 9
437797	Pte.	Banks, E.	K	Vimy Ridge (attack)	Apr. 9
135971	Pte.	Bartle, F. J.	K	Vimy Ridge (attack)	Apr. 9
136637	Pte.	Binsley, E.	K	Vimy Ridge (attack)	Apr. 9
227635	Pte.	Borrow, C.	K	Vimy Ridge (attack)	Apr. 9
116004	Pte.	Bunce, W.	D/W	Vimy Ridge (attack)	Apr. 9
447536	Pte.	Byers, M. V.	K	Vimy Ridge (attack)	Apr. 9
781755	Pte.	Nixon, W. A.	K	Vimy Ridge (attack)	Apr. 9
117176	L/Cpl.	Campbell, D. A.	K	Vimy Ridge (attack)	Apr. 9
781381	Pte.	Clark, C. F.	K	Vimy Ridge (attack)	Apr. 9
180601	Pte.	Clark, F.	K	Vimy Ridge (attack)	Apr. 9
707067	Pte.	Coddington, A. D.	K	Vimy Ridge (attack)	Apr. 9
116913	Pte.	Carlson, C.	K	Vimy Ridge (attack)	Apr. 9
116895	Pte.	Elliott, J.	K	Vimy Ridge (attack)	Apr. 9
183651	Pte.	Gilchrist, W.	K	Vimy Ridge (attack)	Apr. 9
227711	Pte.	Gray, F.	K	Vimy Ridge (attack)	Apr. 9
116823	Pte.	Harwood, G. A.	K	Vimy Ridge (attack)	Apr. 9
706556	Pte.	Hickman, E.	K	Vimy Ridge (attack)	Apr. 9
707102	Pte.	Jones, F.	K	Vimy Ridge (attack)	Apr. 9
447499	Pte.	Landry, W.	K	Vimy Ridge (attack)	Apr. 9
701275	Pte.	Loaring, H. L.	D/W	Vimy Ridge (attack)	Apr. 9
782227	Pte.	Loughrey, J.	K	Vimy Ridge (attack)	Apr. 9
688133	Pte.	McBeath, W.	K	Vimy Ridge (attack)	Apr. 9
116787	Pte.	McKenzie, J. G.	K	Vimy Ridge (attack)	Apr. 9
414307	Pte.	McNeil, A.	K	Vimy Ridge (attack)	Apr. 9
688214	Pte.	McPhail, J.	K	Vimy Ridge (attack)	Apr. 9
440142	Pte.	Ogilvie, R.	K	Vimy Ridge (attack)	Apr. 9
117501	L/Sgt.	Richards, W.	K	Vimy Ridge (attack)	Apr. 9
116039	L/Cpl.	Rooney, T. J.	K	Vimy Ridge (attack)	Apr. 9
706526	Pte.	Roberts, E.	K	Vimy Ridge (attack)	Apr. 9
464166	L/Cpl.	Spears, T. N.	K	Vimy Ridge (attack)	Apr. 9
782052	Pte.	Stemp, H. C.	K	Vimy Ridge (attack)	Apr. 9
118810	Pte.	Stevenson, H. A.	K	Vimy Ridge (attack)	Apr. 9
108570	Pte.	Tammeros, L.	K	Vimy Ridge (attack)	Apr. 9
687665	Pte.	Tyers, S.	K	Vimy Ridge (attack)	Apr. 9
117597	Cpl.	Usherwood, A. E.	K	Vimy Ridge (attack)	Apr. 9
706126	Pte.	Walton, A.	K	Vimy Ridge (attack)	Apr. 9
227661	Pte.	Cadwallader, L. J.	K	Vimy Ridge (attack)	Apr. 10
136305	Pte.	Barber, E.	K	Vimy Ridge (attack)	Apr. 10
687034	Pte.	Caldwell, D. J.	K	Vimy Ridge (attack)	Apr. 10
706697	Pte.	Casey, J.	K	Vimy Ridge (attack)	Apr. 10
2060	Pte.	Craig, W. C.	K	Vimy Ridge (attack)	Apr. 10
781461	Pte.	Dalgleish, W. O.	K	Vimy Ridge (attack)	Apr. 10
781085	Pte.	Elliott, A. F. B.	K	Vimy Ridge (attack)	Apr. 10
781567	Pte.	Gallagher, L.	K	Vimy Ridge (attack)	Apr. 10
700975	Pte.	Hamilton, G. B.	K	Vimy Ridge (attack)	Apr. 10
107337	Sgt.	Jacobs, R. H.	K	Vimy Ridge (attack)	Apr. 10

Appendix II—Killed or Died of Wounds

No.	Rank	Name	Killed or Died of Wounds	Place	Date
					1917
687671	Pte.	Johnston, H. J.	K	Vimy Ridge (attack)	Apr. 10
108334	Pte.	Lang, H. J.	K	Vimy Ridge (attack)	Apr. 10
782326	Pte.	Lindsay, W. S.	K	Vimy Ridge (attack)	Apr. 10
442600	Pte.	Mason, E. H.	K	Vimy Ridge (attack)	Apr. 10
706475	Pte.	Maynard, F. H.	K	Vimy Ridge (attack)	Apr. 10
706906	Pte.	McKeon, P.	K	Vimy Ridge (attack)	Apr. 10
781553	Pte.	Oliver, J.	K	Vimy Ridge (attack)	Apr. 10
832528	Pte.	Parkinson, J.	K	Vimy Ridge (attack)	Apr. 10
464063	Pte.	Rosie, M.	K	Vimy Ridge (attack)	Apr. 10
781452	Pte.	Russell, W. H.	K	Vimy Ridge (attack)	Apr. 10
781383	Pte.	Walker, G.	K	Vimy Ridge (attack)	Apr. 10
706912	Pte.	Watkins, A. D. J.	D/W	Vimy Ridge (attack)	Apr. 10
116735	Pte.	Turnill, E. S.	K	Vimy Ridge (attack)	Apr. 11
781437	Pte.	Thompson, A. E.	D/W	Vimy Ridge (attack)	Apr. 11
706161	Pte.	Carley, S. W.	D/W	Vimy Ridge (attack)	Apr. 12
447552	Pte.	Brown, A.	D/W	Vimy Ridge (attack)	Apr. 13
136376	Pte.	Self, T. W.	D/W	Vimy Ridge (attack)	Apr. 13
116381	Pte.	Murray, A. (alias McGuire, J. A.)	D/W	Vimy Ridge (attack)	Apr. 17
252040	Sgt.	Cameron, L. R.	D/W	Vimy Ridge (attack)	Apr. 17
707211	Pte.	Lipscombe, C. H.	D/W	Vimy Ridge (attack	Apr. 18
116032	Pte.	McGuckie, J.	D/W	Vimy Ridge (attack)	Apr. 22
127257	Pte.	Stubbins, H.	D/W	Vimy Ridge (attack)	May 7
423373	Sgt.	Philip, T.	D/W	Vimy Ridge (attack)	May 8
782045	Pte.	Agar, R. J.	D/W	Vimy Ridge (attack)	Apr. 9
781769	Pte.	Grosart, J.	D/W	Vimy Ridge (attack)	May 12
688217	Pte.	Kennedy, A. D.	D/W	Vimy Ridge (attack)	May 19
135988	Pte.	Bridges, H. B.	D/W	Vimy Ridge (attack)	May 1
706468	Pte.	Duffield, J.	D/W	Vimy Ridge	May 22
781487	Pte.	Padgett, J. R.	K	Vimy Ridge	May 22
136440	Pte.	Vandervoort, S. W.	D/W	Vimy Ridge	May 25
443418	Cpl.	Booker, T.	D/W	Vimy Ridge	June 1
931431	Pte.	Leyland, J.	K	Vimy Ridge	June 2
931051	Pte.	Peet, W.	K	Vimy Ridge	June 2
931372	Pte.	Thorburn, W. A.	K	Vimy Ridge	June 2
688004	Pte.	Foster, H.	D/W	Vimy Ridge	June 6
442384	Pte.	Gold, A. E.	D/W	Villers-au-Bois (accidental)	June 16
931278	Pte.	Thompson, R. E.	K	Vimy Ridge	June 18
781262	Pte.	Smith, R.	K	Vimy Ridge	June 18
707153	Pte.	Penwell, S. J.	K	Vimy Ridge	June 19
116046	Pte.	Sullivan, M.	K	Vimy Ridge	June 19
826665	Pte.	Balcarras, J.	K	Vimy Ridge	June 20
826145	Pte.	McGuire, W.	K	Vimy Ridge	June 24
80128	Pte.	Lyon, I. H.	K	Avion	July 13
826041	Pte.	Dransfield, H.	K	Avion	July 13
826063	Pte.	Clifford, G.	K	Avion	July 16
931843	Pte.	Taylor, H. J.	D/W	Avion	July 17
687809	Pte.	Watt, J. A.	D/W	Avion	July 17
826989	Pte.	Gurling, S. R.	K	Avion	July 18
826088	Pte.	Cooke, J.	D/W	Avion	July 20
135653	Pte.	Bibby, W. G.	K	Loos	Aug. 21

2nd Canadian Mounted Rifles

No.	Rank	Name	Killed or Died of Wounds	Place	Date
					1917
931411	Pte.	Appleby, J.	K	Loos	Aug. 22
931560	Pte.	Deverell, G. H.	K	Loos	Aug. 22
931074	Pte.	Sampson, C.	K	Loos	Aug. 24
827040	Pte.	Brown, J.	K	Loos	Aug. 24
826901	Pte.	Dysart, G. H.	K	Loos	Aug. 24
441139	Pte.	Mourant, A.	K	Loos	Aug. 24
117406	Sgt.	Major, D.	K	Loos	Aug. 25
687505	Cpl.	Skerton, W. H.	K	Loos	Aug. 25
707199	Pte.	Gatti, C.	K	Loos	Aug. 25
781122	Pte.	Heslop, J. W.	D/W	Loos	Aug. 25
136139	Pte.	Smith, W. H.	D/W	Loos	Aug. 27
826086	Pte.	Bonach, J. O. S.	D/W	Loos	Aug. 31
108145	Sgt.	Chapman, W. J.	D/W	Ferfay (accdt)	Sept. 3
931731	Pte.	Yates, A.	D/W	Mericourt	Sept. 5
160813	Sgt.	Huggins, C. O.	K	Mericourt	Sept. 6
707138	Pte.	Stewart, L.	K	Mericourt	Sept. 6
706586	Pte.	McNeil, F. G.	D/W	Caucourt (accdt)	Oct. 9
464098	Pte.	Hughes, H. J.	K	Passchendaele	Oct. 24
440095	Pte.	Ridgewell, B.	D/W	Passchendaele	Oct. 24
826039	Pte.	Burch, A. F.	K	Passchendaele	Oct. 26
447146	Sgt.	McKie, G. M.	K	Passchendaele	Oct. 27
117400	Pte.	McRae, A.	K	Passchendaele	Oct. 28
706585	L/Cpl.	Griffith, W. J.	K	Passchendaele	Oct. 28
706455	Pte.	Dean, A.	D/W	Passchendaele	Oct. 28
782352	Cpl.	Worle, P. C.	K	Passchendaele	Oct. 29
826458	Pte.	Flick, F. W.	K	Passchendaele	Oct. 29
826527	Pte.	Butters, J.	K	Passchendaele	Oct. 29
826137	Pte.	Connelly, J.	K	Passchendaele	Oct. 29
826664	Pte.	Wilson, J.	K	Passchendaele	Oct. 29
931421	Pte.	Dixon, J. J.	K	Passchendaele	Oct. 30
931552	Pte.	Clease, W. J.	D/W	Passchendaele	Oct. 25
706635	Pte.	Cowie, A.	K	Bellevue Spur	Oct. 30
826650	Pte.	Burns, J.	K	Passchendaele	Oct. 30
687847	Pte.	Burbidge, G. J.	K	Passchendaele	Oct. 30
826977	Pte.	Lazenbury, C. J.	K	Passchendaele	Oct. 30
464349	Pte.	Wilson, T. C.	K	Passchendaele	Oct. 30
116246	Sgt.	Mitchell, W. C.	K	Passchendaele	Oct. 30
227689	Pte.	Neal, C. B.	K	Passchendaele	Oct. 30
706527	Pte.	Pike, E.	K	Passchendaele	Oct. 30
826054	Pte.	Fulton, G. J.	K	Passchendaele	Oct. 30
107239	Cpl.	Glasspool, C. J.	K	Passchendaele	Oct. 30
294862	Pte.	Webb, O. M.	K	Passchendaele	Oct. 30
688203	Pte.	Bristow, W. H.	K	Passchendaele	Oct. 30
826666	Pte.	Taylor, W. LaV.	K	Passchendaele	Oct. 30
931205	L/Cpl.	Blaney, W. B.	K	Passchendaele	Oct. 31
117359	L/Cpl.	Loudon, D.	K	Passchendaele	Oct. 31
117456	L/Cpl.	Oxborough, J.	K	Passchendaele	Oct. 31
127409	Pte.	Baker, W. C.	K	Passchendaele	Nov. 1
687129	Pte.	Verity, J. C.	K	Passchendaele	Nov. 1
931359	Pte.	Fuller, T. C.	K	Passchendaele	Nov. 1
826158	Pte.	Attwood, F.	K	Passchendaele	Nov. 2

Appendix II—Killed or Died of Wounds

No.	Rank	Name	Killed or Died of Wounds	Place	Date
					1917
826910	Pte.	Gauthier, J. R.	D/W	Passchendaele	Oct. 25
931270	Pte.	McGuire, W.	K	Passchendaele	Oct. 26
826489	Pte.	Jack, G.	D/W	Passchendaele	Oct. 29
826520	Pte.	Allard, J.	K	Passchendaele	Oct. 30
931535	Pte.	Wade, J.	K	Passchendaele	Oct. 30
117328	Pte.	Jowett, R. N.	K	Passchendaele	Oct. 30
687298	L/Cpl.	Hall, F. S.	K	Passchendaele	Oct. 30
827181	Pte.	Beldham, E.	K	Passchendaele	Oct. 30
826642	Pte.	Barra, C.	K	Passchendaele	Oct. 30
760743	Pte.	Ounstead, A.	K	Passchendaele	Oct. 30
826202	Pte.	Pitello, G.	K	Passchendaele	Oct. 30
107153	Pte.	Coleman, E. H.	K	Passchendaele	Oct. 30
115042	Pte.	Sedgwick, J.	K	Passchendaele	Oct. 30
931007	Pte.	Stephens, F. W.	K	Passchendaele	Oct. 30
706951	Pte.	Butcher, E. J.	K	Passchendaele	Oct. 30
827064	Pte.	Barham, L.	K	Passchendaele	Oct. 30
2015199	Pte.	Bergman, A.	K	Passchendaele	Oct. 30
687450	Pte.	Johnson, A.	K	Passchendaele	Oct. 31
931189	Pte.	Wallace, G.	D/W	Passchendaele	Oct. 31
931630	Pte.	Penson, E. F.	K	Passchendaele	Nov. 1
826678	Pte.	Campbell, F. G.	K	Passchendaele	Nov. 1
931749	Pte.	Smith, H. T.	D/W	Passchendaele	Nov. 1
82630..	Pte.	Evans, F. E.	D/W	Passchendaele	Nov. 2
826312	Pte.	Hanwright, E.	D/W	Passchendaele	Nov. 4
117225	Sgt.	Dick, D.	D/W	Passchendaele	Nov. 4
2015159	Pte.	Carter, E. R.	D/W	Passchendaele	Nov. 5
425447	Pte.	Vincent, W. B.	D/W	Passchendaele	Nov. 6
931640	Pte.	Arnold, R. I.	D/W	Passchendaele	Nov. 8
826817	Pte.	Collier, F.	D/W	Passchendaele	Nov. 15
687392	Pte.	Draper, S. W.	D/W	Passchendaele	Nov. 20
489659	Pte.	Eustace, W. J.	Died	N. E. of Loos	Dec. 29
					1918
706746	L/Cpl.	Richardson, W. G.	D/W	N. E. of Loos	Jan. 6
261054	Pte.	Barrett, J. R.	D/W	N. E. of Loos	Jan. 12
706885	Pte.	Priest, C. F.	K	Merricourt Sector	Feb. 27
781131	Pte.	Harmer, G.	K	Hill 70	Apr. 11
463133	Pte.	Montgomery, A.	D/W	Hill 70	Apr. 16
136451	L/Cpl.	Banfield, J. H.	K	Hill 70	Apr. 17
826794	Pte.	Sovereign, W.	D/W	Les Brebis	Apr. 18
902187	Pte.	Smith, G. H.	D/W	Les Brebis	Apr. 19
853036	Pte.	Donaldson, J. E.	D/W	Mercatel Sector	July 2
916190	Pte.	May, C. P.	K	Mercatel Sector	July 5
443040	Pte.	McMillan, D. D.	K	Mercatel Sector	July 5
					1918
826252	Pte.	Evans, R.	K	Bretencourt	July 21
826542	Pte.	Wright, J. S.	K	Bretencourt	July 21
118051	Pte.	Adlam, L.	D/W	Bretencourt	July 21
916097	Sgt.	Ellison, J. W.	K	Demuin	Aug. 8
916697	Pte.	Howarth, W. R.	K	Demuin	Aug. 8
2020212	Pte.	Davis, W. J.	K	Demuin	Aug. 8

2nd Canadian Mounted Rifles

No.	Rank	Name	Killed or Died of Wounds	Place	Date
					1918
3032149	Pte.	Plato, M. J.	K	Demuin	Aug. 8
931148	Pte.	Halliday, J. G.	K	Demuin	Aug. 8
916737	Pte.	Phillips, H. J.	K	Demuin	Aug. 8
826875	Pte.	Spicer, W.	K	Demuin	Aug. 8
916879	Pte.	Simpson, J. M.	K	Demuin	Aug. 8
3032853	Pte.	Veitch, G. H.	K	Demuin	Aug. 8
227627	Pte.	Funnell, A.	K	Demuin	Aug. 8
135093	Pte.	Atkins, J.	K	Demuin	Aug. 8
916089	Pte.	Egan, S. M.	K	Demuin	Aug. 8
3032876	Pte.	Laue, R. F.	K	Demuin	Aug. 8
440767	Pte.	O'Sullivan, J. L.	K	Demuin	Aug. 8
688070	Pte.	Andrews, J.	D/W	Demuin	Aug. 8
117366	Pte.	Lyle, J.	D/W	Demuin	Aug. 8
931838	Pte.	Nickelby, T.	D/W	Demuin	Aug. 8
180708	Pte.	Young, W.	D/W	Demuin	Aug. 8
796059	Pte.	McNab, C. S.	D/W	Demuin	Aug. 8
116146	Sgt.	Mills, F. H.	D/W	Demuin	Aug. 8
274141	Pte.	Lunn, A. W.	D/W	Demuin	Aug. 9
826184	Pte.	Syer, W. A.	D/W	Demuin	Aug. 9
931369	Pte.	Hadden, W. E.	K	Le-Quesnoy-en-Santerre	Aug. 10
760734	L/Sgt.	Irving, A.	K	Le-Quesnoy-en-Santerre	Aug. 10
931220	L/Cpl.	Ratcliffe, S. H.	K	Le-Quesnoy-en-Santerre	Aug. 10
931432	Cpl.	Woods, T.	K	Le-Quesnoy-en-Santerre	Aug. 10
916139	Pte.	Allen, S.	K	Le-Quesnoy-en-Santerre	Aug. 10
916618	Pte.	Barley, A. H.	K	Le-Quesnoy-en-Santerre	Aug. 10
706335	Pte.	Brough, R. C.	K	Le-Quesnoy-en-Santerre	Aug. 10
7620	Pte.	Nanfan, A. F.	K	Le-Quesnoy-en-Santerre	Aug. 10
931179	Pte.	Slater, H. G.	K	Le-Quesnoy-en-Santerre	Aug. 10
1063139	Pte.	Dixon, W.	K	Le-Quesnoy-en-Santerre	Aug. 10
1063018	Pte.	Faulkner, J. A.	K	Le-Quesnoy-en-Santerre	Aug. 10
255830	Pte.	Harmer, A. R.	K	Le-Quesnoy-en-Santerre	Aug. 10
228491	Pte.	James, R. G.	K	Le-Quesnoy-en-Santerre	Aug. 10
3032644	Pte.	Murless, G. H.	K	Le-Quesnoy-en-Santerre	Aug. 10
931021	Cpl.	Clarke, C.	K	Le-Quesnoy-en-Santerre	Aug. 10
2223310	Pte.	Archer, I.	K	Le-Quesnoy-en-Santerre	Aug. 10
916306	Pte.	Cantwell, W.	K	Le-Quesnoy-en-Santerre	Aug. 10
542495	Pte.	Potts, V. C.	K	Le-Quesnoy-en-Santerre	Aug. 10
916044	Cpl.	Marten, C. McK.	K	Le-Quesnoy-en-Santerre	Aug. 10
136646	Pte.	Abbey, T.	K	Le-Quesnoy-en-Santerre	Aug. 10
916856	Pte.	Ellis, H. C.	K	Le-Quesnoy-en-Santerre	Aug. 10
117402	Cpl.	Mack, J.	D/W	Le-Quesnoy-en-Santerre	Aug. 10
931378	Pte.	Greenwood, F.	K	Le-Quesnoy-en-Santerre	Aug. 10
916749	Pte.	Hanson, J.	K	Le-Quesnoy-en-Santerre	Aug. 10
826303	Pte.	Wilson, J.	K	Le-Quesnoy-en-Santerre	Aug. 10
3032001	Pte.	Wood, F. J.	K	Le-Quesnoy-en-Santerre	Aug. 10
441376	Cpl.	Pell, W. E.	K	Le-Quesnoy-en-Santerre	Aug. 10
916544	Pte.	Wilson, P. H.	K	Le-Quesnoy-en-Santerre	Aug. 10
916780	Pte.	Speight, A.	K	Le-Quesnoy-en-Santerre	Aug. 10
135613	Sgt.	Manders, H. J.	K	Le-Quesnoy-en-Santerre	Aug. 10
117251	Pte.	Frodeen, P. F.	K	Le-Quesnoy-en-Santerre	Aug. 10
681104	Pte.	Mason, G. W.	K	Le-Quesnoy-en-Santerre	Aug. 10

Appendix II—Killed or Died of Wounds

No.	Rank	Name	Killed or Died of Wounds	Place	Date
					1918
707130	Pte.	Smith, E. T.	K	Le-Quesnoy-en-Santerre	Aug. 10
160399	Pte.	Hewitt, F.	K	Le-Quesnoy-en-Santerre	Aug. 10
542093	Pte.	Mitchell, A. T.	K	Le-Quesnoy-en-Santerre	Aug. 10
2334316	Pte.	Stidolph, S. H.	K	Le-Quesnoy-en-Santerre	Aug. 10
706997	Pte.	McNeill, J. R.	K	Le-Quesnoy-en-Santerre	Aug. 10
116585	Pte.	Wright, E. F.	K	Le-Quesnoy-en-Santerre	Aug. 10
440909	Pte.	Robinson, W. C.	K	Le-Quesnoy-en-Santerre	Aug. 10
811921	Pte.	Magee, W.	K	Le-Quesnoy-en-Santerre	Aug. 10
826432	Pte.	Smith, H. C.	K	Le-Quesnoy-en-Santerre	Aug. 10
116980	Pte.	Barnes, A. G.	K	Le-Quesnoy-en-Santerre	Aug. 10
781473	Sgt.	Duxbury, T.	K	Le-Quesnoy-en-Santerre	Aug. 10
916027	Pte.	Wise, R.	K	Le-Quesnoy-en-Santerre	Aug. 10
447179	Pte.	Phillips, W. W.	K	Le-Quesnoy-en-Santerre	Aug. 10
126247	Pte.	Tremain, J. R.	D/W	Le-Quesnoy-en-Santerre	Aug. 10
916094	L/Cpl.	Strathdee, J.	D/W	Le-Quesnoy-en-Santerre	Aug. 10
931327	Pte.	Lehman, J.	D/W	Le-Quesnoy-en-Santerre	Aug. 10
916783	Pte.	Lancaster, G. H.	D/W	Le-Quesnoy-en-Santerre	Aug. 10
464526	Pte.	Gillies, H.	D/W	Le-Quesnoy-en-Santerre	Aug. 11
116369	Pte.	Warman, F. D.	D/W	while ret. from leave	Aug. 11
931818	Pte.	Kinney, F.	D/W	Le Quesnoy	Aug. 11
931216	Pte.	Freer, E. E.	D/W	Le Quesnoy	Aug. 12
916642	Pte.	Wallace, J. R.	D/W	Demuin	Aug. 12
916063	Pte.	Kinkaid, A.	D/W	Le Quesnoy	Aug. 12
760861	Pte.	Cornes, J. K.	D/W	Le Quesnoy	Aug. 18
408791	Pte.	Hammond, B.	D/W	Le Quesnoy	Aug. 22
3033685	Pte.	Johnson, W. D.	K	Orange Hill (E. of Arras)	Aug. 26
707133	Pte.	Baldie, R.	K	Orange Hill (E. of Arras)	Aug. 26
136978	Pte.	Bewsey, B.	K	Orange Hill (E. of Arras)	Aug. 26
542493	Pte.	Ruddick, T. W.	K	Orange Hill (E. of Arras)	Aug. 26
628145	Pte.	Higgins, M.	K	Orange Hill (E. of Arras)	Aug. 26
916685	Pte.	Hunter, I. D.	K	Orange Hill (E. of Arras)	Aug. 26
116121	L/Sgt.	Johnston, W. H.	D/W	Le Quesnoy	Aug. 27
3032971	Pte.	Munslow, S.	K	Orange Hill	Aug. 27
916198	Pte.	Bentley, F. A.	D/W	Orange Hill	Aug. 27
117206	L/Cpl.	Cormack, F. L.	K	Orange Hill	Aug. 28
107542	Pte.	Smith, E.	K	Orange Hill	Aug. 28
463725	Cpl.	McBroom, G.	K	Orange Hill	Aug. 28
916308	Pte.	Brown, F.	K	Orange Hill	Aug. 28
118088	C.S.M.	McRae, K., M.M.	D/W	Orange Hill	Aug. 28
687087	A/Sgt.	Carr, B.	D/W	Orange Hill	Aug. 29
687376	A/Cpl.	Janes, J. S.	K	near Vis-en-Artois	Sept. 9
931777	Pte.	Tomblin, J. C.	D/W	near Vis-en-Artois	Sept. 9
3032616	Pte.	McCorry, T. G.	D/W	Le Quesnoy	Sept. 10
826329	Pte.	McNaughton, R. E.	K	Mill Copse Sector, (E. of Arras)	Sept. 15
136138	Pte.	Smith, A. L.	K	Mill Copse Sector, (E. of Arras)	Sept. 15
916028	Pte.	Ingram, A.	K	Mill Copse Sector, (E. of Arras)	Sept. 17
3031581	Pte.	Class, R. A.	K	Cambrai	Sept. 29
3032648	Pte.	Roberts, A. E.	K	Cambrai	Sept. 29

2nd Canadian Mounted Rifles

No.	Rank	Name	Killed or Died of Wounds	Place	Date
					1918
916179	Pte.	Benjamin, A.	D/W	Cambrai	Sept. 29
2109815	Pte.	Young, H.	D/W	Cambrai	Sept. 29
3032513	Pte.	Colbert, T.	K	Cambrai	Sept. 29
126911	Pte.	Cogger, E.	K	Cambrai	Sept. 29
3231278	Pte.	Rochefort, J.	K	Cambrai	Sept. 29
2458366	Pte.	Thompson, G. H.	K	Cambrai	Sept. 29
116462	Sgt.	Lamport, W. E.	K	Cambrai	Sept. 29
3230923	Pte.	Molan, H.	K	Cambrai	Sept. 29
441474	Pte.	Pilkington, J., M.M.	K	Cambrai	Sept. 29
464144	Cpl.	Millard, W. H.	K	Cambrai	Sept. 29
916849	Pte.	Barres, W. T.	K	Cambrai	Sept. 29
916267	Pte.	Hamilton, A. E.	K	Cambrai	Sept. 29
3031367	Pte.	Lemaire, W.	K	Cambrai	Sept. 29
3030022	Pte.	Sullivan, R. E.	K	Cambrai	Sept. 29
707191	Sgt.	Sivertz, H. G., M.M.	K	Cambrai	Sept. 29
707217	Sgt.	Reardon, H. A.	K	Cambrai	Sept. 29
441062	L/Cpl.	Rudden, P.	K	Cambrai	Sept. 29
117449	A.L/Cpl.	Noell, N. H.	K	Cambrai	Sept. 29
2147327	Pte.	Jackman, G.	K	Cambrai	Sept. 29
405846	Pte.	Rogers, H. E.	K	Cambrai	Sept. 29
3032332	Pte.	O'Hara, S.	K	Cambrai	Sept. 29
3230986	Pte.	McKelvey, E. R.	K	Cambrai	Sept. 29
916473	Pte.	Muringer, F. C.	K	Cambrai	Sept. 29
3033166	Pte.	Glore, D. R.	K	Cambrai	Sept. 29
826953	Pte.	Kelley, H. D.	K	Cambrai	Sept. 29
3031485	Pte.	Wade, J.	K	Cambrai	Sept. 29
928055	Pte.	Winston, G. D.	K	Cambrai	Sept. 29
116701	Pte.	Walker, J. G.	D/W	Cambrai	Sept. 29
931114	Pte.	Phillips, R. A.	K	Cambrai	Sept. 29
2304440	Pte.	Clark, J.	K	Cambrai	Sept. 29
3032362	Pte.	McLean, G. J.	K	Cambrai	Sept. 29
827050	Pte.	Fennell, G.	K	Cambrai	Sept. 29
425330	Pte.	Smith, B.	K	Cambrai	Sept. 29
706001	Sgt.	Miller, R.	K	Cambrai	Sept. 29
781964	Cpl.	Garrod, W., M.M.	K	Cambrai	Sept. 29
827130	Pte.	Barres, J.	K	Cambrai	Sept. 29
1069510	Pte.	Boyce, E.	K	Cambrai	Sept. 29
3231243	Pte.	Savard, R. J.	K	Cambrai	Sept. 29
931721	Pte.	Palmer, T. G.	K	Cambrai	Sept. 29
916889	Pte.	Lord, E. F.	K	Cambrai	Sept. 29
2223305	Pte.	Kerr, W. McL.	K	Cambrai	Sept. 29
916335	Pte.	Verity, H.	K	Cambrai	Sept. 29
441672	Pte.	Primeau, T.	D/W	Cambrai	Sept. 29
916464	Pte.	Robertson, W. C.	D/W	Cambrai	Sept. 29
116568	L/Cpl.	Bushfield, A.	D/W	Cambrai	Sept. 29
826949	Pte.	Moran, O.	K	Cambrai	Sept. 29
706980	Pte.	Cardwell, J. M.	K	Cambrai	Sept. 29
423301	Cpl.	Kinnel, T. N.	K	Cambrai	Sept. 29
916486	Pte.	Thrush, F.	D/W	Cambrai	Sept. 30
285324	Pte.	O'Rourke, M.	D/W	Cambrai	Sept. 30
648661	Pte.	Myers, H. G.	D/W	Cambrai	Sept. 30

Appendix II—Killed or Died of Wounds

No.	Rank	Name	Killed or Died of Wounds	Place	Date
					1918
687694	L/Cpl.	Crouch, F.	D/W	Cambrai	Oct. 1
3251553	Pte.	Watson, R. N.	K	Cambrai	Oct. 2
3034062	Pte.	Durrin, J. E.	D/W	Cambrai	Oct. 2
514144	Pte.	Light, W. A.	D/W	Cambrai	Oct. 2
3033509	Pte.	Fisher, W. R.	D/W	Cambrai	Oct. 2
651824	Pte.	Campbell, D. E.	K	Cambrai	Oct. 2
107306	Sgt.	Hallmark, W.	D/W	Cambrai	Oct. 4
136240	Sgt.	Taylor, S.	D/W	Cambrai	Oct. 5
3031953	Pte.	Prendergast, J. W.	K	Cambrai (Marcoing Line)	Oct. 8
931577	Pte.	Trewhella, J.	D/W	Cambrai	Oct. 8
443006	Pte.	Hickson, W.	D/W	Cambrai	Oct. 31
208247	Pte.	Bannister, J. M.	K	Fresnes	Oct. 30
3313	Cpl.	Dalgleish, T. M., M.M.	K	Quievrain	Nov. 5
3231212	Pte.	Lalonde, A.	K	Quievrain	Nov. 6
135866	Pte.	Smith, T.	K	Quievrain	Nov. 6
464260	Sgt.	McLeod, A. J.	K	Quievrain	Nov. 6
707220	Cpl.	Blackwell, A.	K	Quievrain	Nov. 6
252011	Cpl.	Boyce, G. E.	K	Quievrain	Nov. 6
136512	Cpl.	Simpson, J. J.	K	Quievrain	Nov. 6
707190	Pte.	Gordon, O.	K	Quievrain	Nov. 6
3231152	Pte.	Lundmark, A.	K	Quievrain	Nov. 6
3032273	Pte.	Lawson, T. W.	K	Quievrain	Nov. 6
2355500	Pte.	May, J. P.	K	Quievrain	Nov. 6
931716	Pte.	Coles, P. F.	K	Quievrain	Nov. 6
2562370	Pte.	Sineyr, A. E.	K	Quievrain	Nov. 6
916508	Pte.	Best, T. F.	K	Quievrain	Nov. 6
916445	Cpl.	Gibson, D.	K	Quievrain	Nov. 6
425341	Pte.	Soon, E.	K	Quievrain	Nov. 6
3230854	Pte.	Rennison, G.	K	Quievrain	Nov. 6
3033751	Pte.	Van Hoesen, H. T.	K	Quievrain	Nov. 6
3233524	Pte.	Scott, W. T.	K	Quievrain	Nov. 6
3233558	Pte.	Wood, W. M.	K	Quievrain	Nov. 6
513969	Pte.	Gagnon, J. M.	K	Quievrain	Nov. 6
3032493	Pte.	Mockow, J.	K	Quievrain	Nov. 6
687873	Pte.	Poole, W. C.	K	Quievrain	Nov. 6
3039358	Pte.	Burberry, W.	K	Quievrain	Nov. 6
2355586	Pte.	Armfelt, O. M. W.	K	Quievrain	Nov. 6
3032249	Pte.	Geall, J.	K	Quievrain	Nov. 7
3231481	Pte.	Boulger, T.	D/W	Quievrain	Nov. 7
3234369	Pte.	La Chance, E.	D/W	Fresnes	Nov. 7
225266	Pte.	Fennelly, T.	D/W	Quievrain	Nov. 7
423374	C.S.M.	McKenzie, D., D.C.M.	D/W	Quievrain	Nov. 7
916781	Pte.	Lumb, H.	D/W	Quievrain	Nov. 8
797667	Pte.	Dickson, P.	D/W	Quievrain	Nov. 8
3230999	Pte.	Durrell, W. L.	D/W	Quievrain	Nov. 13
916388	Pte.	Bradley, N. W.	D/W	Quievrain	Dec. 12

APPENDIX III

Nominal Roll of Officers and Other Ranks, Missing or Prisoners of War

No.	Rank	Name	Missing or Prisoner of War	Place	Date
447003	Pte.	Austin, R. C.	Prisoner of War	Hessian Trench	Sept. 29, '16
706759	Pte.	Burgess, G.	Prisoner of War	Vimy Ridge	March 22, '17
180235	Pte.	Hasting, A. F.	Prisoner of War	Vimy Ridge	March 22, '17
826178	Pte.	Jenkinson, J.	Prisoner of War	Passchendaele	Oct. 30, '17

APPENDIX IV

Nominal Roll of Officers, Warrant Officers, N.C.O.'s and Men Wounded

Rank	Name	Place	Date
Lieut.	Worsley, R. S., M.C.	Irish Farm	Dec. 1, '15
Lieut.	Rant, N. W. F.	Irish Farm	Dec. 4, '15
Capt.	Temple, A.	C1-C2 and 142, Trenches	Feb. 10, '16
Maj.	Bapty, W.	Hooge	Mar. 25, '16
Lieut.	Wills, O.	Hooge	Mar. 30, '16
Lieut.	McGuire, M. V.	Ypres	Apr. 5, '16
Lieut.	Pearkes, G. R., V.C., D.S.O., M.C.	Hooge	May 19, '16
Capt.	Edwards, F. B.	Sanctuary Wood	June 3, '16
Maj.	Allen, M. V., D.S.O.	Sanctuary Wood	June 3, '16
Capt.	Le Duc, T.	Sanctuary Wood	June 3, '16
Capt.	Denison, H. R.	Sanctuary Wood (s. o. d.)	June 3, '16
Lieut.	Young, H. C.	Sanctuary Wood	June 3, '16
Lieut.	Strachan, A.	Sanctuary Wood	June 3, '16
Lieut.	Scott, H. G.	Sanctuary Wood	June 3, '16
Lieut.	Pue, W. H.	Sanctuary Wood	June 3, '16
Lieut.	Lewis, C. J.	Sanctuary Wood	June 3, '16
Lieut.	Cruickshank, A., M.C.	Sanctuary Wood	June 3, '16
Lieut.	Latimer, W. R.	Sanctuary Wood	June 3, '16
Capt.	Redpath, S. J., D.C.M.	Sanctuary Wood	June 3, '16
Lieut.	Quanbury, J. H.	Sanctuary Wood	July 24, '16
Capt.	Foster, W. W., D.S.O.	Sanctuary Wood	July 27, '16
Lieut.	Capstick, J. E., M.M.	The Bluff	Aug. 19, '16
Capt.	Le Duc, T.	The Bluff	Aug. 20, '16
Lieut.	Meldrum, J. A.	The Bluff	Aug. 21, '16
Lieut.	Pennie, T. C.	Somme (still on duty)	Sept. 13, '16
Capt.	Asser, R.	Somme	Sept. 13, '16
Lieut.	Heather, F. A., M.C., M.M.	Mouquet Farm (s. o. d.)	Sept. 15, '16
Lieut.	Nicholls, J. W. E.	Mouquet Farm (s. o. d.)	Sept. 15, '16
Lieut.	Foord, J., M.C.	Mouquet Farm	Sept. 16, '16
Lieut.	Spinks, R. C.	Hessian Trench (s. o. d.)	Sept. 28, '16
Capt.	Irving, E. B.	Hessian Trench	Sept. 29, '16
Lieut.	Kennedy, L., M.C.	Hessian Trench	Sept. 29, '16
Lieut.	Pearkes, G. R.	Hessian Trench (s. o. d.)	Oct. 2, '16
Capt.	Asser, R.	Somme	Oct. 11, '16
Capt.	Edwards, F. B.	Somme	Oct. 11, '16
Lieut.	Krauss, C. A.	Somme	Oct. 11, '16
Lieut.	Cruickshank, G.	Somme (s. o. d.)	Oct. 27, '16
Maj.	Van Kleeck, S. B.	Roclincourt (s. o. d.)	Jan. 11, '17
Lieut.	Wilson, W. J.	Roclincourt (s. o. d.)	Jan. 19, '17
Lieut.	Smith, F.	Vimy Ridge (raid)	Mar. 31, '17
Lieut.	Foord, J., M.C.	Vimy Ridge (raid) (s. o. d.)	Mar. 31, '17

s. o. d. Still on duty.

2nd Canadian Mounted Rifles

Rank	Name	Place	Date
Lieut.	Lees, R.	Vimy Ridge (attack)	Apr. 9, '17
Lieut.	Mavor, J.	Vimy Ridge (attack)	Apr. 9, '17
Lieut.	Darcus, R. J.	Vimy Ridge (attack)	Apr. 9, '17
Capt.	Gray, J. L.	Vimy Ridge (attack)	Apr. 9, '17
Lieut.	Heinekey, G. P.	Vimy Ridge (attack)	Apr. 10, '17
Capt.	Armstrong, A. C.	Vimy Ridge (gas)	May 8, '17
Lieut.	Darcus, R. J.	Vimy Ridge (s. o. d.)	May 22, '17
Lieut.	Lewis, C. J.	Villers-au-Bois (accidental)	June 16, '17
Lieut.	Richardson, J. M. S.	Mericourt (gas)	Aug. 22, '17
Lieut.	Warren, W. C.	Passchendaele	Oct. 27, '17
Lieut.	Potter, J. K.	Passchendaele	Oct. 30, '17
Lieut.	Mavor, J.	Passchendaele	Oct. 30, '17
Lieut.	Darcus, R. J.	Passchendaele	Oct. 30, '17
Lieut.	Dexter, F. G.	Passchendaele	Oct. 30, '17
Lieut.	McDermid, G. D.	Passchendaele (s. o. d.)	Oct. 30, '17
Lieut.	Hart, C. L.	Passchendaele	Nov. 1, '17
Lieut.	MacGregor, J., D.C.M.	E. of Loos	Jan. 12, '18
Capt.	Redpath, S. J., D.C.M.	Mericourt (s. o. d.)	Mar. 15, '18
Lieut.	Williams, H. C.	Mericourt (gas)	Mar. 13, '18
Lieut.	Bolt, H. G.	Arleus	Mar. 23, '18
Lieut.	Drew, J. A. C.	Neuville St. Vaast	Apr. 1, '18
Lieut.	Grothe, C. R., M.M.	Hill 70	Apr. 13, '18
Lieut.	Jackson, J. H.	Les Brebis	Apr. 18, '18
Capt.	Breckenridge, C. A.	While on/c 3rd Canadian Division Salvage Co.	Apr. 13, '18
Lieut.	Haigh, A. W.	Hill 70 (s. o. d.)	Apr. 28, '18
Lieut.	Rugg, J. F.	Bretencourt	July 21, '18
Capt.	Rowberry, A. H., M.C.	Demuin	Aug. 8, '18
Lieut.	Campbell, L. G.	Demuin	Aug. 8, '18
Lieut.	Williams, H. D., M.C.	Le Quesnoy	Aug. 10, '18
Lieut.	Trees, A. G.	Le Quesnoy	Aug. 10, '18
Lieut.	Harris, W. M.	Le Quesnoy	Aug. 10, '18
Lieut.	Drew, J. A. C.	Orange Hill (S. E. of Arras)	Aug. 26, '18
Lieut.	Hewetson, H. J.	Orange Hill (S. E. of Arras)	Aug. 27, '18
Lieut.	Gilchrist, N. A. L.	Orange Hill (S. E. of Arras)	Aug. 28, '18
Lieut.	Oxberry, J. R.	Orange Hill (S. E. of Arras)	Aug. 28, '18
Lieut.	Heath, E. F. W.	Orange Hill (S. E. of Arras)	Aug. 26, '18
Capt.	Rant, G. T., D.C.M.	Mill Copse Sector (E. of Arras)	Sept. 15, '18
Lieut.	Manning, H. C., D.C.M.	Cambrai	Sept. 29, '18
Lieut.	Gardiner, W. F.	Cambrai	Sept. 29, '18
Lieut.	Hives, E., M.M.	Cambrai	Sept. 29, '18
Lieut.	Darcus, R. J., M.C.	Cambrai	Sept. 29, '18
Lieut.	Bolt, H. G.	Cambrai	Sept. 29, '18
Lieut.	Smith, F., M.C.	Cambrai	Sept. 29, '18
Lieut.	Bradford, E. E.	Cambrai	Sept. 29, '18
Lieut.	McDermid, G. D., M.C.	Cambrai (s. o. d.)	Sept. 29, '18
Capt.	MacGregor, J., V.C., M.C., D.C.M.	Cambrai (s. o. d.)	Sept. 29, '18
Lieut.	White, E. O.	Quievrain	Nov. 7, '18
Lieut.	Blake, G., M.C.	Quievrain (s. o. d.)	Nov. 7, '18

s. o. d. Still on duty.

Appendix IV—Wounded

DICKIEBUSCH, 1915

October 5
107457 Pte. Nicholson, W. P.
October 6
107577 Pte. Somerset, B.
October 7
107103 Pte. Burden, E. H.

October 8
107575 Pte. Street, F.
107058 Pte. Atkinson, W.
October 18
107607 L/Cpl. †Wilson, J.

BAILLEUL, 1915

November 17
107318 Pte. †Humphreys, D.
107437 Pte. †Marcotte, —

November 22
107592 Pte. †Tozer, W. R.
November 28
107148 Pte. †Carr, E. F.

IRISH FARM, 1915

November 30
107633 Pte. Wilkinson, W.
107406 Sgt. MacBean, R.
December 1
107415 Pte. Melcombe, E. W.
107413 Pte. Malim, K.
107539 Pte. Simpson, H.
107641 L/Cpl. Weir, F.
107058 Pte. Atkinson, W.
107271 Pte. Harrison, J. D.
107113 Pte. Bond, R. M.
107221 Pte. Flowers, W. H.

December 2
107582 Sgt. §Tyler, W.
December 4
107487 Cpl. Potts, J. W.
December 5
107315 Pte. Hutchinson, H.
107374 Cpl. Lees, R.
107481 Pte. Paddon, G. L.
11328 Pte. Cryderman, F. C.
December 7
107357 Sgt. Killick, C. St. J.

RED LODGE, 1916

February 3
107459 Pte. Neill, D. E.
107358 L/Cpl. Kendrew, W.
107438 Pte. Manson, W.
107144 Pte. Coles, A.
107414 Pte. Matterson, G.
108240 Pte. Gibson, E.
115042 Pte. Sedgwick, J.

108289 Pte. Holder, R.
7741 Pte. Caton, E.
108282 Pte. Hawkins, H. G.
108081 Pte. Baverstock, W.
February 4
107110 Pte. Blakey, H. A.
February 5
116056 Pte. Campbell, A.

C1, C2 AND 142 TRENCHES, 1916

February 10
107620 Sgt. Warren, W. C.
107095 Pte. Brown, A. S.
107421 Pte. Malcolm, J. L.

February 12
108394 Pte. Monkman, T.
117108 Pte. Allan, T. W.
February 14
107140 L/Cpl. Cartwright, W. H.

KORTEPYP CAMP

February 15
107571 Pte. Sheret, W.

February 15
107170 Pte. Clark, F.

TRANSPORT LINES, 1916

February 16
107611 Pte. Wheeler, C.

† Working party.

§ Accidentally wounded.

2nd Canadian Mounted Rifles

C1, C2 AND 142 TRENCHES, 1916

February 20
117473	Pte.	Penny, D. G.

February 21
117495	Pte.	Teeling, R. E.

HOOGE, 1916

March 24
117207	Pte.	Coupland, R. S.
107139	Pte.	Carr, W. H.
107473	Sgt.	Pearkes, G. H.
107344	Pte.	Jordan, H. S.
117612	Pte.	Weaver, C. L.
107273	Pte.	Horner, G.
108110	Pte.	Booth, L. E.
107421	Sgt.	Malcolm, J. L.
117331	Pte.	Keep, J. C.
117317	Pte.	Innes, A. E.
107512	Pte.	Coleman, L.
108466	Pte.	Pope, J. L.
107228	Pte.	Fairbairn, L.
117398	Pte.	MacNamara, H.
107559	Pte.	Smith, C. L.
117346	Pte.	Langham, J.
107514	Pte.	Ritchie, D.
107160	Pte.	Chase, D.
117370	Pte.	McKenzie, C. S.

March 25
107170	Pte.	Clark, F.

March 25
117141	Pte.	Bevan, G. A.
107641	L/Cpl.	Weir, F.
116645	Pte.	Swanby, A. O.
116073	Pte.	Kerr, R.
108281	Pte.	Hough, R. S.
107627	Pte.	Willis, H.
107469	Pte.	Partington, E.
117539	Pte.	Smith, P. W.
107381	Pte.	Lee, T. E.

March 26
117514	Pte.	Rogers, J. W.
107189	Pte.	Dennis, R. E.
107511	L/Cpl.	Remnant, S. J.
107286	Pte.	Harrison, J.
112215	Pte.	Elliot, E. W.
435744	Pte.	McIntosh, R. T.

March 27
117202	Pte.	Cooke, H.
107151	Pte.	Champion, J.
107631	Pte.	Wright, W. T.
117522	Pte.	Sangster, A.

YPRES, 1916

March 27
117403	Pte.	†Mahoney, A. P.

March 27
117546	Pte.	†Stafford, R.

HOOGE, 1916

March 27
107354	Pte.	Kenyon, H. H.
116057	Sgt.	Morrison, D.
116007	Pte.	Dunlop, E.

March 28
107104	Pte.	Babbit, H.

March 29
446925	Pte.	Burchinshaw, R.
446643	Pte.	Buckingham, R.
116099	Pte.	Wilson, S.
117276	Pte.	Griffiths, G.
442645	Pte.	Denusik, N.

March 30
423154	Pte.	Chesterman, A.

March 31
108381	L/Cpl.	Meyer, E. R.
107217	Cpl.	Foster, R.
107281	Sgt.	Holmes, A.
107218	Pte.	Farrow, L. W.

April 3
107461	Pte.	Ollerhead, G. A.
108533	Pte.	Shenton, G.
117300	Pte.	Higginson, G. E.
108560	Pte.	St. Dennis, J.
118024	Pte.	Lewis, E.

YPRES CITY, 1916

April 5
107234	B.S.M.	Godfrey, T.
107534	Pte.	Saling, W.
107618	Sgt.	Wilson, W. S.

April 5
107290	Pte.	Hatcher, J. M.
107579	Pte.	Talbot, W. E.

† Working party.

Appendix IV—Wounded

SANCTUARY WOOD, 1916

April 23

117109	Pte.	Allen, F.
107163	Pte.	Crooks, W. D.
442489	Pte.	Stuart, A. L.
108144	Pte.	Chapman, H.

April 25

108238	Cpl.	Garland, E.
107367	Cpl.	Livingstone, G.
107518	Sgt.	Ready, J.
58125	Pte.	Ouimet, P. A.
117434	Pte.	Merkley, F. E.
108551	L/Cpl.	Staines, A.

April 25

435053	Pte.	Moulding, F.
107475	L/Cpl.	Pegg, T. H.
117141	Pte.	Bevan, G. A.
117647	Pte.	Smith, F.
443867	Pte.	Pearce, W. J.

April 28

117401	L/Cpl.	McVicar, J.

April 29

107059	L/Cpl.	Ayles, A.
107086	Pte.	Beveridge, J. W.

YPRES, 1916

May 6

117611	Pte.	Watt, J.
107104	Pte.	Babbit, M.
117435	Pte.	Munsie, E. W.

May 6

117274	Pte.	Green, D. J.
117220	Pte.	Davis, C. D.

HOOGE, 1916

May 11

117478	Pte.	Phillips, J.

May 12

435744	Pte.	McIntosh, G.

May 14

108190	Pte.	Dick, J. C.
107628	Pte.	Winslow, C. A.
117295	Cpl.	Henderson, W.
107278	Pte.	Horner, G.

May 17

117368	Pte.	McDonald, M.
107487	Cpl.	Potts, J. W.
107313	Sgt.	Hazeldine, T.
434652	Pte.	Reid, G.

May 17

107611	L/Cpl.	Wheeler, C.
117165	Pte.	Briggs, A. J.
117383	Pte.	McFayden, J.
117328	Pte.	Jowett, R.

May 18

423373	L/Cpl.	Philip, T.

May 19

117246	Pte.	Fleming, E. B.
117191	L/Cpl.	Clement, R.
107501	Pte.	Randall, R. N.
107425	Pte.	Manning, H. C.
443325	Pte.	Slater, T.

May 26

423178	Pte.	Halliday, J.

SANCTUARY WOOD, 1916

June 2

463901	Pte.	Thomas, G. A.
107363	Pte.	Lance, E.
422135	Pte.	Preston, J.
107494	Pte.	Palmer, G.
435815	Pte.	Woods, A.
107267	Sgt.	Heather, F.
107211	Sgt.	Foord, J.
116037	Sgt.	Richman, R.
464358	Pte.	Willoughby, P.
436800	Pte.	Lillies, W.
117478	Pte.	Phillips, J.
107382	Pte.	Lowery, A.
117481	Pte.	Piper, L. R.
117310	Pte.	Hood, T.

117638	Pte.	Davis, A.
443796	Pte.	Mazur, F.
107434	Pte.	Murray, E.
106284	Pte.	Herman, W.
107605	Sgt.	Whitnall, P.
116027	Sgt.	Morrison, D.

June 3

107623	Sgt.	Whitmore, H.
107558	L/Sgt.	Smith, A. S.
117158	Pte.	Bontillier, N.
442937	Pte.	Berg, C.
443398	Pte.	Barlow, J.
442959	Pte.	Clay, C.
107322	Pte.	Haslam, A.
437796	Pte.	Locke, B.

2nd Canadian Mounted Rifles

SANCTUARY WOOD, 1916

June 3

414307	Pte.	McNeill, A.
414333	Pte.	McLeod, A.
463147	Pte.	Noble, L. W.
463150	Pte.	Newberry, S.
436599	Pte.	Standing, E.
464351	Pte.	Thompson, J.
446158	Pte.	Whillans, F.
117642	Pte.	Yorkland, C.
107248	Sgt.	Gillespie, A.
107371	Cpl.	Lamountaine, L.
107218	L/Cpl.	Farrow, L.
107461	L/Cpl.	Ollerhead, G. A.
422437	Pte.	Carfra, J. W.
443430	Pte.	Gibeau, J.
117317	Pte.	Innes, A. E.
117397	Pte.	McLevin, D.
107404	Pte.	McNamara, W. D.
118087	Pte.	McRae, A.
116035	Pte.	Pollard, R.
117529	Pte.	Sinclair, A.
423144	Pte.	Simmons, P. W.
435300	Pte.	Williams, F.
435422	Pte.	Williams, R.
107651	Pte.	Watson, J. R.
464397	Pte.	Scrimshaw, F.
463902	Pte.	Taylor, A. B.
463829	Pte.	Stant, H.
464349	Pte.	Wilson, T. C.
414185	Pte.	McPhee, A.
117467	Sgt.	Patterson, J. S.
107288	L/Cpl.	Hart, C.
117150	Pte.	Blake, J. A.
107261	Pte.	Gardiner, R.
117431	Pte.	Mortimer, R.
117378	Pte.	McDonald, A.
117113	Pte.	Armstrong, R.
107099	Pte.	Blanchard, L.
463171	Pte.	Ross, J.
463194	Pte.	Urquhart, J.
463148	Pte.	Newnham, J.
463152	Pte.	Norris, F. J.
464677	Pte.	Norris, L.
463452	Pte.	Dooley, J.
117476	L/Cpl.	Perry, C.
117549	L/Cpl.	Stagg, R.
117163	Pte.	Brazil, A.
117172	Pte.	Burchill, C.
118092	Pte.	Quigg, H.
117541	Pte.	Somerville, J.
464620	Pte.	Robertson, D.
443132	Pte.	Fox, G. H.
464437	Pte.	Ross, D. C.

June 3

463383	Pte.	Tolhurst, C.
464608	Pte.	McDonald, J.
463988	Pte.	Skinner, J. W.
117579	Pte.	Teeling, R. E.
118081	Pte.	Massey, L.
442600	Pte.	Mason, E. H.
464560	Pte.	Knox, T. F.
118059	Pte.	Connors, W. D.
447454	Pte.	Fisher, W. G.
464666	Pte.	Hodgkins, S.
117318	Pte.	Innes, T. E.
117222	Pte.	Day, E. B.
463124	Pte.	Appleford, D.
463279	Pte.	Gourley, W.
435517	Pte.	Pearce, D.
463036	Pte.	Clark, A.
108164	Pte.	Convey, C.
107528	Cpl.	Rogers, J.
463954	Pte.	Brown, R. R.
463952	Pte.	Baker, R. P.
107615	Cpl.	Wilson, D. J.
464580	Pte.	Marshall, J.
463324	Pte.	Marshall, K.
463726	Pte.	Ball, J.
107417	Pte.	Milner-Jones, V.
443590	Pte.	Madsen, J.
437235	Pte.	Skeffington, J.
20706	Pte.	Smith, E. G.
443378	Pte.	Menzies, R. P.
117108	Pte.	Allan, T. W.
464477	Pte.	Barr, J. D.
117145	Pte.	Birnie, J.
463959	Pte.	Butts, C. D.
463961	Pte.	Charnley, F.
117311	Pte.	Hope, C.
422915	Pte.	Sturgeon, J.
463252	Pte.	Clark, F.
107535	Cpl.	Saunders, C.
116203	Pte.	Anderton, B.
117238	Pte.	Elford, E. C.
117300	Pte.	Higginson, G.
107349	Pte.	Kermode, W. H.
443023	Pte.	Kennedy, M.
117551	Pte.	Stevens, R.
434296	Pte.	McGravey, J.
442545	Pte.	Haydock, J.
107584	Pte.	Tetlock, H.
463096	Pte.	Highet, J. A.
464283	Pte.	Baker, F. W.
107078	L/Sgt.	Boulton, J.
117289	Pte.	Harvey, W. F.
117577	Pte.	Stewart, A.

Appendix IV—Wounded

SANCTUARY WOOD, 1916

June 3

117334	Pte.	Kershaw, E. J.

117492	Pte.	Raikes, A. C.

MAPLE COPSE, 1916

June 3

464398	Pte.	Fletcher, H. H.	107505	Pte.	Rogers, A. C.
107212	L/Cpl.	Fletcher, C. W.	107387	Sgt.	McCluskey, W. R.
117558	Pte.	Stewart, D. A.	437185	Pte.	Donnelly, J.
442384	Pte.	Gold, A. E.	443467	Pte.	Allen, M. F.
117366	Pte.	Lyle, J.	107085	L/Cpl.	Brown, J. A.
117509	Pte.	Robertson, L. M.	108420	Pte.	McKelvie, R.
117452	Pte.	Newcombe, L.	107272	Pte.	Haskins, E. H.
117533	Pte.	Leppard, C. H.	107327	Pte.	Ibbotson, R.
117585	Pte.	Tooley, J.	108351	Pte.	Love, R. E.
107458	Sgt.	Nash, H. B.	107405	Pte.	Oldershaw, H.
12014	Pte.	Gardiner, H. M.	116039	Pte.	Rooney, T. J.
116016	L/Cpl.	Harding, A.	117457	Pte.	Oxborough, W.
402266	Pte.	Bates, W.	107468	Pte.	Parkyn, G. F.
435819	Pte.	Fraser, A. L.	464526	Pte.	Gillies, H.
117396	Pte.	McLeod, H. E.	118094	Pte.	Sanderson, D.
117373	Pte.	McCarthy, W.	117573	Pte.	Synge, N.
118016	Pte.	McLean, K.	463577	Pte.	Stevens, C. F.
107393	Pte.	McCreight, J. D.	107100	Pte.	Brett, E.
107564	Pte.	Scott, G. W.	117176	Pte.	Campbell, D. A.
117576	Pte.	Taylor, R.	108525	Pte.	Sevior, A. R.
117621	Pte.	White, W.	117627	Pte.	Williams, R. N.
107637	Cpl.	Wallace, G.	118026	Pte.	Lee, J. W.
107332	Pte.	Knight, W. C.	108101	Pte.	Blackmore, H. W.
425282	Pte.	Rutz, E.	117229	Pte.	Doody, K.
115006	Cpl.	Armstrong, J. T.	107517	Pte.	Rowberry, A.
107569	L/Cpl.	Staines, A.	117277	Pte.	Grime, H.
117154	Pte.	Borton, F. G.	107628	Pte.	Winslow, E.
117234	Pte.	Dulton, H. R.	107173	Pte.	Crow, A.
442446	Pte.	McIntosh, C.	107343	Pte.	Jones, E. A.
117200	Pte.	Colwell, L.	117239	Pte.	Ellis, E. E.
7760	Pte.	Foston, H. R.	108528	Pte.	Sharp, A.
108377	Sgt.	Mellor, W.	116029	Pte.	McDonald, F.
435813	Pte.	Blackwell, A. J.	447494	Pte.	Clark, E.
447499	Pte.	Landry, W.	446508	Pte.	Scott, H. A.
117271	Pte.	Graham, A.	117320	Pte.	Jenkins, A. J.
447169	Pte.	Porter, T.	107574	Pte.	Spencer, R. C.
423133	Pte.	Weeks, B. E.	464497	Pte.	Gray, H. C.
447573	Pte.	Dargie, R. E.	117424	Pte.	Mitchell, J.
447513	Pte.	Higgins, R.	118058	Pte.	Butcher, H.
447518	Pte.	McLeod, J.	117372	Pte.	McBride, C. D.
108237	Pte.	Gardiner, A. F.	107541	C.S.M.	Smith, W.
443081	Pte.	Seeman, L.	107611	C.S.M.	Webb, A.
108279	Pte.	Harwood, W.	80128	Pte.	Lyon, J. H.
443112	Pte.	White, N.	117483	Pte.	Pottinger, W. A.
108520	Pte.	Scobie, A. M.	425407	Pte.	Wren, B.
435739	Pte.	Smart, J. E.	118094	Pte.	Sanderson, D.

2nd Canadian Mounted Rifles

GODWAERSVELDE, 1916

June 30
482013 Pte. §Page, E. V.

July 1
117192 Pte. Cobb, B. T.

July 3
16454 Pte. McCaffrey, J.

SANCTUARY WOOD, 1916

July 20
117590 Pte. Turner, C. W.
117142 Pte. Bice, H. V.

July 21
117404 Pte. McVicar, J.
117208 Pte. Cawling, J. T.
107166 Pte. Cockett, L.

July 22
425443 Pte. Venner, G. C.
425335 Pte. Smith, H.
441060 Pte. Robinson, A. F.
118059 Pte. Connors, W. D.
441381 Pte. Pook, G.
117611 L/Cpl. Watt, J.

July 23
463579 Pte. Sprinkling, C. K.
118090 Pte. Patton, G.
127330 Pte. Smart, F. R.
136273 Pte. Wright, W. G.

July 24
108445 Pte. Owens, W. R.
117511 Pte. Robinson, G. F.
136134 Pte. Simmons, W. J.
440767 Pte. O'Sullivan, J.
435443 Pte. Fraser, J.
135873 Pte. Schofield, R. J.
464561 L/Cpl. Diplock, C. B.
126686 Pte. Stinberg, E.
440862 Pte. Rafter, E. J.
136139 Pte. Smith, W. H.
441896 Pte. Pybus, L. J.
464547 Cpl. Boult, E. G.
441130 Pte. Pollard, P. P.
435778 L/Cpl. Jones, G.
447454 Pte. Fisher, W. G.

July 25
107468 Pte. Pelly, G. S.
136242 Pte. Tullet, T.
440492 Pte. Propert, H.
135572 Pte. Smith, J.
107630 Pte. Wood, W. G.
117553 L/Cpl. Stevenson, J. W.
464407 Pte. Andrews, J.
118029 Pte. McLean, A.
440299 Pte. Peck, P.

July 26
414662 Pte. Reid, J.
136508 Pte. Shaw, W. R.

July 27
487489 Pte. Henry, W. R.
118081 Pte. Massey, L. J.
441629 Pte. Noakes, R. E.
440288 Pte. Roy, J. R.
101138 Pte. Barnett, M. D.
440988 Pte. Rutt, J. H.

July 28
117244 Pte. Fewings, L. G.
117226 Pte. Dickens, J. W.
117374 Pte. McCoubrey, H.
463183 Pte. Stevenson, E. H.
117638 Pte. Davis, A. C. W.
135663 Sgt. Brown, W. A.

July 29
425323 Pte. Skinner, E. A.

August 1
107311 Pte. Hepper, J. T.

August 2
464519 Pte. Thomson, A. L.
447169 Pte. Porter, T.

August 12
447461 Pte. Bridges, M. H. o/c

THE BLUFF, 1916

August 16
117261 L/Cpl. Gillies, W. C.
117532 Pte. Smith, C. C.

August 17
117282 Pte. Hainsworth, L.

August 17
135231 Pte. Taylor, J.
126324 Pte. Anderson, W. H.
136448 Pte. Aldridge, C.
136250 Pte. Taylor, S.

§ Accidentally wounded.   o/c On command.

Appendix IV—Wounded

THE BLUFF AND OBSERVATORY RIDGE, 1916

August 17
107164	L/Cpl.	Cross, C. H.

August 18
117635	Pte.	Wormald, J. W.
135415	Pte.	Agnew, R.
441338	Pte.	Reid, W. H.
117624	Cpl.	Whittle, E.
136637	Pte.	Binsley, E.
442769	Pte.	Bishop, H.
443040	Pte.	McMillan, D. D.
126894	Pte.	Shean, J.
108351	Pte.	Gatensburg, A. C.
136646	Pte.	Abbey, T.
435660	Pte.	McKay, A.
108351	Pte.	Love, R. E.

August 19
117106	Pte.	Allen, J.
136239	Pte.	Tapp, F.
464129	Pte.	Dollamore, T. G.
117490	Pte.	Pullen, J.

August 20
136161	Pte.	Walsh, P. J.
440036	Pte.	Pitt, A.
117553	Pte.	Leppard, C. H.

August 21
116026	Pte.	Morgan, O.
107613	Pte.	Wilkinson, T.
126261	Pte.	Sherman, G.
117586	L/Cpl.	Trevenon, W.
464524	Pte.	Bullock, A.

August 22
440766	Sgt.	O'Connor, F. M.
117647	Sgt.	Smith, F. G.
117428	Pte.	Norrish, C.
117154	Pte.	Barton, H.
108138	Pte.	Carr, J. J.
117639	Pte.	Wilson, R. G.
107117	Pte.	Brown, A.
442752	Pte.	Munday, H.
423307	Pte.	Lowe, W. J.
107495	Cpl.	Potter, J. K.
107323	C.S.M.	Hazeldine, T. F.
422933	Pte.	Bedford, F.
447532	Pte.	Bleaken, J. C.

August 23
423330	Pte.	Richards, E. W.

POZIERES TRENCHES AND MOUQUET FARM, 1916

September 11
135420	Pte.	Beamish, B.
436588	Pte.	Standing, E. W.
113046	Pte.	Sullivan, M.
116099	Pte.	Wilson, S.
118074	Pte.	Killip, R. H.
126334	Pte.	Brown, G. H.
441568	Pte.	O'Connor, B. C.

September 12
116040	Pte.	Scott, H.
116037	C.S.M.	Richman, R.
425233	Pte.	Wilson, J. T.
408766	L/Cpl.	Watson, W. H.
107621	L/Cpl.	Whitmore, R. D.
135427	Pte.	Barnes, J. G.
135106	Pte.	Beckett, C. R.
107125	Pte.	Bancroft, W.
126260	Pte.	Boyle, H. A.
117253	Pte.	Gaffney, W. H.
425477	Pte.	Vincent, W. B.
443056	Pte.	McLeod, J.
437634	Pte.	Greenwood, R.
135428	Pte.	Barrett, A.
107268	Cpl.	Howells, E. R.
628479	Pte.	Leask, W.
108073	Pte.	Bavester, F. H.
136197	Pte.	Best, A. E.

September 13
117516	Pte.	Roland, C. E.
117194	L/Cpl.	Caffery, L. C.
464536	Pte.	Taylor, F.
463027	Pte.	Brady, W.
135976	Pte.	Bennett, W. B.
135579	Pte.	Stiff, H.
135250	Pte.	Brooke, H.
443325	Pte.	Slater, T. H.
117290	Pte.	Hawkes, S. T.

September 14
118091	Pte.	Poolman, G. V.
436914	Pte.	Marshall, J.

September 15
117297	Pte.	Herbertson, R.
464458	Pte.	Baker, E. G.
117248	Pte.	Flett, G.
108265	Pte.	Hall, F.

September 16
135086	Pte.	Airhart, L. A.
107069	Pte.	Anson, R.
463212	Pte.	Anderson, B. L.
135640	L/Cpl.	Allen, E.
447011	Pte.	Atkinson, J. W.
135424	Pte.	Bannister, F. E.
64547	Sgt.	Boult, E. G.
135978	Pte.	Bewserf, B.

2nd Canadian Mounted Rifles

POZIERES TRENCHES AND MOUQUET FARM, 1916

September 16

135966	Pte.	Bambough, C. H.	441405	Pte.	Pelkey, A. T.
422769	Pte.	Bishop, H.	117478	Pte.	Phillips, J.
452542	Pte.	Bell, T. G.	441056	Pte.	Patterson, R.
107077	C.S.M.	Bowen, H. T.	440195	Pte.	Patterson, S.
135631	Pte.	Bonser, G.	440584	Pte.	Quinney, H.
117191	Sgt.	Clements, R. A.	107521	Sgt.	Rant, E.
117185	Pte.	Chapman, G. T.	404909	Pte.	Robinson, W.
117231	Pte.	Davison, M.	435402	Pte.	Rhodes, W. E. F.
464299	Pte.	Forsythe, C.	107513	L/Cpl.	Riley, W. J.
107254	Sgt.	Gardiner, E. M.	440626	Pte.	Racicot, T. H.
443648	Pte.	Graham, R.	135858	Pte.	Shaw, G.
107239	Pte.	Glasspool, C. J.	117551	Pte.	Stephen, R.
117318	Pte.	Innes, T.	136129	Pte.	Shultz, J.
443015	Pte.	Jackson, N.	117533	Pte.	Smith, C. H.
435778	L/Cpl.	Jones, G.	464361	Pte.	Summers, V.
117230	L/Cpl.	Jenkins, A. J.	135531	Pte.	Sutherland, J.
117457	L/Cpl.	Lawrence, C. F.	136466	Pte.	Stollard, H. T.
117348	Pte.	Lawrence, V. H.	107539	L/Sgt.	Simpson, H.
463133	Pte.	Montgomery, A.	107573	L/Cpl.	Shipton, B.
464402	Pte.	McTaggart, C. R.	135219	Pte.	Sears, B.
118087	Pte.	McRae, A.	107521	Pte.	Sherritt, W.
107396	Pte.	McLennan, G.	463372	Pte.	Straiton, J.
441698	Pte.	Olsen, J.	463189	Pte.	Todd, C. H.
440441	Pte.	Orton, F.	135389	Pte.	Turp, A. R.
441794	Pte.	Parkinson, W. H.	127090	Pte.	Woods, J. A.
441025	Pte.	Parkyn, E.	464674	Pte.	Williams, B.
440092	Pte.	Parsons, W. A.	117205	Pte.	Corbell, F. D.
441747	Pte.	Page, E.			

MOUQUET FARM, 1916

September 12			September 16		
107356	Cpl.	°Kildahl, B.	107557	Cpl.	Shuttleworth, R.
107269	Pte.	°Hughes, J. T.			

LA BOISELLE, 1916

September 23

117115	Pte.	Atkinson, G. S.

BOUZENCOURT, 1916

September 24

443270	Pte.	Knox, F. W.	108598	Sgt.	Vayro, G.
136289	Pte.	Summers, H. G.	127046	Pte.	Brooks, R. W.
136639	Pte.	Barnaby, T.	115429	Pte.	Harper, H. J.
126209	Pte.	Black, J. A.	107141	Pte.	Clarke, E. W.
127015	Pte.	Lynch, J. W.	446759	Pte.	Roberts, C. E.
108546	C.S.M.	Sneddon, T.	136131	Pte.	Shaw, F. H.
108213	C.Q.M.S.	Farmer, A. E.	107304	Pte.	†Hines, J.
108113	Pte.	Brand, W.	117604	Pte.	†Stephen, W.
447362	Pte.	Carmichael, A. C.	434540	Pte.	†Ainge, A. C.
437358	Pte.	Lorrimer, W. K.	117496	Pte.	†Rawlings, W. L.
I36379	Pte.	Smith, H. C.			

° Trench Mortar Battery.
† Working party.

Appendix IV—Wounded

HESSIAN TRENCH, 1916

September 27

463798	Pte.	Hedley, R.
135253	Pte.	Vickery, W.
135902	Pte.	Watson, J.

September 28

161201	Pte.	Armstrong, T. L.
135100	Pte.	Bird, H.
100584	Pte.	Brasnett, C. H.
447558	Pte.	Beales, R. E.
108147	Pte.	Chapman, C. T.
117206	Pte.	Cormack, F. L.
446143	Pte.	Davison, J. W.
117247	Pte.	Fletcher, J. J.
464638	Pte.	Hogland, O.
107309	Cpl.	Hartley, J. M.
446139	Pte.	Hardie, J. M. O.
117330	Pte.	Keating, B. T.
107370	Pte.	Loftus, K.
700999	Pte.	Lee, G.
117400	Pte.	McRae, A.
117391	Pte.	McKinnon, J. P.
150170	Pte.	McQuade, T. F.
447765	Pte.	Park, J.
441376	Pte.	Pell, E. W.
160190	Pte.	Pickard, J. R. V.
700255	Pte.	Renning, T. J.
180525	Pte.	Roberts, E.
135574	Pte.	Smith, R. G.
136382	Pte.	Sullivan, J. F.
117570	Pte.	Sutherland, E. P.
464175	Pte.	Travis, A. J.
446401	Pte.	Trigg, C.
446421	Pte.	Tabbener, A. J.
160438	Pte.	Wilson, W.

September 29

136546	Pte.	Bishop, H. E.
135440	Pte.	Boyt, F.
136198	Pte.	Brearley, A.
127407	Pte.	Bowd, A.
127705	Pte.	Bower, D. E.
135655	Pte.	Barrow, W.
136543	Pte.	Brabson, H. S.
135327	Sgt.	Borland, A. G.
135463	Pte.	Coulter, W.
180198	Pte.	Cochrane, P.
107139	L/Cpl.	Carr, W. H.
446153	Pte.	Caffelle, N.
700992	Pte.	Dahlbury, O.
117242	Pte.	Evans, J.
447066	Pte.	Falconer, J. L.
700454	Pte.	Harris, F.
107306	Pte.	Hollmark, W.
108311	Pte.	Joblin, R.
447617	Pte.	Jackson, H. R.
118073	Pte.	Kerr, R.
180490	Pte.	Kingston, R.
436210	Pte.	Lailey, A. W.
117429	Pte.	Morris, E. J.
464403	Pte.	McKenzie, J. M.
107388	Pte.	McEwan, G. B.
700014	Pte.	McMahony, E. T.
435660	Pte.	McKay, A.
440195	Pte.	Patterson, S.
180514	Pte.	Paine, J.
118092	Cpl.	Quigg, H.
440149	Pte.	Robinson, A. J.
117497	Pte.	Reinholt, F. L.
107535	Sgt.	Saunders, C. G.
770929	Pte.	Saunderson, R.
135575	Pte.	Squirrel, H.
107573	Cpl.	Shipton, B.
107539	A/Sgt.	Simpson, H.
46943	Pte.	Seager, S. G.
159559	Pte.	Sokoloski, V.
108528	A/Cpl.	Sharp, A.
107581	Sgt.	Tyler, S. S.
135236	Pte.	Tomsett, A. J.
136159	Pte.	Walkling, A.
117613	Pte.	Weatherhead, B.
464675	Pte.	Williams, T.
136245	Pte.	Waldron, W. E.
160873	Pte.	Watt, G. L.
423240	Pte.	Wright, E. J.
447003	Pte.	Austin, R. C.
160195	Pte.	Heasleton, A.
107456	L/Cpl.	Neish, J. D.
446158	Pte.	Willans, F.

September 30

409317	Pte.	Ambrose, W.
135963	Pte.	Aston, T. G.
136301	Pte.	Abel, H. J. T.
135964	Pte.	Aylward, A. V.
117156	L/Cpl.	Boulter, P. P.
117129	Pte.	Beech, K.
135442	Pte.	Bacon, T.
107081	L/Cpl.	Baverstock, W.
180180	Pte.	Blasson, B.
117159	Cpl.	Bowie, J. B.
107174	Pte.	Crow, A. O.
117224	Pte.	Deforas, F. F.
464049	Pte.	Denligh, A.
464294	Pte.	Edkins, S. L.
435524	Pte.	Edwards, J.
107212	L/Cpl.	Fletcher, C. W.
464398	Pte.	Fletcher, H. H.

2nd Canadian Mounted Rifles

HESSIAN TRENCH, 1916

September 30

107257	Cpl.	Grant, C. F.
423445	Pte.	Gordon, C.
117281	Pte.	Hainstock, C. L.
442834	Pte.	Hall, S.
117289	Sgt.	Harvey, W. F.
117312	Pte.	Hopkins, N. R.
116017	Pte.	Harper, J. M.
107338	L/Cpl.	Jacombs, M. H. L.
443013	Pte.	Jackson, A.
136482	Pte.	Jowett, F. D.
456900	Pte.	Lillis, W.
446914	Pte.	Moran, E.
116032	Pte.	McGuckie, D. N.
117401	L/Cpl.	McVicar, A. R.
443863	Pte.	Nichol, W. G.
441824	Pte.	Penrose, M. G.
440053	Pte.	Pickard, A.
160991	Pte.	Rutherford, G.
107565	Pte.	Shiers, J.
701185	Pte.	Sheppard, C. E.
425287	Pte.	Saunders, G. H.
135877	Pte.	Shields, G.
136154	Pte.	Turner, A. E.
136390	Pte.	Tubbs, W. G.
447247	Pte.	Wallace, B.
464679	Pte.	Crompton, F.
464560	Pte.	Knox, T. F.

September 30

136163	Pte.	Ward, T.

October 1

135971	Pte.	Bartle, F. J.
135432	Pte.	Berry, W.
446960	Pte.	Baker, W. E.
447973	Pte.	Clarke, A. W.
108254	L/Cpl.	Grigg, E. J.
463484	Pte.	Keith, N.
441062	A/Sgt.	Rudden, P.
422774	Pte.	Robertson, F.
136134	Pte.	Simons, W. J.
136584	Pte.	Smith, L. F.
136137	Pte.	Smith, H.

October 2

436166	Pte.	Bergeron, T. A.
447532	Pte.	Brown, M.
107215	Pte.	°Fowle, J. T.
434944	Pte.	Gittins, J.
441367	Pte.	Pack, E.
441498	Pte.	Rooney, H. N.
135218	Pte.	Scott, J.
108649	Pte.	°Warder, G. R.
116050	Sgt.	Wright, E. J.
443646	Pte.	Burt, G.
107478	Sgt.	Palmer, E.
107383	Sgt.	McCarvell, J. J.

SOMME, VANCOUVER AND SUDBURY TRENCHES, 1916
[Between E. and W. Miraumont Road]

October 9

107350	Pte.	Knight, G.
700490	Pte.	Loner, W.
107439	Pte.	Marcotte, H.
464786	Pte.	McEwan, J.
441629	Pte.	Noakes, R. E.
117479	L/Cpl.	Phizackerly, A. O.
108491	Pte.	Roberts, H. S.
441065	Pte.	Read, E. C.
180679	Pte.	Stone, W. G.
136586	Pte.	Staley, H. F.
136517	Pte.	Tilbe, A. V.
126247	Pte.	Tremain, J. R.
135642	Pte.	Addy, R. W.

October 10

136808	Pte.	Barclay, A. F.
180614	Pte.	Goddard, A.
463681	L/Cpl.	Goodship, L. A.
107268	Cpl.	Howells, E. R.
107354	L/Cpl.	Kenyon, H. H.
464403	Pte.	McKenzie, J. M.
443877	Pte.	McMahon, J. G.
117414	Pte.	Menzies, A. A.
107434	Pte.	Murray, E. E.
117479	Pte.	Miller, T. L.
108466	Pte.	Pope, J. S.
117517	L/Cpl.	Ross, A.

SOMME, 1916

October 10

108493	Pte.	Roberts, W.
425293	Pte.	Scott, J. R.
117563	L/Sgt.	Strickland, F. C.
126579	Pte.	Simms, A. E.
425323	Pte.	Skinner, A. E.

October 10

425335	Pte.	Smith, H.
136583	Pte.	Thomas, G.
446946	Pte.	Torrens, W.
446421	Pte.	Tabbener, A. J.
158698	Pte.	Veremuchik, J.

° Trench Mortar Battery.

Appendix IV—Wounded

SOMME, 1916

October 10
180970	Pte.	Young, C. McP.
425517	Pte.	Youngman, E. A.
447611	Pte.	York, B. F.

October 11
118051	Pte.	Adlam, L.
135972	Pte.	Baxter, R.
136312	Pte.	Bolton, W.
107117	L/Cpl.	Brown, A.
106004	Pte.	Barrett, A.
446162	Pte.	Brookes, E. H.
135988	Pte.	Bridges, B. H.
108152	Pte.	Clark, G.
107180	A/Cpl.	Duncan, J.
464654	Pte.	Douglas, H. R. E.
434262	Pte.	Dower, W.
161337	Pte.	Doney, A.
463884	L/Cpl.	Goode, T. W.
160007	Pte.	Huggins, R. B.
442705	Pte.	Kennedy, P. N.
108345	Pte.	Littleford, T. J.
107405	Cpl.	Miller, D.
160945	Pte.	Morey, G.
446030	Pte.	McCarthy, L. G.
112253	Pte.	Markle, J.
117393	Pte.	McLeod, A.
437068	Pte.	Martin, R. C.
160309	Pte.	Nicol, J. A.
441305	Pte.	Noakes, L. A.
440582	Cpl.	Pratt, C. F.
441234	Pte.	Pascoe, A. H.
700255	Pte.	Renning, J.
464063	Pte.	Rosie, M.
108478	Pte.	Reade, H. J.

October 11
441400	Pte.	Rees, A. L.
107557	A/Sgt.	Shuttleworth, L.
126428	Pte.	Sherwood, G.
135571	Pte.	Smalley, G.
135578	Pte.	Stiff, A. F.
442780	Pte.	Smith, F.
422832	Pte.	Sommerville, E. A. R.
414280	Pte.	Shankley, R.
108527	Cpl.	Sharland, W.
443134	Pte.	Trevor, H. R.
463205	Pte.	Woolsey, G. G.
107607	Sgt.	Wilson, J. C.

October 12
135418	Pte.	Andrew, T.
135425	Pte.	Bannister, T. S.
135980	Pte.	Birks, C.
117192	Pte.	Cobb, B. T.
117224	Pte.	DeForas, F. J.
441309	Pte.	Parlee, J. P.
180701	Pte.	Patterson, H. M.
107228	Pte.	Fairburn, L. E.
112178	Pte.	°Bell, T. J.

October 13
135965	Pte.	Baine, J. W.
117156	L/Cpl.	Boulter, P. P.
107280	Pte.	Huntley, C. E.
136144	Pte.	Stephens, W. G.
446023	L/Cpl.	Slipp, L. L.

October 14
107170	Pte.	°Clarke, F.
135433	Pte.	°Blackhall, A.

October 16
160854	Pte.	Cohl, R.

ROCLINCOURT, 1916

October 26
117301	Pte.	Hives, J. E.

October 28
135879	Pte.	Sherman, W. J.
180664	Pte.	Pugh, W.

November 4
441183	Sgt.	Rowlette, J. I.
425476	Pte.	Westover, F.
425330	Pte.	Smith, B.

November 17
414920	Pte.	°Neary, P. J.

November 20 (Raid)
117313	Pte.	Cullen, W.
108443	Pte.	Osenton, C.
107256	L/Cpl.	Graham, G. W.

° 8th Trench Mortar Battery.

November 20 (Raid)
425326	Pte.	Slater, W. P.
107065	Pte.	Armit, T. N.
126065	Pte.	Scott, F.
100374	Pte.	Wells, P. W.
440091	Pte.	Pritchard, R. S.
113017	Pte.	Gervin, W.
107428	Pte.	Maxwell, G. S.
135636	Pte.	Addy, E. R. N.
117597	L/Cpl.	Usherwood, A. E.

December 1
117452	Pte.	°Nurcombe, E. L.

December 3
435764	Pte.	Blackwell, F. H. (Tunnelling Co.)
440588	Pte.	Ross, L.

2nd Canadian Mounted Rifles

ROCLINCOURT, 1916

December 11
161267	Pte.	Sherman, C.
135980	Pte.	Birks, C.
135966	Pte.	Bamborough, C. H.

December 15
181022	Pte.	Irvine, C. W.
440588	Pte.	Ross, L.
117412	Pte.	Meers, H.
136145	Pte.	Stiff, F.
441183	Sgt.	Rowlett, J. T.
441672	Pte.	Primeau, T.
464284	Pte.	Chapman, J. F.
108257	A/Cpl.	*Gunness, W. C.
160404	Pte.	*Murray, J. L.
463252	Pte.	*Clark, C. F.
108527	A/Sgt.	*Sharland, W.
117303	L/Cpl.	*Hives, E.

December 16
117226	Pte.	Dickens, J. W.

December 20
117232	Cpl.	°Duckworth, F.
117509	Pte.	°Robertson, L. M.

December 23
435524	Pte.	Edwards, J.

December 24
135435	Pte.	*Booker, H. G.
136637	Pte.	*Binsley, E.

December 26
440529	Pte.	Peterson, A.
107512	Pte.	*Ricketts, D.

December 28
135966	Pte.	Bamborough, C. H.

ROCLINCOURT, 1917

January 14
425341	Pte.	Soan, E.

January 17
116950	Pte.	Reid, W. C.
107541	Pte.	Smith, A. C.
113057	Sgt.	Anderson, J.

January 18
116246	A/Sgt.	Mitchell, C.

January 20
628479	Pte.	Leask, W.

January 21
117225	Sgt.	Dick, D.
782074	Pte.	Watkins, G.
160410	Pte.	Dunlop, J.
117555	L/Cpl.	Stevenette, W. A.
136584	Pte.	*Smith, L. F.
117465	Pte.	*Patchett, H.
117281	Pte.	*Hainstock, C. D.

MONT ST ELOI, 1917

February 1
136639	Pte.	Barnaby, F.
135091	Pte.	Angus, J.

February 1
464657	Pte.	Jackson, W.
700929	Pte.	Sanderson, R.

ADRIANE, 1917

February 7
116249	Pte.	Price, D. W.

VIMY RIDGE, 1917

March 24
135082	Sgt.	°Trueman, G.

March 25
425162	Pte.	Nesteruk, F.
706489	Pte.	*Riley, W. G. S.

March 26
463893	Sgt.	Smythe, A. H.

March 29
136584	Pte.	Smith, L. F.
136145	Pte.	Stitt, F.
500533	Pte.	Glass, J.
107126	Sgt.	°Brett, W.

March 31 (Raid)
135988	Pte.	Bridges, B. H.
441916	L/Cpl.	Whiting, J. R.
116146	A/Sgt.	Mills, F. H.
781481	Pte.	Hall, J. A.
227689	Pte.	Neal, C. B.

* Still on duty.
° Trench Mortar Battery.

Appendix IV—Wounded

VIMY RIDGE, 1917

March 31 (Raid)
707253	Pte.	Dasher, A. J.
781033	Pte.	Boyle, G. A.
116412	L/Cpl.	Cluse, E.

March 31
252005	Pte.	Angus, W. M.
781473	Pte.	Duxbury, T.
687606	Pte.	Clark, J.
181022	Pte.	Irvine, C. W.

April 6
108324	Pte.	Kight, E.

April 8
408791	Pte.	Hammond, B.
760909	Pte.	Archibald, J. G.

April 9 (Attack
116452	A/Sgt.	Glover, W.
227669	Pte.	Armstrong, J.
464034	L/Cpl.	Booker, R. D. B.
706414	Pte.	Rule, A.
135980	Pte.	Birks, C.
781422	Pte.	Eley, G. M.
107289	Pte.	Harvey, J. W.
706544	Pte.	Evans, C. S.
781923	Pte.	Wales, A. T.
441916	L/Cpl.	Whiting, J. R.
707208	Pte.	Burns, R. S.
687061	Pte.	Crossetta, F.
781450	Pte.	Thompson, H. F.
107433	Pte.	Mortimer, V.
116302	Pte.	Edwards, E.
117490	L/Sgt.	Pullen, J. S.
707178	Pte.	Burns, R. M.
136621	Pte.	Boorman, J.
832334	Pte.	Goodwin, J. A.
687069	Pte.	Wisson, R. C. A.
687064	Pte.	Mahoney, W. J.
227649	Pte.	Terry, J.
706624	Pte.	Evans, E.
781888	Pte.	Welch, J.
781942	Pte.	Webb, D. J.
227692	Pte.	Keith, F.
707242	Pte.	Armstrong, W. R. C.
116785	Pte.	Price, A. G. F.
687592	Pte.	Stewart, W. B.
781151	Pte.	Killien, M.
447234	Pte.	Trerise, W. J.
688057	Pte.	Ruddock, E. B.
116128	Pte.	Burgess, J.
706448	Pte.	Howe, J. E.
687083	Pte.	Monk, W. H.
781337	Pte.	Smith, F.

* Still on duty.

April 9 (Attack
116769	Pte.	Lambert, J.
706761	Pte.	Liddell, W. K.
135640	Cpl.	Allen, E.
136248	Pte.	Appleby, J.
463951	Pte.	Amos, A.
116776	Pte.	Baggs, W. F.
252382	L/Cpl.	Bowes, A.
116568	Pte.	Bushfield, A.
687087	Pte.	Carr, B.
116562	Pte.	Corrigan, J. T.
116839	Pte.	Champion, E.
116990	Pte.	Curts, E. H.
135473	L/Cpl.	Duncan, T.
227743	Pte.	Fletcher, F. J.
116106	L/Cpl.	Gavin, J.
463681	Cpl.	Goodship, L. A.
116723	Pte.	Grant, D.
706801	Pte.	Handlen, J. W.
117289	Sgt.	Harvey, W. F.
117416	Pte.	Meredith-Browne, S. E.
706733	Pte.	Parlee, G. M.
426370	Pte.	Pearcey, H.
117471	L/Sgt.	Pegler, A. W.
441406	Pte.	Pilkington, W.
687257	Pte.	Pritchard, R.
135553	Pte.	Pugh, W. J.
687648	Pte.	Smith, J. G.
117559	Pte.	Stewart, W.
687031	Pte.	Stocking, G. H.
135882	Pte.	Train, N.
136440	Pte.	Vandervoort, S. W.
782315	Pte.	Young, F.
832087	Pte.	Trenholme, W. C.
706804	Pte.	Peck, T. E. L.
706590	Pte.	James, T.
706693	Pte.	Brown, J.
463252	Pte.	Clarke, C. F.
464524	Pte.	Bullock, A.
687707	Pte.	Evans, J.
707213	Pte.	Franklin, E.
688073	Pte.	Grantham, V. F.
117300	Pte.	Higginson, G.
707209	Pte.	Boskovitch, V.
440909	Pte.	*Robinson, W. C.
624318	Cpl.	Davey, E. J.
116045	L/Cpl.	Swanby, A. O.
117297	Cpl.	Herbertson, R.
117644	Cpl.	Zuehlke, F.
116153	Pte.	Bridgeman, W.
781021	Pte.	Belleghem, E.
116738	Pte.	Hannah, C. H.

2nd Canadian Mounted Rifles

VIMY RIDGE, 1917

April 9 (Attack)

181200	Pte.	Patterson, T.
707312	Pte.	Rourke, W.
180876	Pte.	Stollery, E.
227701	Pte.	Yoll, J.
135875	L/Cpl.	Scorgie, J.
117154	Pte.	Barton, H.
706565	Pte.	Butters, W.
181688	Pte.	Watson, W. D.
116020	Sgt.	James, S. G.
117425	L/Cpl.	Moffatt, J. K.
116832	Pte.	Banning, J.
227660	Pte.	Evans, D. J.
707123	Pte.	Hurst, H. J.
116320	Pte.	Stanton, H. F.
116701	Pte.	Walker, J. G.
707025	Pte.	McDonald, A.
706997	Pte.	McNeil, J. R.
116691	Pte.	Rennie, P. M.
441063	Pte.	Roberts, T. H.
135879	Pte.	Sherman, W. J.
117261	Cpl.	Gillies, W. C.
116323	Cpl.	Lawrence, E. M.
116782	L/Cpl.	King, J.
116471	Pte.	Beard, W. K.
160789	Pte.	Forest, M.
116475	Pte.	Hutchinson, A.
463133	Pte.	Montgomery, A.
706953	Pte.	McColl, J.
227752	Pte.	Walton, A. T.
782433	Pte.	Raymer, H.
116744	Pte.	Taylor, J.
116369	Pte.	Warman, F. D.
706757	Pte.	Scott, J. A.
441415	Pte.	Rudolph, C. P.
781687	Pte.	Squires, T. F.
707210	Pte.	Sivertz, G.
160443	Pte.	Gunn, J.
160087	Pte.	McKenzie, J.
117247	Pte.	Fletcher, J. J.
117553	Sgt.	Stevenson, J. W.
108587	Sgt.	Trembley, H. C.
108527	L/Sgt.	Sharland, W.
108584	Cpl.	Treece, A. E.
252431	Cpl.	Keir, T. G.
117206	L/Cpl.	Cormack, F. L.
781010	Pte.	Arnett, F. H.
781031	Pte.	Bentley, A. C.
781542	Pte.	Claydon, P. L.
160854	Pte.	Cohl, R.
687694	Pte.	Crouch, F.
447573	Pte.	Dargie, R. E.
116011	Pte.	Foster, T. D.
782089	Pte.	Flock, A. J.
108324	Pte.	Kight, E.
781152	Pte.	Knoll, H. H.
160809	Pte.	McLean, R.
781645	Pte.	Midler, W. H.
781681	Pte.	McNutt, S. B.
447735	Pte.	McCleary, L. P.
116985	Pte.	O'Reilly, A.
687451	Pte.	Olson, O.
442760	Pte.	Palmer, J. L.
447179	Pte.	Phillips, W. W.
687413	Pte.	Quinn, C.
687892	Pte.	Reed, C.
136634	Pte.	Smith, R.
706914	Pte.	Stillwell, W. B.
447608	Pte.	Taylor, C. J.
781774	Pte.	Goodwin, W. E.
437068	Pte.	Martin, R. C.
227698	Pte.	Bradley, J.
782248	Pte.	Wade, J.
707168	Pte.	Wallace, A.
706484	Pte.	Thompson, B. T.
252041	Pte.	Cameron, D.
441574	Pte.	Reid, H. W.
116737	Pte.	McLean, H.
116343	Pte.	Hicks, E. P.
688177	Pte.	Page, H.
791156	Pte.	DeHollis, R. C.
706729	Pte.	Taylor, W.
781852	Pte.	Bryan, L. A.
117412	Pte.	Meeres, H.
706980	Pte.	Cardwell, J.
706633	Pte.	Snowden, E.
706858	Pte.	Watson, W.
707099	Pte.	Corble, W. S.
687988	Pte.	Smith, W.
447247	Pte.	Wallace, B.
227664	Pte.	Robins, A.
687476	Pte.	Bennett, A. G.
136156	Pte.	Veness, E. T.
107131	Pte.	Brown, W. R.
		(8th M. G. C.)

April 10 (Attack)

706335	Pte.	Brough, R. C.
117317	Sgt.	Innes, A. E.
227613	Pte.	Innes, T.
781737	Pte.	Brown, H. C.
135438	L/Cpl.	Boyd, J.
252652	Pte.	McLaughlin, H.
436599	Pte.	Standing, E. W.
107555	Cpl.	Shields, C.
181039	Pte.	Eaton, W. M.
781295	Pte.	Wright, J. E.
687616	Pte.	Spooner, F.
107560	Pte.	Swadden, J. A.

Appendix IV—Wounded

VIMY RIDGE, 1917

April 10 (Attack)			**April 10 (Attack)**		
782306	Pte.	Wilkins, P. L.	108051	L/Cpl.	Adams, J. S.
687723	Pte.	Carter, A.	**April 11**		
687779	Pte.	Mennell, J. A.	107368	Pte.	Lancaster, C.
687751	Pte.	*Pizzolato, A.	107368	Pte.	Lancaster, C.
464679	Pte.	*Crompton, F.	464643	Pte.	Hazell, E.
227762	Pte.	*Birch, O.	116995	Pte.	Osborne, J.
116707	Pte.	*Johnston, C.	136239	L/Cpl.	Tapp, F.
707237	Pte.	*Purser, E.	706554	Pte.	Webster, D.
116862	Pte.	Dyer, E.	116911	Pte.	Roells, S. S.
706673	Pte.	Cheslyn, W. H.	706580	Pte.	Thornton, D. R.
107309	Cpl.	Hartley, J. M.	117303	Cpl.	Hives, E.
781470	Pte.	Duxbury, G.	706813	Pte.	Gillan, F. H.
160410	Pte.	Dunlop, J.	116819	Pte.	Watson, A. F.
422269	Pte.	Lamb, A.	117383	Pte.	McFayden, J.
687620	Pte.	McCall, H. A.	107273	Pte.	Hayhurst, A.
487680	Pte.	Penny, A. F.			(Brigade Signals)
441369	Pte.	Ringrose, J. F.	**April 23**		
136141	Pte.	Staden, J.	706205	Pte.	Bentley, E.
181022	Pte.	Irvine, C. W.	127043	Pte.	Sherwood, G. R.
108381	Cpl.	Meyer, E. R.	**April 27**		
706861	Pte.	Hayward, C. E.	706805	Pte.	‡Bobbett, T.

CHAUDIERE, 1917

May 6		
161097	L/Cpl.	Jones, J. R.

TRENCHES IN FRONT OF AVION, 1917

May 6			**May 8**		
136196	Pte.	Baker, C. W.	116786	Pte.	‡Dawley, H. B.
443023	Pte.	Kennedy, N. N.			(attached Corps Light Ry.)
May 8			**May 9**		
135964	Pte.	Aylward, A.	116029	Pte.	MacDonald, F.
116869	Pte.	‡Jones, T. M.	**May 10**		
		(attached Corps Light Ry.)	116196	L/Cpl.	‡Hope, J. A.

VIMY RIDGE, 1917

May 12			**May 12**		
931449	Pte.	Billsborough, R.	252012	Pte.	Bain, C.
931767	Pte.	Donagan, R.			(attached 8th Bde. carrying party)
688217	Pte.	Kennedy, A. D.			

TRENCHES IN FRONT OF AVION, 1917

May 22			**May 28**		
706928	Pte.	Neill, J.	687723	Pte.	Carter, A.
425447	Pte.	Vincent, W. B.	**May 29**		
May 25			931078	Pte.	Precious, F.
136440	Pte.	Vandervoort, S. W.	931740	Pte.	Rowe, T. H.
May 27			707169	Pte.	Creber, H. H.
136146	Pte.	Stollard, H. T.	706690	Pte.	Flett, A. L. M.
‡ Gassed.			**June 6**		
* Still on duty.			687348	Pte.	Woods, J. B.

2nd Canadian Mounted Rifles

TRENCHES IN FRONT OF AVION

May 30
107623	C.S.M.	Whitmore, H. A.
135428	L/Cpl.	Barrett, A.
931612	Pte.	McIllwraith, T. H.

May 31
688004	Pte.	Foster, H.

June 1
116411	L/Cpl.	Ellis, C. S.
135645	L/Cpl.	Broomhead, T. V.
707133	Pte.	Baldie, R.
116950	Pte.	Reid, W. C.
435778	Pte.	Jones, G.
116926	Pte.	Matveichuk, J.

June 2
107076	Sgt.	Berwick, R.
782352	L/Cpl.	Worle, P. G.
931160	Pte.	Lindblad, H. J.
227762	Pte.	*Birch, O.

June 3
931101	Pte.	Watt, C. F.
441721	A/Cpl.	Parker, S. H.

117390	Cpl.	McKenzie, R. W.
706489	Pte.	Riley, W. G. S.
463150	Pte.	Newbery, G.
688097	Pte.	Coombs, J.

June 5

June 6
706239	Pte.	Matthews, R. H.
687995	Pte.	‡Dick, J.

June 7
931600	Pte.	Geddes, E. R.
931505	Pte.	Healey, H.
931726	Pte.	Kent, G. S.

June 8
100115	Pte.	*Darlington, T. T.
180919	Pte.	*Palmer, W. J.

June 9
707156	L/Cpl.	*Bowler, P. J.

June 10
116869	Pte.	Jones, T. M., o/c

VILLERS-AU-BOIS, 1917

June 16
108445	Cpl.	§Owens, W. R.
688017	Pte.	§Funk, L.

VIMY RIDGE-AVION, 1917

June 18
826703	Pte.	Rutherford, T.
826524	Pte.	Kyle, R.
687064	Pte.	Mahoney, W. J.
687500	Cpl.	Brown, O. W.
760175	Pte.	McIntyre, W.
826370	Pte.	Marr, W. N.
446936	L/Cpl.	Jempson, J.

June 19
116297	Cpl.	Moore, T.
180701	Cpl.	Patterson, H. M.
443038	Pte.	McLeod, M. A.
116097	Pte.	McInnery, A.
116334	Pte.	Welch, J.
931143	Pte.	Gridley, H. C.
446914	Pte.	Moran, P.

827017	Pte.	Horton, R.
422769	Pte.	Bishop, H.

June 21

June 22
135898	Pte.	Ward, A.

June 24
826033	Pte.	Biggan, J.
826262	Pte.	Dowell, W. W.
826530	Pte.	Fraser, W. B.
826934	Pte.	Hemsill, R.
826153	Pte.	Bonden, C. B.
706477	Pte.	*Potter, J. F.

June 25
687119	Pte.	*Marchinia, B.
781089	Pte.	Fletcher, J.

ZOUAVE VALLEY, 1917

July 1
160834	Pte.	Rigg, T. W.

July 2
826029	Pte.	§Canning, P.

* Still on duty.
§ Accidentally wounded.
‡ Gassed.

464679	Pte.	§Crompton, F.
790500	Pte.	§Sullivan, P.

July 6

o/c On command.

Appendix IV—Wounded

AVION, 1917

July 12
826713 Pte. *Meunier, C.

July 13
931468 Pte. *Laderonte, C. E.
826036 Pte. Barrett, E.
826057 Pte. §Judd, J. H.

July 15
116121 Pte. Johnson, W. H.
440299 Pte. *Peck, P.
931843 Pte. Taylor, H. J.
931376 Pte. Gave, G. B. M.
116008 Pte. Elliot, J.

July 15
464358 Pte. Willoughby, P.
687740 Pte. Phinney, W. E.

July 16
135549 Sgt. Pogue, W. E.

July 17
826916 Pte. *Gops, A.

July 18
826903 Pte. Heath, A.
931133 Pte. Bourne, G. S.
826205 Pte. Shaw, J. G.

RAIMBERT, 1917

August 5
116097 Pte. §McInery, A.

August 5
931320 Pte. §Walker, H.

LOOS, 1917

August 20
688246 Pte. Richley, G. E.

August 21
931067 Pte. Regan, J.
827045 Pte. Anderson, F.
255830 Pte. Harmer, A. R.
 (with 46th Bn.)

August 22
707242 Pte. Armstrong, W. R. C.

August 23
826599 Pte. *Sanders, W.
760734 Pte. *Irving, A.
931275 Pte. ‡Greenwell, N. A.
826252 Pte. *Evans, R.
136505 Pte. Smylie, J.
931260 Pte. Kana, J.

August 24
687858 Pte. *Palmer, A. S.
422769 Pte. Bishop, H.

August 24
463884 Sgt. Goode, T. W.
826270 Pte. Potter, H.
826138 Pte. Collins, J.
931291 Pte. Womack, T. W.
931022 Pte. Robichaud, M. F.
931112 Pte. McNicholas, J. M.
446649 Pte. Brown, J. W.
829259 Pte. Padgham, A.
931247 Pte. Pinkerton, J.
826302 Pte. McWilliams, R.
781122 Pte. Heslop, J. W.
117586 L/Sgt. Trevenen, W. G.
107505 Pte. *Rogers, A. C.

August 25
136139 Pte. Smith, W. H.
707015 Pte. Dobie, J. L.
826814 Pte. Bulloch, A.
826516 Pte. Mercier, R. J.
707156 L/Cpl. Bowler, P. J.

CITE ST. PIERRE, 1917

August 30
687447 Pte. Manery, G. F.
826086 Pte. Bonach, J. O. S.
931799 Pte. Dyer, W.
826686 Pte. Erickson, A.
827034 Pte. Lane, J. R.
826716 Pte. §Brock, C. E.
108507 Pte. *Rylander, C. A.
435660 Pte. Mackay, A.

August 31
826436 Pte. Saunders, F.
826505 Pte. Stride, L. C. W.
826033 Pte. *Biggan, J.
442774 L/Cpl. *Robertson, F.

November 2
825601 Pte. Clark, G.
 (with 7th F.C.C.E.)

* Still on duty.
‡ Gassed.
§ Accidentally wounded.

2nd Canadian Mounted Rifles

MERICOURT, 1917

August 24
227666 Pte. Olson, A.
(with entrenching battalion)

September 3
423359 Sgt. ‡Ivy, J.

September 4
463798 Pte. ‡Hedley, R.

September 5
931302 Pte. Danielson, D.
826561 Pte. Scorgie, C. A.
931731 Pte. Yates, A.
931197 Pte. Krall, L.
116691 Pte. Rennie, P. N.
826093 Pte. Harwood, A. A.
443038 Pte. McLeod, M. A.
431020 Pte. Buxton, E.
931198 Pte. Krall, A.
931279 Pte. Kotek, J.
760360 Pte. Smith, Z. C.

September 6
252639 Pte. Rennie, A.
781930 Cpl. ‡Overy, A. W.

September 8
117533 Pte. Smith, C. H.

September 10
931121 Pte. ‡Coulliard, H. E.

September 15
826526 Pte. Davidson, J. C.
107066 Sgt. *Aspray, O. T.

September 29
931479 Pte. Smith, H. T.
(with 182nd Tunnelling Co.)
826649 Pte. Brodie, G. P.
(with 182nd Tunnelling Co.)

October 5
826809 Pte. Hart, S. S.
(with 182nd Tunnelling Co.)
826711 Pte. Lewis, W.
(with 182nd Tunnelling Co.)

PASSCHENDAELE, 1917

October 24
116040 Pte. Scott, H.
117188 Pte. Church, A.
440095 Pte. Ridgewell, B.
117395 Pte. McLeod, A.
447997 Pte. Downs, J.
117396 Pte. McLeod, H. E.
706568 Pte. Anderson, S. R.
136298 Pte. Brearly, A.
826163 Pte. Rand, J. G.
826160 Pte. Proctor, S. A.
441405 Pte. Pelky, A. J.
931496 Pte. *Conrad, J. A.

October 25
827036 Pte. Burnie, R.
826022 Pte. Sutherland, W. J. S.
707237 Pte. Purser, E. P.
781819 Pte. Hill, W. P.
2015196 Pte. Ekminko, J.
826304 Pte. Philliphant, F.
107066 Sgt. Aspray, O. T.
117449 Cpl. Noell, N. H.
826910 Pte. Gauthier, J. R.
107461 L/Cpl. Ollerhead, G. A.

161068 Pte. Clugston, H.
931552 Pte. Clease, W. J.

October 26
440299 Pte. *Peck, P.
826742 Pte. Barnes, W.
464051 Pte. Stride, H. A.
706740 Cpl. Kelly, D. E.
700492 Pte. Thomas, E.
294832 Pte. Lamon, E.
160410 Pte. Dunlop, J.
116097 Pte. McInnery, A.

October 27
135589 Cpl. Turp, A. R.
645691 Pte. Wilson, J.
826321 Pte. Skinner, D.
826489 Pte. Jack, G.
931216 Pte. Freer, E. E.
827036 Pte. Burnie, R.
447513 Pte. Higgins, R.
931821 Pte. White, W.
826917 Pte. Hart, R.
706455 Pte. Dean, A.
446485 Pte. Symons, A.
463579 Pte. Sprinkling, C. K.
826064 Pte. Moss, W. G.
931388 Pte. Nicholls, S. J.

‡ Gassed.
* Still on duty.

Appendix IV—Wounded

PASSCHENDAELE, 1917

October 28

826637	Pte.	Campbell, L. N.
826254	Pte.	Whigham, R.
437796	Pte.	Locke, B.
687892	Pte.	Reed, C.
116452	L/Sgt.	Glover, W.
687061	Pte.	Crossetta, F.
687847	Pte.	*Burbridge, G. J.
706625	Pte.	Sherman, D. H.

October 29

116016	L/Cpl.	Harding, J. S.
826760	Pte.	Denicola, A.
826483	Pte.	Nickerson, H. S.
117171	Cpl.	*Bryan, R. D.
826784	Pte.	*Hurst, N. L. R.
442647	Pte.	Davidovitch, —
931289	Pte.	*Grant, J.
441806	Sgt.	Rogers, M. E.
425447	Pte.	Vincent, W. B.
706729	Pte.	Taylor, W.
117579	Pte.	Teeling, R. E.
706858	Pte.	Watson, W. M.
931202	Pte.	Webster, J. T.
826331	Pte.	Downie, J.
931577	Pte.	Trewhilla, J.
931294	Pte.	Murdoch, W.
931260	Pte.	Kana, J.
931058	Pte.	Ravin, J.
447577	Pte.	*Feary, P.

October 30

781453	Pte.	Anderson, J.
931334	Pte.	Cookson, J.
107557	Sgt.	Shuttleworth, R.
931829	Pte.	Lee, R.
486686	Pte.	Bailey, W. N.
826928	Pte.	Wilcox, W.
931014	Pte.	Billy, J.
706800	Pte.	Nairn, J.
931113	Pte.	Tripp, L. E.
227611	Pte.	Mason, J. C.
826720	Pte.	Field, J.
931035	Pte.	Forbister, F. B.
781371	Sgt.	Waud, W. O.
294879	Pte.	Kruger, A.
706489	Pte.	Riley, W. G. S.
826066	Pte.	Abbott, L.
931338	Pte.	Williamson, E.
781089	Pte.	Fletcher, J.
701163	Pte.	Lester, W.

* Still on duty.

October 30

294844	Pte.	Jacobson, J. E. H.
706481	Pte.	Orchard, L.
931640	Pte.	Arnold, R. I.
826312	Pte.	Hanwright, E.
931749	Pte.	Smith, H. T.
826703	Pte.	Rutherford, T.
107117	Pte.	Brown, A.
760942	Pte.	Whaley, G.
463725	Pte.	McBroom, G.
782306	Pte.	Wilkins, P. L.
706951	Pte.	Butcher, E. J.
826406	Pte.	Shaw, G.
781888	Pte.	Welch, J.
707178	Pte.	Burns, R. M.
826463	Pte.	Spencer, G. P.
782471	Pte.	Schamahorn, S. J.
227672	Pte.	Holt, T.
116013	Pte.	Grimes, J. W.
931449	Pte.	Billsborough, R.
2142321	Pte.	Ryan, W.
116790	Cpl.	Scott, H.
931800	Pte.	Hogan, D.
707032	Pte.	Johnson, S.
931835	Pte.	McCallum, M.
931208	Pte.	Gilmour, R.
463951	Pte.	Amos, A.
227762	Pte.	Burch, O.
126322	Sgt.	Tremaine, W.
826144	Pte.	Matthews, G. W.
117380	Pte.	Tildesley, W.
2025157	Pte.	Davison, T.
2020168	Pte.	Ulasoff, J.
931374	Pte.	Elliott, T. J.
136248	Pte.	Appleby, J. H.
442832	Pte.	Crossley, W.
706798	Pte.	Harper, C. J.
2015159	Pte.	Carter, E. R.
180701	Cpl.	Patterson, H. M.
826651	Pte.	Ferguson, D. R.
931157	Pte.	Keatley, G. E.
629443	Pte.	Simard, R.
706390	Pte.	McIntosh, H.
827064	Pte.	Barham, L.
442774	Cpl.	Robertson, F.
826033	Pte.	Biggan, J.
826572	Pte.	Stares, J. H.
826270	Pte.	Potter, H.
706303	L/Cpl.	Masters, R.
687097	Pte.	McGregor, C.
931735	Pte.	Phillips, W.
826969	Pte.	Franklin, J.
760756	Pte.	Baxter, C. J.

2nd Canadian Mounted Rifles

PASSCHENDAELE, 1917

October 30
707093	Pte.	Platt, F. C.
422933	Cpl.	Minter, F. A.
931007	Pte.	Stephens, F. W.
136403	Pte.	*Troutman, N. J.
781592	Pte.	*Beattie, J.

October 31
826725	Pte.	Bryenton, C. N.
782379	L/Cpl.	Gillies, A. C.
464634	Pte.	Stant, H.
706930	Pte.	Watkins, G.
826522	Pte.	Ross, G.
760053	Pte.	Reed, R.
625294	Pte.	Clicteur, H.
826462	Pte.	Sherman, W. E.
826090	Pte.	Hoita, R.
706552	Pte.	Knox, F.
688187	Pte.	Wood, G. B.
826412	Pte.	Turner, T. S.
160834	Pte.	Rigg, T. W.
687119	Pte.	Marchenia, A.
116845	Pte.	Henderson, J.
441391	Pte.	Oliver, N. J.
107458	Sgt.	Nash, H. B.
706791	L/Cpl.	Armstrong, F.
782248	Pte.	Wade, J.
446715	Pte.	Davidge, A.
781804	Pte.	Betson, T.
826050	Pte.	Nicholson, R.
826393	Pte.	Thew, F. W.
706450	Pte.	Betton, E.
107334	Pte.	Jessop, J. R.
108224	Pte.	Flemming, W.
434540	Pte.	Ainge, A. C.
827050	Pte.	Fennell, G.

November 1
117225	Sgt.	Dick, D.
931520	Pte.	Seaman, F.
116929	Pte.	Barr, A.
2025193	Pte.	Bailey, D. J.
443877	Pte.	McMahon, J. D.
826851	Pte.	Frewin, F.
706551	Pte.	Gough, G.
826626	Pte.	Skolberg, A.
781551	Pte.	Herd, A.

November 2
180198	Pte.	Cochrane, P.
687250	Pte.	Garcia, A.
706616	Pte.	Lang, W.
108721	Pte.	Fairhurst, W.
931401	Pte.	Harrison, F. E.
931095	Pte.	McDonald, A.
116382	Pte.	Lord, O. K.
446139	Pte.	Hardie, J. M. O.
252639	Pte.	Rennie, A.
116950	Pte.	Reid, W. C.
107117	Pte.	Brown, A.
441367	Pte.	Pack, E.

November 3
135596	Pte.	Watson, G. P.
826360	Pte.	Howard, W. H.
441749	Pte.	Pearce, G.
425461	Pte.	Warner, G. W.
464638	Cpl.	Hogland, O.
688009	Pte.	*Cook, A. G.

November 8
107634	C.Q.M.S.	Warren, J.
180313	Pte.	Silver, D.

November 14
931460	Pte.	Marnock, A.
200165	Pte.	Woods, T. S.
425368	Pte.	Stickney, C.
116832	Pte.	Banning, J.

FERFAY, 1917

December 4
117596	Pte.	§Urquhart, C. J.
464536	Pte.	§Taylor, F.

ESTREE BLANCHE, 1917

December 5
782266	Pte.	§McNamee, W. J.

NORTH-EAST OF LOOS, 1917

December 22
135565	Cpl.	Shearer, A.

December 25
108493	Pte.	Roberts, W.

December 29
464497	Pte.	§Gray, H. C.
931117	Pte.	McRae, A. F.

§ Accidentally wounded. * Still on duty.

Appendix IV—Wounded

NORTH-EAST OF LOOS, 1918

January 1
687090	L/Sgt.	Carr, F.
707187	Pte.	Downie, G.
790500	Pte.	Sullivan, P.

January 2
117222	Pte.	Day, E. B.

EAST OF LOOS, 1918

January 8
706493	Pte.	Cooley, R.

January 9
7753	Cpl.	§Ellidge, W.

January 11
116016	L/Cpl.	Harding, J. S.

January 12
827072	L/Cpl.	White, A. D.
687751	Pte.	Pizzolato, A.
826530	Pte.	Fraser, W. B.
117142	Pte.	Bice, H. V.

January 12
116179	Pte.	*Ross, D.

January 14
931101	Pte.	*Watt, C. F.
826379	Pte.	*McLuckie, J.
116770	Pte.	*Laurent, E. St. L.
931484	Pte.	*Kemball, A.
422796	Pte.	*Munroe, R.

January 19
487657	A/L/Cpl.	*Belton, W. G.

MERICOURT, 1918

March 9
426370	Pte.	Pearcey, H.
181139	Pte.	‡Lock, C.
135880	Pte.	‡Theodore, H. J.
916760	Pte.	‡Spiers, R. E.
916664	Pte.	‡Scott, J. C.
916506	Pte.	‡Hunter, S. J.
916624	Pte.	‡Smith, J. A.
916160	A/Cpl.	‡Rowe, J. A.

March 10
116839	Pte.	Champion, E.

March 11
107289	Pte.	*Harvey, J. W.

March 13
116845	Pte.	Henderson, J.

March 16
441787	Pte.	Rowland, H. F.
180113	Pte.	Palmer, R.

March 18
832334	Sgt.	Goodwin, J. A.
116576	Cpl.	Bracken, F.
827050	Pte.	‡Fennel, G.

ARLEUX, 1918

March 25
826764	Pte.	*Hencher, L.
916120	Pte.	Williamson, R.
916261	Pte.	Wilcock, L.
441062	Cpl.	Rudden, P.
931012	Pte.	Jenkinson, H.

March 28
760175	Pte.	‡McIntyre, W.

March 29
464283	L/Cpl.	‡Baker, F. W.

HILL 70, 1918

April 11
781803	Pte.	Jolin, N.

April 13
118090	Sgt.	Patton, I. P.

April 14
116179	Pte.	Ross, D.
117425	C.Q.M.S.	*Moffatt, J. K.
463012	Pte.	*Brown, H. W.

April 15
706729	Pte.	Taylor, W. W.
117251	Pte.	Frodeen, P. F.
463133	Pte.	Montgomery, A.
441466	A/Sgt.	Ross, J. E.
706956	Pte.	Margetts, P.
447577	Pte.	*Feary, P.
117429	Pte.	*Morris, E. J.

‡ Gassed.
* Still on duty.
§ Accidentally Wounded.

2nd Canadian Mounted Rifles

HILL 70, 1918

April 16
826267	Pte.	Laybourne, H.
827071	Pte.	Prager, W.
108257	Sgt.	Gunness, W. C.

April 17
931800	Pte.	Hogan, D.
931771	Pte.	Garbutt, R.
2142325	Pte.	Phillips, D.
916816	Pte.	Shook, R. C.

April 23
707133	Pte.	*Baldie, R.
440861	Sgt.	*Oram, D.

510285	Pte.	Lee, W.

April 26

April 27
706490	Pte.	Copas, R.
228497	Pte.	Wilson, J.
687222	Pte.	Clark, D.
542303	Pte.	Tighe, J. E.
525308	Pte.	Galbraith, H. W.
706909	Pte.	*Parkinson, I.

April 28
430974	Sgt.	Humphrey, T.

LES BREBIS, 1918

March 11
687386	Pte.	Wall, W. (while attached 8th T. M. By.)

April 18
1063118	Pte.	Gunther, W. G.
136141	Pte.	Staden, J.

MERCATEL SECTOR, 1918

July 4
707144	Pte.	Veitch, W.

July 5
116743	A/Sgt.	Hale, P. S.
14876	Pte.	McTeer, A.
126310	Pte.	Shaw, A. H.
916191	Pte.	Brabbs, L.

117500	Pte.	*Reid, W.
2334316	Pte.	*Stidolph, S.
916730	Pte.	*McCann, W. A.

July 16
135879	Pte.	Sherman, W. J. (On/Cmd 3rd C.M.G. Bn.)

BRETENCOURT, 1918

July 21
706545	Pte.	Willson, H. J.

July 22
108138	Pte.	Carr, J. J. (On/Cmd 3rd C.M.G. Bn.)

GENTELLES TRENCH, 1918

August 7
826231	Pte.	Geldard, G. F.
274085	Pte.	Strebig, D. L.

August 10
3032369	Pte.	Bulger, W. R. (wounded whilst en route to join battalion as reinforcement)

August 10
447611	Sgt.	York, B. F. (wounded whilst en route to rejoin battalion from course)

DEMUIN (SOUTH-EAST OF AMIENS), 1918

August 8
127090	Cpl.	Woods, J. A.
107304	Pte.	Hine, J.
916077	Pte.	Lang, F. G.
916499	Pte.	McLellan, A.
196368	Pte.	Stanley, P.

August 8
542299	Pte.	Scales, C. G.
451994	Pte.	Grant, J. T.
687723	Pte.	Carter, A.
916825	Pte.	Switzer, W. G.
760668	L/Cpl.	Renwick, E. J.

* Still on duty.

Appendix IV—Wounded

DEMUIN (SOUTH-EAST OF AMIENS), 1918

August 8

916319	Pte.	Binks, W. C.
826029	Pte.	Canning, P.
916475	Pte.	Broughton, E.
706805	L/Cpl.	Bobbitt, T.
228459	Pte.	Coxwell, E. G.
136154	Pte.	Turner, A. E.
2137535	Pte.	Charters, R.
778876	Pte.	Carney, R. J.
706446	Cpl.	Martin, J. H.
435660	Pte.	McKay, A.
916718	Pte.	Mackerell, R. R.
117592	Pte.	Tutt, H.
135649	Pte.	Ball, R.
115006	Sgt.	Armstrong, J. T.
118081	Cpl.	Massey, L.
135856	Pte.	Shaw, G.
916771	Pte.	Allard, H. J.
228210	Pte.	Airth, I. T.
180630	Pte.	Herd, T. H. D.
931693	Pte.	Knowles, J.
916212	Pte.	Mulhern, J. B.
916604	Pte.	Nolloth, W. R.
117496	Pte.	Rawlings, W. L. R.
916135	Pte.	Stephenson, H. G.
916323	Pte.	Stevens, M. H.
3032258	Pte.	Skingle, B. F.
2245503	Pte.	Lundeborg, F. H.
491372	Pte.	Bennett, J. W.

August 8

916700	Pte.	Harwood, A. E.
814572	Pte.	Holden, P.
916523	Pte.	Hollingsworth, G. R.
200164	Pte.	Howse, P.
108101	Pte.	Blackmore, H. W.
707099	Pte.	Corble, W. S.
814424	Pte.	Kirkpatrick, N.
542414	Pte.	Smith, F. L.
136584	L/Cpl.	Smith, L. F.
916714	Pte.	Sherry, G. J.
706722	Pte.	Townsend, G.
108209	Sgt.	Ellis, J. P.
706633	Pte.	Snowden, E.
706144	Pte.	Province, G.
440882	L/Cpl.	Pratt, A.
868294	Pte.	Craig, G. J.
470144	L/Cpl.	McDonald, C. R.
117131	Pte.	Beatty, J. H.
931025	Pte.	Gregory, L.
441573	Pte.	Rustige, D., M.M.
541235	Pte.	Booth, W. G.
264392	Pte.	Cowan, A.
264495	Pte.	Thornton, E.
1263345	Pte.	Richardson, H.

August 9

916734	Pte.	Johnston, E.
853457	Pte.	Hibberd, H. J.

LE QUESNOY (SOUTH-EAST OF AMIENS), 1918

August 10

707001	Pte.	Cuthell, G. W.
3032380	Pte.	McDougall, W. J.
107388	Sgt.	McEwan, G. D.
135438	Sgt.	Boyd, J.
135436	Pte.	Borthwick, J.
531132	Pte.	Barrie, C.
136277	Pte.	Blakely, J.
706403	Pte.	Bracken, W. T.
295002	Pte.	Barclay, W.
649406	Pte.	Brown, B. H.
135250	Pte.	Brooks, H.
274002	Pte.	Crane, P.
916563	Pte.	Conacher, R. B.
2142341	Pte.	Paul, H.
760053	Pte.	Reed, R.
826481	Pte.	Thrippleton, A.
931185	Pte.	Talbot, G. J.
136245	Pte.	Waldron, W. E.
826236	Pte.	Louch, G. T.
931290	Pte.	Dolstra, C.
228481	Pte.	Dunstall, J. R.

August 10

931446	Pte.	Hyde, H. H.
916963	Pte.	Maxwell, J.
101415	Pte.	Maiman, H.
916796	Pte.	Morgan, F. E.
826448	Pte.	Morrison, G. E.
3031458	Pte.	Merpaw, W. A.
136545	Pte.	Bestwick, H.
540102	Pte.	Dwyer, A. J.
447086	Sgt.	Harris, K. M. W.
116970	L/Cpl.	Watson, G. B.
916193	Pte.	Bosanquet, H. E.
916033	Pte.	Hughes, J.
160991	Pte.	Rutherford, G.
931641	Pte.	Barnes, E. E.
916595	Pte.	Catton, H. E.
916795	Pte.	Coope, E. L.
1027040	Pte.	Greenfield, V. R.
826764	Pte.	Hencher, L.
3032488	Pte.	Levi, C.
931363	Pte.	Watson, J. M.
916716	Pte.	Yates, H. P.

2nd Canadian Mounted Rifles

LE QUESNOY (SOUTH-EAST OF AMIENS), 1918

August 10

117077	Sgt.	Lewis, R.
2025156	L/Cpl.	Beattie, J.
687755	Pte.	Brett, F. J.
931213	Pte.	Hollis, C. E.
228321	Pte.	Baker, R.
853622	Pte.	Chalmers, R. A.
916622	Pte.	Forest, J.
228530	Pte.	Harrison, A. H.
916845	Pte.	Busby, C. D.
916473	Pte.	Muringer, F. C.
107193	L/Cpl.	Dollemore, D.
200043	Pte.	Reid, J. L.
826562	Pte.	Taylor, J. S.
116953	Pte.	Doane, H. L.
931206	Pte.	Holmes, J. W.
443038	Pte.	McLeod, M. A.
931509	Pte.	Hammond, J.
826087	Pte.	Harwood, C. N.
707223	Pte.	Grexton, E.
781924	Pte.	Bagshaw, H.
160854	Pte.	Cohl, R.
931455	Pte.	McDonald, C. R.
161007	Sgt.	McDonald, A.
916204	Pte.	Chalmers, J.

August 10

447606	Pte.	Fleetwood, E.
916477	Pte.	Gardner, W. C.
707225	Pte.	Scott, J.
463147	Pte.	Noble, L. W.
425487	Pte.	Wilkinson, S.
706693	Pte.	Brown, J., M.M.
3033353	Pte.	Morris, A.
931816	Pte.	McGuire, J. G. (reinforcement wounded en route to battalion)
425461	Pte.	Warner, G. W. (wounded while on command 8th C. I. Brigade Signals)
116295	Pte.	McDonald, R. W. (wounded while on command A. P. M. 3rd Division Battle Post duty)

August 11

107289	Cpl.	Harvey, J. W.
107633	Pte.	Wilkinson, W. J.

ORANGE HILL (SOUTH-EAST OF ARRAS), 1918

August 25

3230956	Pte.	Levesque, H.
180113	Pte.	Palmer, R.

August 26

117363	Sgt.	Lowe, D., M.M.
706900	Pte.	Elkerton, W.
2528367	Pte.	Anderson, F.
117407	Cpl.	Peterson, J. S.
2142329	L/Cpl.	Richards, E. S.
3030669	Pte.	Bertelson, V. L.
782411	Pte.	Willey, B. E.
2355500	Pte.	May, J. P.
116452	L/Sgt.	Glover, W.
3231289	Pte.	Cook, G.
2334335	Pte.	Miller, G.
3033164	Pte.	Ferguson, S. J.
2448374	Pte.	Walcarins, H.
228504	Pte.	Benzie, J. W.
687090	Sgt.	Carr, F.
3031441	Pte.	Courtice, C. S.
797667	Pte.	Dickson, P.
931799	Pte.	Dyer, K. W.
651995	Pte.	Dibson, W. M.
826169	Pte.	Grant, J. M.
706946	Pte.	Hill, H. A.
273821	Pte.	Jones, W.

August 26

3032460	Pte.	Parkes, M. H.
3132146	Pte.	Reede, R. H.
2334378	Pte.	Reynolds, E. N.
116809	A/Sgt.	McGibbon, D. L.
116790	Sgt.	Scott, H.
701185	Pte.	Sheppard, G. E.
2517380	Pte.	Schiebel, G.
3033138	Pte.	Thibodau, P. L.
931131	Pte.	Buckingham, A.
117462	Pte.	Pearkes, W. E.
931101	Pte.	Watt, C. F.
706489	L/Cpl.	Riley, W. G. S.
802499	Pte.	Raylor, H.
657771	Pte.	Wice, R.
826631	Cpl.	Simpson, A. W.
931840	Cpl.	Kay, W. B.
160443	Cpl.	Gunn, J.
491323	Pte.	Borrowman, W. W.
3032513	Pte.	Colbert, T.
826472	Pte.	Gray, S.
916420	Pte.	Hansuld, J. H.
228108	Pte.	Young, T. C.
654658	Pte.	Wray, G.
654567	Pte.	Westlake, W. M.
3032713	Pte.	Turner, F. M.

Appendix IV—Wounded

ORANGE HILL (SOUTH-EAST OF ARRAS), 1918

August 26

116801	Pte.	Watson, T.
706928	Pte.	Neill, J.
826313	Sgt.	Lowe, T. W.
916215	Pte.	Toms, H.
3230478	Pte.	Altavista, J. P.
441405	L/Cpl.	Pelkey, A. J.
3033919	Pte.	Gomme, P. W.
916147	Pte.	Mein, E.
3033171	Pte.	Hicks, T. W.
844212	Pte.	Carey, A. M.
602993	Pte.	Williamson, H.
116056	L/Cpl.	Campbell, A.
916525	Pte.	Harrington, H. C.
3230851	Pte.	Allen, R. C.
3032808	Pte.	Boott, H.
1045301	Pte.	Love, G. H.
441367	Pte.	Pack, E.
916105	Pte.	Hay, J. G.
916736	Pte.	Patterson, A.
916263	Pte.	Sellors, J. R.
730443	Pte.	Shoesmith, A.
916510	Pte.	Ansell, H. G.
135069	Pte.	Tanner, L. F., M.M.
108240	L/Cpl.	*Gibson, E.

August 27

687254	Pte.	Harris, S. C.
853676	Pte.	Banks, W. T.
3033428	Pte.	Brown, J. R.
2413311	Pte.	McDonald, S.
2355336	Pte.	Acker, E.
2355809	Pte.	Lee, M. E.
2015158	Pte.	Cartier, R. E.
2378346	Pte.	Hopley, O.
2497934	Pte.	Bloomberg, J.
760410	Pte.	Cullen, J.
2517356	Pte.	Flower, A. W.
651112	Pte.	Arnold, J.
853459	Pte.	James, H.
3032262	Pte.	Murphy, J.
3032905	Pte.	Heron, A. B.
1012725	Pte.	Webster, G.
3231037	Pte.	Robinson, C. E.
116770	Pte.	Laurent, E. St. L.

August 27

706762	Pte.	McIntosh, G.
651994	Pte.	Waechter, F. J.
651236	Pte.	Threndyle, H. A.
928041	Pte.	Tate, J. S.
651771	Pte.	Kennedy, A. W.
116789	Pte.	McKenzie, H. V.
3231559	Pte.	*Mask, A.
931644	Pte.	*Battershall, W. G.
707135	Pte.	*Whitley, W. R.
3033318	Pte.	Sherratt, O.

August 28

654602	Pte.	Carpenter, R. H.
931158	Pte.	Kennedy, C. H.
916243	Pte.	McLellan, D.
832087	Pte.	Trenholme, W. G.
117171	Sgt.	Bryan, R. D.
916547	A/Cpl.	Paton, T. A.
425335	Pte.	Smith, H.
707145	Pte.	Wilson, W.
916086	Pte.	McGillivray, D. A.
916611	Pte.	Collins, A. A.
116407	Pte.	Graham, R.
651148	Pte.	Willaugham, H.
916128	Pte.	Wilson, A.
916729	Pte.	Jones, E.
2137304	Pte.	George, A.
200165	Pte.	Woods, T. S.
784040	Pte.	Cross, B. W.
916451	Pte.	Ainsworth, T.
826560	Pte.	Maloney, W.
687447	Pte.	Manery, F.
107338	Sgt.	Jacombs, M. H. L.
117505	Pte.	Robbie, J. D.
826147	Pte.	Tose, P.
862256	Pte.	Dewey, A. G.
469444	Pte.	Owens, W.
2004150	Pte.	Quilty, C. R.

August 29

2448432	Pte.	Normandy, A. P.

September 7

108619	Pte.	Webb, T.
		(near Vis-en-Artois, east of Arras)

MILL COPSE SECTOR (EAST OF ARRAS), 1918

September 12

2448447	Pte.	Ryan, R. J.
3034065	Pte.	*Givins, F.
916267	Pte.	*Hamilton, A. E.

* Still on duty.

September 14

3232956	Pte.	Fawcett, J. H.
707190	Pte.	Gordon, O.
916416	Pte.	Francis, J.
3032303	Pte.	Potter, E. H.
3032559	Pte.	Newson, E.

2nd Canadian Mounted Rifles

MILL COPSE SECTOR (EAST OF ARRAS), 1918

September 15
116572 Sgt. Shipley, J. W., M.M.

September 17
853182 Pte. McGill, J. E.

September 17
931693 Pte. Knowles, J.
3231272 Pte. St. Armour, A.
2529321 Pte. Goodyear, T. L.

CAMBRAI, 1918

September 29

117513	L/Sgt.	Robinson, R.
3230999	Pte.	Durrell, W. L.
3032070	Pte.	Flear, T. J.
274155	Pte.	Grandin, H. D.
3032959	Pte.	Freshour, C.
602582	Pte.	Hubbard, S.
931559	Pte.	Deverell, S. J.
294262	Pte.	Larson, J. B.
687799	A/Cpl.	Merrell, J. A.
117363	Sgt.	Lowe, I., M.M.
117378	Pte.	McDonald, A.
916170	Pte.	Cast, G.
916742	Pte.	Anderson, J. M.
3231094	Pte.	Dubie, L.
226072	Pte.	Cumming, J.
916143	Pte.	Hopkins, R. G.
3230493	Pte.	Baker, C. F.
3230971	Pte.	Morris, G. F.
928422	Pte.	Cole, A. E.
3033845	Pte.	Dewdney, S. P.
3033136	Pte.	Pigeon, A.
916142	Pte.	Hollocks, F.
688148	Pte.	Campbell, D.
781930	L/Sgt.	Overy, A. W.
827071	Cpl.	Prager, W.
3231032	Pte.	Maxted, W.
116995	Cpl.	Osborne, J.
3231279	Pte.	Levigne, G.
1263345	Pte.	Richardson, H.
833441	Pte.	Lightfoot, E.
3033442	Pte.	Roberts, G.
443378	Cpl.	Menzies, R. P.
931144	Pte.	Greyson, R.
3030592	Pte.	Wotherspoon, T.
652270	Pte.	Hodge, R.
3231205	Pte.	Primeau, O.
464536	Pte.	Taylor, F.
853663	Pte.	Paxton, A.
441406	Sgt.	Pilkington, W.
3055568	Pte.	Ladoncour, H.
2499335	Pte.	Leake, G. H.
3034065	Pte.	Givins, F. M.
3231714	Pte.	Scafe, F.
853479	Pte.	Johnson, E.
706805	L/Cpl.	Bobbett, T.

September 29

3231472	Pte.	Laderonte, A.
916718	Pte.	Mackerell, R. R.
3032534	Pte.	Wallace, J. F.
931379	Pte.	Hare, J. J.
3032143	Pte.	Lollo, M.
651010	Pte.	McWhinney, C. V.
916807	Pte.	Harris, G. W.
3231026	Pte.	Miller, J.
3032992	Pte.	Masterton, J. B.
117190	Sgt.	Clement, N.
3032957	Pte.	Fitzgerald, M.
706804	L/Cpl.	Peck, T. E. L.
644668	Pte.	McIndoo, J. B.
651898	Pte.	Greig, A. J.
916613	Pte.	Pirie, W. A.
228296	Pte.	Purdue, A. E.
826692	Pte.	Marrington, T. F.
1063136	Pte.	French, J. R.
3231057	Pte.	Frazer, E. P.
827011	Pte.	Chapman, G.
3231251	Pte.	St. Orge, B. J.
251395	Pte.	Ott, C. N.
3231502	Pte.	Ritchie, D. S.
116418	Cpl.	Dorman, G.
2378530	Pte.	Beauchamp, L.
2355727	Pte.	Moore, J.
751328	Pte.	Saxton, I. H.
916042	Pte.	Sharp, R.
3033443	Pte.	Schuler, P.
916330	Pte.	Smith, H.
853184	Pte.	Breedon, W. H.
916692	Pte.	Cordner, W. E.
440861	Sgt.	Oram, D. McH.
115006	Sgt.	Armstrong, J.
781021	Cpl.	Belleghem, E.
826938	Cpl.	Bolton, N.
116153	A/Cpl.	Bridgeman, W.
931574	Cpl.	Bridger, J.
760672	Pte.	Bradley, L. A.
916827	Pte.	Barker, E.
3033157	Pte.	Contois, J. H.
3231062	Pte.	Johnston, C. W.
811695	Pte.	Kenny, W. H.
916195	Pte.	Long, J.
3033444	Pte.	Toohey, E. J.

Appendix IV—Wounded

CAMBRAI, 1918

September 29

3033821	Pte.	Webster, W.
443361	Pte.	McDonald, P., M.M.
2245504	Pte.	Lundeborg, J. A.
114280	Pte.	Shankley, R.
931819	Pte.	Lavigeur, D.
320998	Pte.	White, R.
542413	Pte.	St. Orge, J. J.
2355442	Pte.	Rider, D.
3231256	Pte.	Bezley, C.
136131	Pte.	Shaw, F. H.
3032367	Pte.	Sanders, F.
814708	Pte.	Mason, M. J.
3033611	Pte.	Mooney, J.
441660	Pte.	Olsen, S.
3231119	Pte.	Baillod, W. E.
916135	Pte.	Stephenson, H. G.
116337	Pte.	Nicholls, C. S.
706548	Pte.	McKinnon, A.
3032318	Pte.	Searles, P. A.
3033174	Pte.	Lecocq, J. T.
3034057	Pte.	Harvey, H.
1003981	Pte.	Lemap, L.
3033625	Pte.	Wilson, A.
3033537	Pte.	MacDonald, C. E.
3033661	Pte.	Montgomery, O. W.
3032584	Pte.	Murray, A. H.
916819	Pte.	Marchant, W.
3033810	Pte.	Goddard, E. W.
3230973	Pte.	McCartney, G. W.
916547	A/Cpl.	Paton, T. A.
2134833	Pte.	Sykes, F. J.
706800	Pte.	Nairn, J.
320988	Pte.	Shields, P. C.
3033597	Pte.	Keetch, W. B.
3231580	Pte.	Armitage, R.
443112	Pte.	White, N.
931606	Pte.	Hugh, L.
3031954	Pte.	Primrose, A.
826109	Cpl.	O'Connor, S.
931697	Pte.	Morgan, D.
706039	Pte.	Quarnby, L.
826392	Pte.	Canary, J. N.
826568	Pte.	Moley, T. V.
430144	Cpl.	Fisher, W. E.
117132	Pte.	Beatty, J.
117301	Pte.	Hives, J. E.
916778	Pte.	Godfrey, C.
117492	Pte.	Raikes, A. C.
2115330	Pte.	Reid, G.
916980	Pte.	Petherick, W. H.
435737	Cpl.	Bennett, W. T., M.M.

September 29

463029	Pte.	Craig, J.
2020211	Pte.	Dobie, F. G.
928015	Pte.	Durr, J.
931443	Pte.	Lewis, W. H.
422924	Pte.	Newman, C. W.
687994	Pte.	Pierrish, W.
931278	Pte.	Podrasky, A.
916047	Pte.	Hogan, G. E.
3032364	Pte.	Skinner, A. F.
826969	Pte.	Franklin, J.
117357	Sgt.	Logan, M. J.
136584	L/Cpl.	Smith, L. F.
916490	Pte.	Exley, C. E.
3033450	Pte.	Berg, L.
916790	Pte.	Lowry, T. R.
916061	Pte.	Sayers, A. S.
706626	Pte.	Snape, G. B.
2355382	Pte.	Rigden, C. E.
784149	Pte.	Stonehouse, G. M.
3231541	Pte.	Bouchard, J. B.
3032946	Pte.	Bond, G. J.
3031500	Pte.	Rentner, A. A.
931544	Pte.	McCammon, T.
228301	Pte.	Osborne, J.
3031544	Pte.	Powell, C. L.
826781	Pte.	Ward, H.
651680	Pte.	Arnold, M.
931391	Pte.	Tanner, H. W. G.
3032953	Pte.	Dukes, G. A.
651090	Pte.	Gillen, W. L.
916949	Pte.	Lambie, G.
3033076	Pte.	Brown, F. R.
525309	Pte.	Rines, L. A.
826286	Pte.	Stephenson, H.
3033038	Pte.	Smith, A.
108118	L/Sgt.	Brown, V. L.
525015	Pte.	McArdle, B.
463961	Sgt.	Charnley, F.
931388	Pte.	Nicholls, J.
135104	Pte.	Bogg, C. G.
916852	Pte.	Pidduck, E. W. R.
446080	Pte.	Woods, H. B.
916188	Pte.	Perrin, W. J.
463195	Pte.	Vinall, F. C.
602389	Pte.	Allen, H.
116061	Pte.	Cryderman, H.
707187	Pte.	Downie, G.
473085	Cpl.	*Paul, H.
916521	Pte.	*Coe, F. W.

* Still on duty.

2nd Canadian Mounted Rifles

CAMBRAI, 1918

September 30
3230836	Pte.	Erb, W. O.
916385	Pte.	Robb, H.
3231548	Pte.	Mallett, J.

October 1
916407	Sgt.	Watson, C. F.
136198	Pte.	Brearley, A.
107135	Pte.	Carter, A. C.

October 2
3231083	Pte.	Bazinet, L. D.
351388	Pte.	Moore, M.
3033665	Pte.	Whitney, A. R.
706815	Pte.	Scott, G. M.
3033500	Pte.	Buttonshaw, J. E.
739675	Pte.	Henry, E. J.

October 3
931264	Pte.	Pollard, E. J.
2378508	Pte.	Isaac, E.
3231217	Pte.	Lafontaine, S.

October 4
784319	Pte.	‡Woodward, H. P.

FRESNES, 1918

October 28
916032	Pte.	Evis, A. A.
285459	Pte.	Heeps, J. E.

October 31
3231084	Pte.	Hussey, J. A.

QUIEVRAIN, 1918

November 5
760668	Cpl.	Renwick, E. J.

November 6
2590979	Pte.	Doyle, J. E.
2355421	Pte.	Deline, G.
3033483	Pte.	Jackson, J. H.
916324	Pte.	Tomlins, W. S.
3033474	Pte.	Bisson, J. L.
2355591	Pte.	Faulkner, J. R.
654183	Pte.	Hillson, F. R.
916723	Pte.	Patterson, D. B.
931345	Pte.	Anderson, C.
916077	Pte.	Long, O.
916395	Pte.	Heyes, S.
136544	Sgt.	Beynon, G. M.
440988	Cpl.	Rutt, J. H.
931644	Pte.	Battershall, W. G.
916738	Pte.	Holding, C.
3032391	Pte.	Agius, J.
3231344	Pte	Delano, H.
3036161	Pte.	Gilmartin, M.
117465	Pte.	Patchett, H.
916241	Sgt.	Gray, F. G.
3035265	Pte.	Ferguson, J. W.
3233874	Pte.	Flesher, S.
781723	Pte.	Johnson, C. W.
931726	Pte.	Kent, G. S.
826036	Pte.	Barrett, F.
116569	Pte.	Fielding, F. J.
687751	Pte.	Pizzolato, A., M.M.
853729	Pte.	Holden, A.
3107156	Pte.	Pritchard, R. C.
928111	Pte.	Black, D.
2355381	Pte.	Fry, C. R.
688275	Pte.	Freault, L.
136151	Pte.	Thorpe, P.
434944	Cpl.	Gittings, G.
3234036	Pte.	*Studholme, N. E.

November 7
3231096	Pte.	Alderson, J.
405097	Pte.	Osborne, E. R.
805091	Pte.	King, F.
826084	Pte.	Henry, J. R.
3031474	Pte.	Kliskey, S.
3233761	Pte.	Furlong, G. H.
3107397	Pte.	Vail, C. L.
931289	Pte.	Grant, J.
2537437	Pte.	*Lovell, J. B.
3030072	Pte.	*Kane, J.
3231209	Pte.	*Caron, R.
3033286	Pte.	*Mullin, J. K.
1027688	Pte.	Jennings, A. W.

November 8
3107540	Pte.	‡McClintock, R. L.
707025	L/Cpl.	‡MacDonald, A.
3037847	Pte.	McDonald, W.

‡ Gassed.
* Still on duty.

APPENDIX V

Nominal Roll of Officers, Warrant Officers, N.C.O'S and Men

Officers

Officers marked * were granted Commissions from the ranks of the Battalion.

	22-9-14
Lieut.-Col.	Bott, C. L.
Major	Mutrie, R. J.
Major	Allen, M. V., D.S.O.
Major	Bardolph, J. T.
Major	Bapty, W.
Capt.	Johnston, G. C., D.S.O., M.C.
Capt.	Foster, W. W., D.S.O.
Capt.	Leduc, T.
Capt.	Temple, A.
Hon. Capt.	Brooke, P.
Lieut.	Agnew, J. C.
Lieut.	Barlee, W. R.
Lieut.	Bell, A. H.
Lieut.	Bennett, R. O. G., M.C.
Lieut.	Denison, H. R.
Lieut.	Edwards, F. B.
Lieut.	Evans, A. V., M.C.
Lieut.	Irving, E. B.
Lieut.	Moncreiff, N. H.
Lieut.	McGuire, M. V.
Lieut.	Rant, N. W. F.
Lieut.	Routh, P. G., M.C.
Lieut.	Wood, W. W.
Lieut.	Worsley, R. S., M.C.
Capt.	McAskill, J. E., M.C. (attd.), C.A.M.C.
Capt.	Evans, D. S. (attd.), C.A.P.C.
	11-1-16
Hon. Capt.	Fallis, A.
	3-1-16
Lieut.	McIntosh, W.
Lieut.	Wills, J. R. O.
Lieut.	Brick, A. L.
Lieut.	Thomson, D. C.
Lieut.	Taylor, H. S.
Lieut.	Breckenridge, C. A.
Lieut.	Fennell, T. H.
Lieut.	Weir, G. P., M.C.
Lieut.	Crothers, V. B.
Lieut.	Latimer, W. R.
Lieut.	Brichta, G. J. O.
Lieut.	Pue, W. H.
Lieut.	Lewis, C. J.
Lieut.	Quanbury, J. R.
	3-2-16
Lieut.	Krauss, C. A.
	2-4-16
Lieut.	Haigh, A. W.
Capt.	Redpath, S. J.
	15-4-16
Lieut.	Davis, D. W.
Lieut.	Scott, H. G.
Lieut.	Birkenshaw, E. L.
	23-4-16
Lieut.	Chisholm, C. G.
Lieut.	*Hogg, J. C., M.C.
	27-4-16
Lieut.	Brown, J. S.
Lieut.	Audy, P. J. T.
Lieut.	Cruikshank, G., M.C.
	30-4-16
Lieut.	*Worrall, J.
Lieut.	*Joyce, W. B.
Lieut.	*Heinekey, G. P.
Lieut.	*Pearkes, G. R., V.C. D.S.O., M.C.
	6-5-16
Lieut.	Strachan, A. K.
	5-5-16
Lieut.	Cameron, D. U.
	9-6-16
Lieut.	Pearson, R. W.
Lieut.	Newman, T. L.

2nd Canadian Mounted Rifles

Rank	Name
Lieut.	Mitchell, J. H.
Lieut.	Wilson, W. J.

22-6-16
Capt.	Van Kleeck, S. B.

18-6-16
Capt.	Miller, L. W., D.S.O.
Capt.	Asser, R.
Major	Mowat, J. A. McD.
Lieut.	Moran, P. J.
Lieut.	Meldrum, J. A.
Lieut.	Nicholls, J. W. E.
Lieut.	Brown, T. D.
Lieut.	Spinks, R. C.
Lieut.	Kennedy, L. A., M.C.
Lieut.	Temple, C. C.
Lieut.	Dunk, S.
Lieut.	Dickinson, J.

10-6-16
Capt.	Cote, A. E. (attd.), C.A.M.C.

12-6-16
Capt.	Perras, J. H. F. (attd.), C.A.M.C.

27-6-16
Lieut.	Pennie, T. C.
Major	Murray, L. R. (attd.), C.A.M.C.

8-7-16
Lieut.	Baird, R. P. H.

29-6-16
Lieut.	*Morrison, D.
Lieut.	*Capstick, J. E., M.M.
Lieut.	*Heather, F. A., M.C., M.M.
Lieut.	*Foord, J., M.C.

9-7-16
Lieut.	*Gray, J. L., M.C.

25-7-16
Lieut.	*Godfrey, T., M.C.

2-8-16
Capt.	McQueen, —
Capt.	Cooper, F. B.
Capt.	Gray, A. C. B.
Lieut.	Franks, H.
Lieut.	Sievewright, C. W.
Lieut.	Jefferson, C.
Lieut.	McKenzie, J. M.
Lieut.	Evans, H. H.

15-8-16
Capt.	Armstrong, A. C., M.C. (attd.), C.A.M.C.

10-9-16
Lieut.	*Board, A. W., M.M.

25-9-16
Hon. Capt.	Colwell, T. C.,M.C., Chaplain

12-10-16
Lieut.	*Haseldine, T. F.

26-10-16
Lieut.	Elkins, F. D.

22-11-16
Capt.	Walsh, C. R. (attd.)

4-11-16
Lieut.	*Douglas, C. F. H. K., M.C.

18-11-16
Lieut.	*Gardiner, H. M.
Lieut.	*Smith, F., M.C.
Lieut.	*Darcus, R. J., M.C.

24-11-16
Hon. Major	Wilson, T. A. (attd.)

2-12-16
Lieut.	*Rowberry, A. H., M.C.

13-1-17
Lieut.	*Lees, R.
Lieut.	*Steer, C. P.
Lieut.	*Potter, J. K., M.C.

30-1-17
Lieut.-Col.	Lang, N. (attd.)
Major	Adams, R. W. (attd.)
Major	Elliott, A. E. (attd.)
Major	Nation, H. T. (attd.)
Major	Shortreed, W. J. (attd.)
Major	Taylor, T. A. (attd.)

19-2-17
Lieut.	*Pimm, A. G.

21-2-17
Lieut.	Christie, J. H. H.

20-2-17
Lieut.	Mulholland, P. C.

8-3-17
Lieut.	*Wasson, T. C.

10-3-17
Lieut.	Richardson, J. M. S.
Lieut.	Jackson, J. H.
Lieut.	Hanna, D. B.
Lieut.	Mavor, D., M.C.

20-3-17
Major	Raynes, S. H. (attd.)

13-4-17
Lieut.	*Monteith, J. I.

26-4-17
Lieut.	Allen, C. C.

Appendix V—Nominal Roll

Lieut.	Whitlow, F. M.		9-11-17
Lieut.	*Blake, G., M.C.	Lieut.	Harris, W. M.
Lieut.	*Rant, G. T., M.C., D.C.M.	Lieut.	Gardiner, W. F.
Lieut.	*Gardiner, E. M., M.M.		12-11-17
Lieut.	*Hart, C. L., M.C.	Lieut.	Drew, J. A. C.
	2-5-17		22-11-17
Lieut.	Howard, P.	Lieut.	Heath, E. F. W.
Lieut.	Foot, E. D.		24-11-17
Lieut.	Bolt, H. G.	Lieut.	Bradford, E. E.
	7-5-17	Lieut.	Cook, J.
Lieut.	*Williams, H. C., M.C.		7-12-17
Lieut.	*Hammerton, N.	Lieut.	Alsen, G. O.
Lieut.	*MacGregor, J., V.C., M.C., D.C.M.	Lieut.	Williams, H. C.
Lieut.	*Apps, C.	Lieut.	*Bowen, H. T.
	9-5-17		13-12-17
Capt.	Malcolm, D. C. (attd.)	Lieut.	Fraser, R.
	14-5-17		10-1-18
Lieut.	*McLeod, G. W. L.	Lieut.	Barker, W. J.
	17-5-17	Lieut.	Pye, F., M.C.
Lieut.	*Lyle, H. S., M.C.		17-1-18
	16-6-17	Lieut.	*Robertson, J. R.
Major	Lloyd, R. E. A.		13-2-18
	4-7-17	Lieut.	*Baverstock, W.
Lieut.	*McDermid, G. D., M.C.	Lieut.	*Hinckesman, G. F.
	30-7-17	Lieut.	*Grothe, C. R., M.M.
Lieut.	*Warren, W. C.		1-3-18
	2-8-17	Lieut.	Trees, C. F.
Lieut.	*Whitehead, W. R.	Lieut.	Trees, A. G.
	8-8-17		8-3-18
Lieut.	Dexter, F. G.	Lieut.	Stewart, P.
Lieut.	Martin, J. J.		13-3-18
Lieut.	*Manning, H. C., M.C., D.C.M.	Capt.	Gunn, R. E.
	18-8-17		11-4-18
Lieut.	Stewart, T. C.	Lieut.	Boothe, C. H.
	22-9-17	Lieut.	Webber, J. E.
Lieut.	*Gilchrist, N. A. L.	Lieut.	Hudd, F.
Lieut.	*Gough, D. C., M.C.	Lieut.	Palmer, B. M.
	6-10-17	Lieut.	Palmer, W. S.
Lieut.	*Stubbs, I. H.		14-5-18
Lieut.	*Griffiths, G. H.	Lieut.	Campbell, L. G.
Lieut.	*Shipton, B., M.C., M.M.		17-4-18
Lieut.	*Price, H. E.	Lieut.	Skirrow, H. E.
	15-10-17		30-4-18
Lieut.	Hewetson, H. J.	Lieut.	*Scarnakia, D. A.
Lieut.	*Sprague, F. A., M.C.		8-5-18
	8-11-17	Lieut.	*Rugg, J. F.
Lieut.	Archer, C. J.	Lieut.	*Whitmore, H. A., M.C., D.C.M.
			15-5-18
		Lieut.	*Castle, A. J., M.M.

127

2nd Canadian Mounted Rifles

	3-6-18			8-9-18
Lieut.	*Hayward, W., D.C.M., M.M.		Lieut.	*McCoubrey, J. L., D.C.M.
	4-6-18			26-9-18
Lieut.	*Goodship, L. A., D.C.M.		Lieut.	*Hewlett, H., M.C.
	11-6-18			12-10-18
Capt.	Robb, W. M., M.C. (attd.), C.A.M.C.		Lieut.	*Oxborough, W.
			Lieut.	*Rankin, J.
	23-6-18			9-10-18
Lieut.	*Robbins, L. M., M.C.		Lieut.	*Spratt, M.
	8-7-18			20-10-18
Lieut.	*Oxberry, J. R.		Capt.	Petrie, G. A. (attd.)
	2-9-18			27-10-18
Lieut.	*Harris, F. W.		Lieut.	*Bond, H. P.
Lieut.	*Langhorne, T. H.		Lieut.	*Brown, W. W.
Lieut.	*Hereron, C., M.M.			30-10-18
	7-9-18		Lieut.	*Mellett, W. J.
Lieut.	*Francis, A.			
Lieut.	*Hives, E., M.M.			
Lieut.	*White, E. O.			

Appendix V—Nominal Roll

W.O.'S., N.C.O.'S and Men

Rank	No.	Name
	22-9-14	
S.Q.M.S.	107077	Bowen, H. T.
S.Q.M.S.	107089	Bradford, H. C.
Cpl.	107078	Bailey, G.
Cpl.	107102	Bayntun, A. E.
Cpl.	107094	Bostock, L. S.
S. S. Cpl.	107132	Bremner, W.
Cpl.	107126	Brett, W.
L/Cpl.	107080	Barr, P. S.
L/Cpl.	107079	Boulton, J.
Tpr.	107090	Baum, W. J.
Tpr.	107111	Brockett, L. C.
Tpr.	107087	Brixton, J.
Tpr.	107071	Barber, F., M.C., D.C.M.
Tpr.	107105	Barraclough, P. E.
Tpr.	107081	Baverstock, W., M.M.
Tpr.	107104	Babbitt, M.
Tpr.	107092	Baxter, W. H.
Tpr.	107091	Baylis, W.
Tpr.	107076	Berwick, R., M.M.
Tpr.	107082	Berard, A. W.
Tpr.	107083	Bessette, C. J.
Tpr.	107086	Beveridge, J. W.
Tpr.	112178	Bell, T. J.
Tpr.	107107	Beattie, A.
Tpr.	112179	Birchall, S.
Tpr.	107130	Blackwood, J.
Tpr.	107109	Blakeway, W. E.
Tpr.	107099	Blanchard, S. G.
Tpr.	107110	Blakey, H. A.
Tpr.	107093	Bogert, H. A.
Tpr.	107113	Bond, R. M.
Tpr.	107112	Bond, L. M.
Tpr.	107115	Booth, H.
Tpr.	107114	Boond, S.
Tpr.	107129	Bourne, A. E.
Tpr.	107072	Boyd, W. G.
Tpr.	107098	Boyd, W. G.
Tpr.	107116	Branford, E. J.
Tpr.	107084	Brett, R.
Tpr.	107100	Brett, E.
Tpr.	107088	Brown, J. R.
Tpr.	50484	Board, A. W., M.M.
Tpr.	107073	Brown, J. C.
Tpr.	107085	Browne, J. A.
Tpr.	107095	Brown, A. S.
Tpr.	107117	Brown, A.
Tpr.	107131	Brown, W. R.
Tpr.	107118	Browne, A. E.

Rank	No.	Name
Tpr.	107075	Bull, F.
Tpr.	107103	Burden, E. H.
Tpr.	112188	Burrows, F. W.
Tpr.	107074	Bussell, F. O.
S/Sgt.	107128	Beckett, L.
Tpr.	107097	Butler, J. W.
S. S. Cpl.	107063	Adkins, F.
	107051	Alexander, J.
Tpr.	107057	Arnott, W.
Tpr.	107052	Allison, A.
Tpr.	107054	Anderson, L. M., M.M.
		Allen, A.
Tpr.	107060	Allen, A.
Tpr.	116003	Anderton, R. A.
Tpr.	107069	Anson, R. N.
Tpr.	107057	Armstrong, E. C.
Tpr.	107065	Armit, T. N., D.C.M.
L/Cpl.	115006	Armstrong, J. T.
Tpr.	107070	Arnold, R. C.
L/Cpl.	107066	Aspray, O. T.
Tpr.	107058	Atkinson, W.
L/Cpl.	107059	Ayles, A. J.
L/Cpl.	107181	Drake, P. W.
	22-9-14	
Cpl.	107183	Drake, H. A.
Tpr.	107182	Drake, W. R.
Tpr.	107184	Dunbar, A.
Tpr.	107177	Dickson, G. H.
Tpr.	107178	Dobbs, J.
L/Cpl.	107190	Douglas, C. F. K.
Tpr.	107180	Duncan, J.
Tpr.	116007	Dunlop, E.
Tpr.	107185	Davidson, W. W.
Tpr.	107186	Davies, G. L.
Tpr.	107176	Dram, J. A.
Tpr.	107187	Davis, H. E.
Tpr.	107189	Dennis, R. E.
Tpr.	116006	Delmonico, H. N.
Tpr.	107179	De Pass, C.
Tpr.	115009	Davies, W. H.
Sad. Sgt.	107133	Cooper, H. C.
Sgt.	107138	Cather, A. M.
Sgt.	107137	Clark, T. G. M.
Tpr.	107135	Carter, A. C.
Tpr.	107134	Castle, C. H.
Tpr.	107139	Carr, W. H.
Tpr.	107140	Cartwright, W. H.
Tpr.	107150	Chambres, R. N.
Tpr.	107171	Chapman, F.

2nd Canadian Mounted Rifles

Rank	No.	Name
Tpr.	107141	Clark, E. W.
Tpr.	107161	Child, R. F.
Tpr.	107142	Clark, K. C.
Tpr.	107143	Coates, E.
Tpr.	107144	Coates, A., M.M.
Tpr.	107145	Cullen, E.
Tpr.	107146	Carew, H.
Tpr.	107147	Carew, T.
Tpr.	107148	Carr, E. F.
Tpr.	107151	Champion, J. P.
Tpr.	107170	Clark, F.
Tpr.	107172	Coleman, C.
Tpr.	107152	Coleman, L. S.
Tpr.	107153	Coleman, H.
Tpr.	107154	Cooper, F.
Tpr.	107155	Corbett, E. C.
Tpr.	107156	Coxall, J.
Tpr.	107157	Cull, N.
Tpr.	107158	Cargill, J.
Tpr.	107162	Clarke, W. J.
Tpr.	107166	Cockett, L. N.
Tpr.	107167	Coppinger, M.
Tpr.	107163	Crooks, W. D.
Tpr.	107164	Cross, C. H.
Tpr.	107173	Crow, A. A.
Tpr.	107174	Crow, P. J.
Tpr.	107165	Cruikshank, F. R.
Tpr.	107175	Crerar, R.
Tpr.	116061	Cryderman, F. J.
Tpr.	50485	Carter, W. L.
Tpr.	116056	Campbell, A.
Tpr.	107197	Elloart, F. O.
Tpr.	107200	Ehlers, L. B.
Tpr.	107205	Ellam, R. A.
Tpr.	107199	Erskine, D.
Tpr.	107202	Elliott, J. E.
Tpr.	107207	Eccleston, C.
Tpr.	107201	Elgood, J. E. B.
Tpr.	107203	Ellis, H.
Tpr.	107198	Ekins, J. D.
Tpr.	107206	Edge, R. E.
Tpr.	107196	Ellison, P.
Tpr.	116008	Elliott, J.
Tpr.	116009	Emery, J. A.
Tpr.	112215	Elliott, E. W.
Tpr.	7753	Ellidge, W.
Sgt.	107216	Fitzgerald, R. O.
Sgt.	107209	Fleet, W. T.
L/Sgt.	107211	Foord, J., M.C.
Cpl.	107217	Forster, R.
Tpr.	107212	Fletcher, C. W.
Tpr.	107226	Fleming, J. A.
Tpr.	107213	Ford, F.

Rank	No.	Name
Tpr.	107214	Forsyth, J.
Tpr.	107215	Fowle, J. T.
Tpr.	107230	Fulton, R. B.
Tpr.	107221	Flowers, W. H. F.
Tpr.	107222	Frampton, E. R.
Tpr.	107223	Fryer, D. B.
Tpr.	107228	Fairbairn, L. E.
Tpr.	107224	Fletcher, H. A.
Tpr.	107120	Fleming, T. A.
Tpr.	107225	Flynn, R. J.
Tpr.	107229	Fisher, A. J.
Tpr.	116011	Foster, T. D.
S. S.	107231	Frank, T.
L/Cpl.	107218	Farrow, L.
Tpr.	107219	Findlay, F.
Tpr.	107220	Fleming, J. B.
R. S. M.	107234	Godfrey, T., M.C.
S. S. M.	107232	Gray, J. L., M.C.
Sgt.	107245	Gammon, P.
Cpl.	107236	Graves, P.
Cpl.	107237	Grantham, H.
Cpl.	107244	Glenn, D. K.
Sig. Cpl.	107246	Griffiths, E. W.
L/Cpl.	107248	Gillespie, A.
Tpr.	107262	Gillett, A.
Tpr.	107238	Giles, A. H.
Tpr.	107239	Glasspool, C. J.
Tpr.	107240	Greaves, W.
Tpr.	107241	Goldie, W. S.
Tpr.	107242	Green, J. P.
Tpr.	107252	Groves, J. S.
Tpr.	107243	Gynne, W.
Tpr.	107247	Gammon, R. E.
Tpr.	107261	Gardiner, R. W.
Tpr.	107249	Good, J. M.
Tpr.	107263	Gough, D. C., M.C.
Tpr.	107250	Green, V. de B.
Tpr.	107251	Griffiths, G. H.
Tpr.	107253	Gainer, W. G. C.
Tpr.	107258	Gadsden, B.
Tpr.	107254	Gardiner, E. M., M.M.
Tpr.	107255	Gardin, J.
Tpr.	107256	Graham, G. W., M.M.
Tpr.	116012	Grandy, A. C.
Tpr.	107257	Grant, C. F.
Tpr.	113017	Gervin, W.
Tpr.	12014	Gardiner, H. M.
Sgt.	107323	Hazeldine, T. F.
Sgt.	107263	Heather, F. A., M.C., M.M.
Sgt.	107298	Holland, J. J.
Sgt.	107299	Heinekey, G. P.
Far. Sgt.	107297	Holmes, A. E.

Appendix V—Nominal Roll

Rank	No.	Name	Rank	No.	Name
Sgt.	107281	Holmes, A. O.	Tpr.	107327	Ibbottson, R.
Cpl.	107282	Hallam, C.	Tpr.	107324	Ibbottson, G. F.
Cpl.	107300	Hewlett, H., M.C.	Tpr.	107325	Impett, W., M.M.
L/Cpl.	107312	Hilleard, E.	Tpr.	116019	Ingraham, L. H.
L/Cpl.	107268	Howells, E. R.	Tpr.	107326	Innocent, A.
Tpr.	107273	Hayhurst, A., M.M.	Tpt. Sgt.	107330	Jones, K. F.
Tpr.	107274	Haywood, G. F.	Sig. Sgt.	107329	Joyce, W. P.
Tpr.	107264	Holmes, F.	Cpl.	107340	Joyce, J. P.
Tpr.	107269	Hughes, J. T.	Tpr.	107331	Jacob, C. F.
Tpr.	107265	Hagerman, N.	Tpr.	107332	Jacob, F. B.
Tpr.	107266	Hill, J.	Tpr.	107335	Jephson, A. M.
Tpr.	107271	Harrison, J. D.	Tpr.	107334	Jessop, J. R.
Tpr.	107272	Haskins, C. H.	Tpr.	107335	Johnson, G.
Tpr.	107275	Hett, R. M.	Tpr.	107341	Jobson, R. N.
Tpr.	107278	Horner, G.	Tpr.	107342	Johnstone, F. D.
Tpr.	107294	Hogg, J. C., M.C.	Tpr.	107348	Johnson, C. W.
Tpr.	107279	Hulme, A. E.	Tpr.	107337	Jacob, R.
Tpr.	107280	Huntley, C. E., M.M.	Tpr.	107338	Jacombs, M. H. L.
Tpr.	107283	Hamilton, G.	Tpr.	116020	James, S. G.
Tpr.	107284	Hammerton, N.	Tpr.	107339	Jones, T.
Tpr.	107285	Hardy, G. H.	Tpr.	107347	John, K. K.
Tpr.	107286	Harrison, J. A.	Tpr.	107343	Jones, E. W.
Tpr.	107287	Hartley, G. A.	Tpr.	107344	Jordan, H. S.
Tpr.	107288	Hart, C. L., M.C.	Sgt.	107357	Killick, C. St. J.
Tpr.	107322	Haslam, E. W.	L/Cpl.	107358	Kendrew, W.
Tpr.	107290	Hatcher, J. M.	Tpr.	107351	Kay, C.
Tpr.	107291	Hayes, T. J.	Tpr.	107352	Knight, W. C.
Tpr.	107292	Hayward, W., D.C.M., M.M.	Tpr.	107350	Knight, G.
			Tpr.	107349	Kermode, W. H.
Tpr.	107295	Holden, C. W.	Tpr.	107353	Keith, F. G. A. St. C.
Tpr.	107296	Holden, F. C.	Tpr.	107354	Kenyon, H. H.
Tpr.	107302	Hodding, A. V.	Tpr.	107356	Kildahl, B., M.M.
Tpr.	107306	Hallmark, W. H., M.M.	Tpr.	107360	Leslie, R. O.
			Cpl.	107374	Lees, H.
Tpr.	116014	Hall, R.	Cpl.	107363	Lance, E.
Tpr.	116016	Harding, J. S.	Tpr.	107364	Lane, R. O.
Tpr.	107307	Harris, G. A.	Tpr.	107365	Lane, F.
Tpr.	107316	Hayne, H. L.	Tpr.	107366	Lintern, J. E. W.
Tpr.	107311	Hepper, J. T.	Cpl.	107367	Livingstone, S. H.
Tpr.	107313	Hindle, C. S.	Cpl.	107371	Lamountaine, C.
Tpr.	107318	Humphreys, D. D.	Tpr.	107368	Lancaster, C.
Tpr.	107314	Howard, A. C.	Tpr.	107380	Lee, A. A.
Tpr.	107315	Hutchinson, H.	Tpr.	107373	Langley, S. P.
Tpr.	107309	Hartley, J. M.	Tpr.	107381	Lee, T. E.
Tpr.	116015	Handley, H. J.	Tpr.	107370	Loftus, K.
Tpr.	50486	Hall, C. E. R.	Tpr.	107382	Lowery, A. J. H.
Tpr.	115026	Hamilton, A. M.	Tpr.	107375	Lewis, H. M.
Tpr.	115029	Harper, H. J.	Tpr.	107376	Liddiard, H.
S. S.	107304	Hine, J.	Tpr.	107377	Livsey, H.
Tpr.	107303	Hargreaves, J.	Tpr.	114032	Lumb, T. P.
Tpr.	107293	Hewlett, S. J.	S. S.	107362	Lee, J. F.
Tpr.	107276	Hinckesman, G. F.	Tpr.	107372	Lamb, G. P. H.
Tpr.	107277	Hinckesman, J. W.	Tpr.	107369	Lefevre, N.
Tpr.	107328	Ibbottson, E.	Sgt.	116027	Morrison, S.

2nd Canadian Mounted Rifles

Rank	No.	Name
Cpl.	107421	Malcolm, J. E.
L/Cpl.	107437	Marston, R. S., D.C.M.
L/Cpl.	107405	Miller, D.
Tpr.	107408	Moody, H. A.
Tpr.	107406	Maclean, R. F.
Tpr.	107410	Mace, W. G.
Tpr.	107411	Major, M.
Tpr.	107412	Malan, J. C.
Tpr.	107413	Malim, K.
Tpr.	107414	Matterson, G. S.
Tpr.	116024	Montgomery, W. T.
Tpr.	116413	Melcombe, E. W.
Tpr.	107416	Miller, J.
Tpr.	107417	Milner-Jones, V.
Tpr.	107418	Mills, C. E. L.
Tpr.	107419	Mutchison, K.
Tpr.	107424	Maddock, A. J.
Tpr.	107425	Manning, H. C., M.C., D.C.M.
Tpr.	107426	Mason, P. S.
Tpr.	107428	Maxwell, G. S., M.M.
Tpr.	107432	Montgomery, D.
Tpr.	107435	Meadows, R. R.
Tpr.	107429	Miller, A. O.
Tpr.	107431	Morrison, R.
Tpr.	107447	Moir, D. N.
Tpr.	107451	Morgan, F. W.
Tpr.	107433	Mortimer, V.
Tpr.	107420	Murison, G. J.
Tpr.	107434	Murray, E. E.
Tpr.	116028	Morton, J., M.M.
Tpr.	107438	Manson, W. F.
Tpr.	112253	Morkle, J.
Tpr.	107440	Marston, E. P.
S. S. M.	107436	Marshall, J. T.
Tpr.	107450	Marshall, B. R.
Tpr.	107442	Mawhinney, C. H.
Tpr.	107444	Mitchell, W. W. B.
Tpr.	107445	Monteith, J. I.
Tpr.	107423	Mowatt, P. K., M.M.
Tpr.	116026	Morgan, O.
Tpr.	112255	Matthews, H. C.
Tpr.	107430	Milne, A.
Tpr.	116022	Mahoney, J. F., M.M.
Tpr.	107427	Matthews, P.
Sgt.	107384	McBain, H.
Sgt.	107383	McCarvell, J. J.
Sgt.	107403	McMinn, R. E.
L/Cpl.	107389	McLeod, G. W. L.
Tpr.	107390	McSweeney, H. M.
Tpr.	107387	McCluskey, W. R.
Tpr.	107394	MacDonnell, A. K.
Tpr.	107388	McEwen, G. D.
Tpr.	116033	McLeod, H. J.
Tpr.	107392	McCallum, A.
Tpr.	107393	McCreight, J. D.
Tpr.	107401	McEwan, A.
Tpr.	116031	MacGregor, J., V.C., M.C., D.C.M.
Tpr.	107396	McLennan, E. A.
Tpr.	107385	McWilliams, T. F.
Tpr.	107386	McDonald, J. C.
Tpr.	107402	MacDonald, R.
Tpr.	107404	MacNamara, W. D.
Tpr.	107409	MacCoubrey, J. L., D.C.M.
Tpr.	116029	Macdonald, F.
Far. Sgt.	107453	Newman, W. J.
Cpl.	107458	Nash, H. B.
S. S. Cpl.	107454	Neil, J.
Tpr.	107455	Newton, B.
Tpr.	107456	Neish, J. D.
Tpr.	107459	Neil, D. E.
Tpr.	107457	Nicholson, W. P. P.
Tpr.	107460	Nickson, J. R.
Tpr.	107466	Oldershaw, A.
Tpr.	107461	Ollerhead, G. A.
Tpr.	107463	Oxberry, J. R.
Sgt.	107478	Palmer, E., M.M.
Trp.	107428	Paquette, F.
Tpr.	107479	Pimm, A. G.
Tpr.	107473	Pearkes, G. R., V.C., D.S.O., M.C.
Tpr.	107475	Pegg, T. H.
Tpr.	107487	Potts, J. W.
Tpr.	107467	Pomeroy, J.
Tpr.	107468	Parkyn, G. P.
Tpr.	107469	Partington, E. L., M.S.M.
Tpr.	107470	Pearson, G. W.
Tpr.	107471	Phillips, S. L.M.
Tpr.	107472	Pochin, W. F.
Tpr.	107497	Peters, F. W.
Tpr.	107494	Palmer, A.
Tpr.	107474	Pangbourne, A. G.
Tpr.	107476	Pelly, G. S.
Tpr.	107477	Phillips, F. J.
Tpr.	116035	Pollard, R. J.
Tpr.	107481	Paddon, G. M.
Tpr.	107483	Park, A.
Tpr.	107484	Pearce, F. A.
Tpr.	107485	Pearce, W.
Tpr.	107490	Parry, T. R.
Tpr.	107489	Price, H. E.
Tpr.	107486	Pollard, E. H.
Tpr.	107496	Ponder, H. A.

Appendix V—Nominal Roll

Rank	No.	Name	Rank	No.	Name
Tpr.	107493	Peacock, W. G.	Tpr.	107545	Speechley, T. M.
Tpr.	107495	Potter, J. K., M.C.	Tpr.	107546	Speeden, R.
Tpr.	112277	Palmer, C. A.	Tpr.	115042	Sedgewick, J.
Tpr.	116036	Quintan, J. L.	Tpr.	116042	Somerville, R.
Tpr.	118092	Quigg, H.	Tpr.	107547	Sprague, F. A.
R.Q.M.S.	107499	Rankin, J.	Tpr.	107575	Street, F.
Sgt.	107518	Ready, J.	Tpr.	116044	Stuart, E. V.
Sgt.	107500	Rugg, J.	Tpr.	107576	Sullivan, T. E.
Cpl.	116037	Richman, R., M.M.	Tpr.	107554	Scholte, F. X.
L/Cpl.	107519	Rayment, V. C.	Tpr.	107573	Shipton, B. W.
L/Cpl.	107511	Remnant, S. J.			M.C., M.M.
Tpr.	107516	Rootham, A. E.	Tpr.	107556	Silsby, C. J.
Tpr.	107501	Randall, R. N.	Tpr.	107557	Shuttleworth, R.
Tpr.	107502	Raymer, B. H.	Tpr.	116040	Scott, H.
Tpr.	107503	Richardson, F. N.	Tpr.	107563	Scott, B. E.
Tpr.	107528	Rogers, J. N. F.	Tpr.	107564	Scott, G. N.
Tpr.	107507	Rogers, L. P.	Tpr.	107560	Swadden, J. H.
Tpr.	107508	Ryan, H.	Tpr.	107562	Sanderson, G.
Tpr.	107505	Rogers, A. C.	Tpr.	107553	Sadler, J. W.
Tpr.	107506	Rogers, H. A., M.M.	Tpr.	107571	Sheret, W.
Tpr.	107510	Rea, C.	Tpr.	107565	Shires, J.
Tpr.	107512	Ricketts, D.	Tpr.	107566	Simpson, J. S.
Tpr.	107513	Riley, W. J., M.M.	Tpr.	107569	Strang, A.
Tpr.	107514	Ritchie, D. W.	Tpr.	116046	Sullivan, M.
Tpr.	107515	Rogers, H. L.	Tpr.	107552	Sunington, R.
Tpr.	107517	Rowberry, A. H., M.C.	Tpr.	107574	Spencer, R. L. L.
Tpr.	107520	Renouf, R. J.	Sgt.	107581	Tyler, S. S.
Tpr.	107521	Rant, G. T., M.C., D.C.M.	L/Sgt.	107582	Tyler, W.
			Tpr.	107592	Thomson, A. T.
Tpr.	107522	Ritchie, D. V.	Tpr.	107580	Tozer, W. R.
Tpr.	107523	Roberts, Z.	Tpr.	107579	Talbot, W. E.
Tpr.	107527	Robinson, T.	Tpr.	107591	Taylor, W.F.
Far. Sgt.	107529	Sargent, P.	Tpr.	116047	Taylor, W.
Sgt.	107532	Smith, W., M.M.	Tpr.	107584	Tetlock, H. H.
Far. Sgt.	107551	Sutherland, R.	Tpr.	107593	Thompson, H. G.
Sgt.	107561	Steer, C. P.	Tpr.	107583	Todd, C.
Cpl.	107533	Stillingfleet, H. C.	Tpr.	107595	Vaughan, F. H.
L/Cpl.	107550	Steward, C. A. C.	Tpr.	107598	Vernon, J. A.
Cpl.	107558	Smith, A. S.	Tpr.	107596	Verleysen, M.
Tpr.	116043	Stacey, F.	Tpr.	116049	Venell, W.
Tpr.	107534	Saling, W.	S. S. M.	107619	Webb, A. W.
L/Cpl.	107535	Saunders, C. G.	Sgt.	107635	Worrall, J.
Tpr.	107536	Seon, A. E.	S.Q.M.S.	107634	Warren, J.
Tpr.	107537	Sharpe, W. R.	O. R. S.	107600	Walley, S.
Tpr.	107538	Sigalet, P.	Sgt.	107620	Warren, W. C.
Tpr.	107539	Simpson, H. M.M.	Sgt.	107636	Wasson, T. C.
Tpr.	107540	Smith, A.	Sgt.	107618	Wilson, W. S.
Tpr.	107541	Smith, A. C.	Sgt.	107605	Whitnall, P.
Tpr.	107542	Smith, E.	Sgt.	116050	Wright, F. T.
Tpr.	107559	Smith, C. L.	Cpl.	107606	Wright, D. S.
Tpr.	107577	Somerset, B.	Cpl.	107637	Wallace, G. I.
Tpr.	107530	Somerset, L.	L/Cpl.	107624	Ward, H. C.
Tpr.	107544	Sootheran, L. G.	L/Cpl.	107641	Weir, F. P.

2nd Canadian Mounted Rifles

Rank	No.	Name	Rank	No.	Name
L/Cpl.	107603	White, E. O.	Tpr.	116030	McGowan, J.
L/Cpl.	107623	Whitmore, H. A., M.C., D.C.M.	Tpr.	107526	Roberts, J. W.
			Tpr.	107531	Smith, G.
L/Cpl.	107646	Wood, C. V.	Tpr.	107555	Shield, C.
L/Cpl.	107607	Wilson, W. C., D.C.M.			23-12-15
Tpr.	107608	Waite, W.	L/Cpl.	107301	Hodgkin, W. L.
Tpr.	107602	White, J. F.	Tpr.	107361	Lockhart, E.
Tpr.	107610	Ward, G. J.	Tpr.	116032	McGuckie, D. N.
Tpr.	107611	Wheeler, C. H.	Tpr.	116045	Swanby, A. O., D.C.M.
Tpr.	107616	Whyte, B. M.			
Tpr.	107614	Wilmot, F. B.	Tpr.	116048	Tring, T. J.
Tpr.	107612	Wheeler, J.	Tpr.	118058	Butcher, H.
Tpr.	107613	Wilkinson, T.	Tpr.	118051	Adlam, L.
L/Cpl.	107622	Williams, H. L.	Tpr.	118057	Bowker, G. D.
Tpr.	107617	Wright, W.	Tpr.	118054	Bishop, O.
Tpr.	107615	Wilson, D. J.	Tpr.	118009	Brown, G. G.
Tpr.	107601	White, J. R.	Tpr.	118059	Connors, W. D., M.M.
Tpr.	107625	Warren, O. Q.	Tpr.	118063	Foulds, R.
Tpr.	107626	Wickham, J. B.	Tpr.	118062	Farrell, W.
Tpr.	107628	Winslow, C. A.	Tpr.	118019	Heatherington, F. W.
Tpr.	107651	Watson, J. R.	Tpr.	118067	Harland, M. S.
Tpr.	107627	Willis, H.	Tpr.	118074	Killip, R. H.
Tpr.	107630	Wood, W. J.	Tpr.	118073	Kerr, R.
Tpr.	107629	Wood, E. F.	Tpr.	118026	Lee, J. W.
Tpr.	107599	Worsley, G. N.	Tpr.	118024	Lewis, F.
Tpr.	107631	Wright, W. T.	Tpr.	118081	Massey, L.
Tpr.	107632	Wright, C. H.	Tpr.	118079	MacFarlane, W.
Tpr.	107638	Ward, A. E.	Tpr.	118085	McEwen, A.
Tpr.	107639	Warren, E. H.	Tpr.	118086	McLean, K.
Tpr.	107642	Westlake, H., M.M.	Tpr.	118087	McRae, A., D.C.M., M.M.
Tpr.	107644	Wheatley, S. T.			
Tpr.	107645	Woodward, W. H.	Tpr.	118088	McRae, K.
Tpr.	107650	Weatherstone, W. G.	Tpr.	118092	Quigg, H.
Tpr.	107633	Wilkinson, W. J.	Tpr.	116091	Reid, A.
Tpr.	107621	Whitmore, R.	Tpr.	116092	Rose, H. G.
Tpr.	107653	Zettergreen, A. L.	Tpr.	118050	Watson, J.
		2-11-15	Tpr.	118094	Sanderson, T. O.
Tpr.	107160	Chase, D.			6-1-16
Tpr.	107193	Dollemore, D.	Pte.	106023	Horton, C. A.
Tpr.	116013	Grimes, J. W.	Pte.	108237	Gardner, A. F.
Tpr.	107289	Harvey, J.	Pte.	106002	Allnutt, S.
Tpr.	107336	Jackson, D. B. M.	Pte.	106011	Dorman, H.
Tpr.	107439	Marcott, H.	Pte.	106117	Browne, J. A.
Tpr.	116023	Meany, J.	Pte.	106025	Jamieson, Alex.
Tpr.	107391	McLeod, N.	Pte.	106030	Layton, C. B.
Tpr.	116039	Rooney, T. J.			11-1-16
		10-11-15	Pte.	106004	Barratt, A.
Tpr.	107055	Armstrong, C. H.			3-1-16
Tpr.	116004	Bunce, W.	Pte.	108051	Adams, J. S.
Tpr.	15115	Doyle, G.	Pte.	108057	Allison, W. H.
Tpr.	117017	Harper, J. M.	Pte.	108067	Asquith, G. L.
Tpr.	107308	Hart, H. P.	Pte.	108073	Bavester, F. H.
Tpr.	14876	McTeer, A.	Pte.	108079	Bamborough, G. W.

Appendix V—Nominal Roll

Rank	No.	Name
Pte.	108083	Barnes, R. F.
Pte.	108084	Bartlett, J.
Pte.	108088	Bear, C. S.
L/Cpl.	108090	Beeton, O.
Pte.	108101	Blackmore, H. W. F.
Pte.	108103	Bland, W. G.
Pte.	108110	Booth, L. E. W.
Pte.	108113	Brand, W. C.
Cpl.	108114	Bray, C.
L/Cpl.	108115	Breakel, H. A.
Pte.	108118	Brown, V. L.
Pte.	108120	Bull, S. J.
Pte.	108123	Burden, T.
Pte.	108124	Burdett, T.
Sgt.	108128	Capstick, J. F., M.M.
Pte.	7741	Caton, E.
Pte.	108138	Carr, J. J.
Pte.	108139	Cates, M. L.
Pte.	108144	Chapman, H. H.
Sad. Sgt.	108129	Carpenter, W.
Pte.	108137	Carr, J. W.
Pte.	108145	Chapman, W. J.
Pte.	108147	Chapman, C. T.
Pte.	108148	Chegwin, J. F.
Pte.	108149	Chinneck, C. G.
Pte.	108151	Clark, T. H.
Pte.	108152	Clark, G. P.
L/Sgt.	108160	Coles, A. H.
Pte.	108164	Convey, C.
Pte.	108170	Cousins, G. A.
L/Sgt.	50487	Culp, R. E.
L/Cpl.	108183	Darcus, R. J., M.C.
Cpl.	108184	Davidson, W.
L/Cpl.	108190	Dick, J. C., D.C.M., M.M.
Pte.	108194	Dryden, J.
Pte.	50488	Easton, A.
Pte.	108195	Dryden, J. G.
L/Cpl.	108208	Elliott, F. H.
Cpl.	108209	Ellis, J. P.
Pte.	108211	Emslie, C. G.
C.Q.M.S.	108213	Farmer, A. E.
F.Q.M.S.	108215	Foy, W.
Pte.	108216	Ferguson, J.
Pte.	108218	Ferrier, W. F.
Pte.	108225	Fleming, W.
Pte.	108228	Foster, W. L.
Pte.	7760	Foxten, H. R.
Pte.	108229	Fraser, A. C.
Pte.	7761	French, G.
Pte.	108224	Flemming, W. W.
Sgt.	108232	Gordon, J
B. S. M.	108235	Griffith, C. J.
Cpl.	108238	Garland, E.
Pte.	108240	Gibson, E.
Pte.	108241	Gilchrist, N. A. L.
Pte.	108248	Graham, J. S.
Pte.	108250	Grayson, W. B.
Pte.	108254	Grigg, E. J.
Pte.	108257	Gunness, W. C.
C. S. M.	108258	Hallworth, J. H.
Sgt.	108259	Hays, T. R. O.
S/Sgt.	108260	Hilton, F. W. C.
Pte.	108263	Hall, H. T.
Pte.	108265	Hall, F.
Pte.	108266	Hamlet, W. F.
Pte.	108281	Haugh, R.
Pte.	108274	Harrop, F. T.
Pte.	108279	Harwood, W.
Pte.	108278	Hartland, W. J.
Pte.	108282	Hawkins, H. G.
Pte.	108285	Holmkay, G.
Pte.	108289	Holder, R.
Pte.	108293	Horner, C.
Pte.	108294	Hughes, R. G.
Pte.	108299	Huntington, A. L.
Pte.	108300	Hurst, N. C.
Pte.	108301	Hulmes, F.
Pte.	108302	Howard, M.
Pte.	108311	Joblin, R., D.C.M.
Pte.	108312	Johnson, H. H.
Sgt.	108317	Keynes, A. V.
B.Q.M.S.	108318	Krauss, C. A.
Pte.	108319	Kelly, J.
Pte.	108323	Keynes, R.
Pte.	108324	Kight, E.
Pte.	108330	Knight, G. C.
Pte.	108334	Lang, H. T.
Pte.	108345	Littleford, J. T.
Pte.	108348	Longworth, T.
Pte.	108349	Loughlan, R. C.
Pte.	108351	Love, R. E.
Pte.	108352	Love, T. H.
Pte.	108355	Luscombe, H. A.
Cpl.	108356	Lyle, H. S., M.C.
Sgt.	7706	Little, J. W.
Sgt.	108358	Morley, H. F.
S/Sgt.	108357	Marchant, A.
Pte.	108367	Mallock, E. C. St. J.
Sgt.	108377	Mellor, W., M.M.
L/Cpl.	108381	Meyer, E. R.
Pte.	108387	Miller, F. R.
Pte.	108394	Monkman, T. N.
Pte.	108401	Mullins, J.
Pte.	50489	Morden, J. E.
Pte.	108403	Munroe, A. P.

2nd Canadian Mounted Rifles

Rank	No.	Name	Rank	No.	Name
Pte.	108407	Murray, W.	Pte.	108581	Tombling, A.
Pte.	108408	Myksenaar, A.	Pte.	108588	Trembley, H. C.
Pte.	108411	McCullough, F. L.	L/Cpl.	108598	Vayro, C.
Pte.	108414	McEwan, H. G.	Pte.	108584	Treeco, A. E.
Pte.	108420	McKelvie, R.	Pte.	108611	Waight, L.
Pte.	108421	McKenzie, J. T.	Pte.	108614	Warder, G. R.
Pte.	108424	McKinnon, M.	Pte.	108615	Wardle, J.
Pte.	108427	McLaughlin, G.	Pte.	108619	Webb, T.
Pte.	108431	McLennan, A. D.	Pte.	108623	White, W. P.
Pte.	108433	McRae, W.	Pte.	108627	Williams, D. J.
Pte.	108434	McWilson, W.	Pte.	108638	Wood, A. C.
Pte.	108029	McLean, A.	Pte.	116099	Wilson, S.
Pte.	108443	Osenton, C.	Pte.	108207	Edward, D. B.
Pte.	108444	Ostler, J.			29-1-16
Pte.	108445	Owens, W. R.	Pte.	117104	Adkins, W. F.
Pte.	108455	Paterson, A. C.	Pte.	117106	Allan, J.
Pte.	108466	Pope, J. S.	Pte.	117108	Allan, T. W.
Pte.	108464	Pieroth, P.	Pte.	117109	Allen, F.
Pte.	108090	Patton, I. P.	Pte.	117113	Armstrong, R.
Pte.	108091	Poolman, G. V.	Pte.	117115	Atkinson, G. S.
Cpl.	108478	Reade, M. J.	Pte.	117120	Bailey, H.
Pte.	108479	Reade, T.	Pte.	117121	Bailey, P. M.
Pte.	108488	Rivett, J.	Pte.	117125	Bancroft, W.
Pte.	108491	Roberts, H. S.	Pte.	117128	Brass, H. E.
Pte.	108493	Roberts, W.	Pte.	117129	Beach, K.
Pte.	108497	Robinson, J.	Pte.	117130	Beasley, F.
Pte.	108498	Robinson, R. W.	Pte.	117132	Beatty, J.
Pte.	108501	Rooke, J. V. H.	Pte.	117133	Beckett, G.
Pte.	108507	Rylander, C. A.	Pte.	117134	Bennett, A. F.
Sgt. Ck.	108508	Seggie, W. P.	Pte.	117139	Berry, L.
Sgt. Tptr.	108510	Smart, F. O.	Pte.	117141	Bevan, G. A.
Far. Sgt.	108511	Smilie, R. M.	Pte.	117145	Birnie, J.
Arm. Sgt.	108512	Snowdon, J. D.	Pte.	117146	Beack, W. B.
Pte.	108520	Scobie, A. M.	Pte.	117148	Beake, G.
Pte.	108523	Scrivens, W. J.	Pte.	117150	Blake, J. A. T.
Pte.	108525	Sevior, R.	Pte.	117151	Beencowe, C. A.
Pte.	108527	Sharland, W., M.M.	Pte.	117153	Borton, F. G.
Pte.	108528	Sharpe, A.	Pte.	117154	Borton, H.
Pte.	108533	Shenton, G.	Pte.	117157	Boutillier, N. D., M.M.
Pte.	108534	Short, W. S.			
Pte.	7836	Simons, W.	Pte.	117158	Bowe, S. R.
Pte.	108537	Smedley, C. S.	Pte.	117159	Bowie, J. B.
Cpl.	108541	Smith, F.	Pte.	117162	Bray, E. N.
Pte.	108543	Smith, S.	Pte.	117163	Brazil, A.
Sgt.	108546	Sneddon, T.	Pte.	117165	Briggs, A. J.
Pte.	108551	Stainer, A. T.	Pte.	117171	Bryan, R. D.
Pte.	108554	Stewart, J.	Pte.	117176	Campbell, D. A.
Pte.	108560	St. Denny, J.	Pte.	117181	Cashore, R. D.
A/Sgt.	108563	Stubbs, I. H.	Pte.	117184	Cambon, H.
Pte.	108567	Swan, J.	Pte.	117185	Chapman, S. T.
Pte.	118097	Smith, J.	Pte.	117187	Chessor, J.
Pte.	108570	Tammeros, L.	Pte.	117189	Clark, H. C.
Pte.	108572	Taylor, C. St. J.	Pte.	117190	Clement, N.

Appendix V—Nominal Roll

Rank	No.	Name	Rank	No.	Name
Pte.	117191	Clements, R. A.	Pte.	117301	Hives, J. E.
Pte.	117192	Cobb, B. T.	Pte.	117303	Hives, E.
Pte.	117194	Coffey, L. O.	Pte.	117310	Hood, T.
Pte.	117195	Coglin, G.	Pte.	117311	Hope, C. E.
Pte.	117197	Collinson, H.	Pte.	117312	Hopkins, N. R.
Pte.	117200	Colwell, C.	Pte.	117313	Home, F. J.
Pte.	117202	Cook, H.	Pte.	117317	Innes, A. E.
Pte.	117203	Cookson, W.	Pte.	117318	Innes, T.
Pte.	117205	Corbell, F.	Pte.	117320	Jenkins, A. J.
Pte.	117206	Cormack, F. L.	Pte.	117328	Jowett, R. N.
Pte.	117207	Coupland, R. S.	Pte.	117330	Keating, B. T.
Pte.	117208	Cowling, J. T.	Pte.	117331	Keep, J. C.
Pte.	117212	Crees, R.	Pte.	117334	Kershaw, E. J. K.
Pte.	117213	Cullin, W. P.	Pte.	117335	Kerstens, A. B.
Pte.	117218	Davidson, T.	Pte.	117338	Kilroy, R. A.
Pte.	117220	Davies, C. S.	Pte.	117340	Knight, C. H.
Pte.	117221	Davison, M.	Pte.	117342	Knott, A. R.
Pte.	117223	Dracon, L. F.	Pte.	117343	Kilvington, B.
Pte.	117225	Dick, D.	Pte.	117344	Kyle, C. M.
Pte.	117226	Dickens, J. W.	Pte.	117346	Langham, J.
Pte.	117238	Davis, A. C. W.	Pte.	117347	Lawrence, C. F.
Pte.	117229	Doody, K.	Pte.	117348	Lawrence, V. H.
Pte.	117232	Duckworth, F.	Pte.	117350	Leckie, W.
Pte.	117233	Duke, C. W.	Pte.	117351	Lee, A. E.
Pte.	117236	Dutton, W. H. R.	Pte.	117353	Leppard, C. H.
Pte.	117237	Edwards, H.	Pte.	117355	Littleworth, A.
Pte.	117238	Edwards, J.	Pte.	117357	Logan, M. J.
Pte.		Elford, E. C.	Pte.	117359	Loudon, D.
Pte.	117239	Ellis, E. E.	Pte.	117366	Lyle, J.
Pte.	117240	Ellison, R. H.	Pte.	117368	MacDonald, M.
Pte.	117242	Evans, J.	Pte.	117369	McLean, T.
Pte.	117243	Farquhar, D. C.	Pte.	117370	MacKenzie, C. S.
Pte.	117244	Fewings, L. G.	Pte.	117372	McBride, C. D.
Pte.	117247	Fletcher, J. J.	Pte.	117373	McCarthy, Wm.
Pte.	117248	Flett, G.	Pte.	117374	McCoubery, H.
Pte.	117250	Frankish, J. A.	Pte.	117378	McDonald, Alex
Pte.	117270	Forbes, J. G.	Pte.	117379	McDougall, Colin
Pte.	117252	Froment, W. J.	Pte.	117380	McDermott, J. E.
Pte.	117253	Gaffney, W. H.	Pte.	117384	McFayden, R. S.
Pte.	117254	Garom, F.	Pte.	117383	McFayden, J.
Pte.	117261	Gillies, W. C.	Pte.	117386	McGlashan, H. D.
Pte.	117271	Graham, W. A.	Pte.	117390	McKenzie, R. W.
Pte.	117274	Greene, D. I.	Pte.	117391	McKinnon, J. P.
Pte.	117276	Griffith, G.	Pte.	117392	McKay, F. A.
Pte.	117277	Grime, H.	Pte.	117394	McLeod, H. E.
Pte.	117281	Hainstock, C. D.	Pte.	117398	McNamara, H. L.
Pte.	117282	Hainsworth, R.	Pte.	117399	McQuinn, N.
Pte.	117289	Harvey, W. F.	Pte.	117400	McRae, Alex
Pte.	117290	Hawkes, S. T.	Pte.	117401	McVicar, J. W.
Pte.	117291	de la Haye, C. W. F.	Pte.	117403	Mahoney, A. P.
Pte.	117292	Heatley, T. W. B.	Pte.	117405	Mainwaring, J.
Pte.	117295	Henderson, W.	Pte.	117411	Medlicott, W. F.
Pte.	117297	Herbertson, R.	Pte.	117412	Meeres, H.

2nd Canadian Mounted Rifles

Rank	No.	Name
Pte.	117414	Menzies, A. A.
Pte.	117418	Massender, R. C.
Pte.	117419	Miller, T. L.
Pte.	117420	Michie, A.
Pte.	117421	Miles, B. A.
Pte.	117425	Moffatt, J. K.
Pte.	117429	Morris, E. J.
Pte.	117431	Mortimer, R.
Pte.	117432	Moore, L.
Pte.	117438	Nash, F.
Pte.	117441	Nelson, F. M.
Pte.	117442	Nelson, J.
Pte.	117444	Nethercot, H. J.
Pte.	117428	Norrish, Chas.
Pte.	117450	Norton, C. J.
Pte.	117451	Notman, R.
Pte.	117452	Nurcombe, L. J. N.
Pte.	117456	Oxborough, J.
Pte.	117457	Oxborough, W.
Pte.	117458	Palmer, B. S.
Pte.	117460	Parker, G.
Pte.	117462	Park, J.
Pte.	117465	Patchett, H.
Pte.	117467	Paterson, J. S.
Pte.	117468	Patterson, L.
Pte.	117471	Pegler, A. W.
Pte.	117473	Penny, D. G.
Pte.	117475	Perraton, P. R.
Pte.	117476	Perry, C. L.
Pte.	117478	Phillips, J.
Pte.	117479	Phizackerley, A. O.
Pte.	117481	Piper, L. R.
Pte.	117482	Pool, P. R.
Pte.	117483	Pottinger, W. A.
Pte.	117484	Prevel, P. E. J.
Pte.	117487	Prime, W.
Pte.	117491	Quantz, D.
Pte.	117492	Raikes, A. C.
Pte.	117496	Rawlings, W. L. R.
Pte.	117497	Reinholt, F. L.
Pte.	117500	Reid, W.
Pte.	117501	Richards, W.
Pte.	117503	Ritchie, H. S.
Pte.	117505	Robbie, J. J.
Pte.	117506	Roberts, G.
Pte.	117509	Robertson, L. M.
Pte.	117511	Robinson, G. E.
Pte.	117512	Robinson, Hugh
Pte.	117514	Rogers, I. W.
Pte.	117515	Rogers, P., D.C.M.
Pte.	117516	Roland, C. E.
Pte.	117517	Ross, A.
Pte.	117518	Russell, J.
Pte.	117522	Sangster, A.
Pte.	117523	Scott, John
Pte.	117527	Shiedel, R. W.
Pte.	117528	Shouldice, D. R. M.
Pte.	117530	Sinclair, W.
Pte.	117532	Smith, C. C.
Pte.	117533	Smith, C. H.
Pte.	117534	Sinnott, E. E.
Pte.	117537	Smith, John
Pte.	117538	Smith, Stephen
Pte.	117539	Smith, P. W.
Pte.	117540	Smith, F. G.
Pte.	117541	Somerville, J. C.
Pte.	117546	Stafford, R.
Pte.	117547	Stanton, A. S.
Pte.	117548	Stark, A. J., D.C.M.
Pte.	117549	Stagg, R. C.
Pte.	117550	Steedman, J. K.
Pte.	117551	Stephen, R.
Pte.	117553	Stephenson, J. W., D.C.M.
Pte.	117555	Stevenett, W. A.
Pte.	117557	Stewart, A.
Pte.	117558	Stewart, D. A.
Pte.	117559	Stewart, W.
Pte.	117563	Strickland, F.C., M.M.
Pte.	117564	Stringer, W. E.
Pte.	117570	Sutherland, P. R.
Pte.	117571	Swanwick, H.
Pte.	117572	Synge, N. H.
Pte.	117604	Stephen, W.
Pte.	117576	Taylor, P.
Pte.	117579	Teeling, R. E.
Pte.	117580	Tildesley, W.
Pte.	117581	Tillier, L. J.
Pte.	117582	Timms, J. R.
Pte.	117583	Thomas, B. B. H.
Pte.	117584	Thomson, J. R.
Pte.	117587	Trimble, R. C.
Pte.	117590	Turner, C. W.
Pte.	117593	Underwood, J.
Pte.	117594	Unwin, A. N.
Pte.	117596	Urquhart, C. J.
Pte.	117597	Usherwood, A. E.
Pte.	117601	Waldock, W. H.
Pte.	117602	Wallace, J.
Pte.	117605	Walters, R. L.
Pte.	117606	Warren, D. S.
Pte.	117607	Warren, L. W.
Pte.	117611	Watt, J.
Pte.	117612	Weaver, C. L., M.M.
Pte.	117613	Weatherhead, B.

Appendix V—Nominal Roll

Rank	No.	Name
Pte.	117615	Webster, J.
Pte.	117616	Webster, T. H.
Pte.	117619	Weston, T. H.
Pte.	117621	White, J. W.
Pte.	117623	Whiteside, Wm.
Pte.	117624	Whittle, E.
Pte.	117629	Wilson, R. G.
Pte.	117631	Winder, E. A.
Pte.	117632	Winder, H. W.
Pte.	117627	Williams, R. N.
Pte.	117635	Wormald, J. W.
Pte.	117642	Yorkland, C.
Pte.	117643	Young, E.
Pte.	117644	Zuehlke, F.
Pte.		Woolway, A. J.
Pte.	117424	Mitchell, J.
Pte.	117433	Moor, W.
Pte.	117101	Abrahamson, P. A.
Pte.	117116	Attrell, R. H.
Pte.	117122	Baird, S. R.
Pte.	117131	Beatty, J. H.
Pte.	117142	Bice, H. V.
Pte.	117156	Boulter, P. P.
Pte.	117172	Burchell, C.
Pte.	117188	Church, A.
Pte.	117222	Day, E. B.
Pte.	117224	de Foras, F. J.
Pte.	117246	Fleming, E. J.
Pte.	117255	Gatensbury, A. C.
Pte.	117300	Higginson, G. E.
Pte.	117321	Jeffers, J. W.
Pte.	117337	Kidder, H. L.
Pte.	117363	Lowe, D., M.M.
Pte.	117381	McElroy, A.
Pte.	117385	McGarity, D. P.
Pte.	117397	McLevin, D.
Pte.	117406	Major, D.
Pte.	117408	Marles, J. C.
Pte.	117415	Meredith-Brown, R.
Pte.	117416	Meredith-Brown, S. E.
Pte.	117434	Merkley, F. E.
Pte.	117435	Munsie, E. W.
Pte.	117123	Baker, F.
Pte.	117126	Barnes, D. H.
	2-3-16	
Pte.	442932	Banks, W.
Pte.	442933	Bard, H.
Pte.	442033	Bateman, C.
Pte.	442939	Bere, R.
Pte.	442937	Berg, C. W.
Pte.	42327	Bjerke, K. O.
Pte.	422769	Bishop, H.
Pte.	442347	Carfra, J.
Pte.	423154	Chesterman, A.
Pte.	442959	Clay, C. H.
Pte.	442356	Cook, W.
Pte.	442832	Crossley, W.
Pte.	442647	Davidsvich, N.
Pte.	442645	Denusik, N.
Pte.	432025	Gay, C. F.
Pte.	442384	Gold, A. E.
Pte.	442677	Gregory, J. P.
Pte.	442999	Hanna, P.
Pte.	443006	Hickson, W.
Pte.	443013	Jackson, A.
Pte.	443015	Jackson, N.
Pte.	423169	Johnstone, B. E.
Pte.	443023	Kennedy, M. N.
Pte.	442705	Kennedy, P. N.
Pte.	423301	Kinnie, J. H.
Pte.	44327	Knox, F. V.
Pte.	422269	Lamb, A.
Pte.	423412	LeMeuir, P. J.
Pte.	442902	Lee, E. J.
Pte.	442725	Mundy, H.
Pte.	443361	McDonald, P.
Pte.	442446	McIntosh, C.
Pte.	423374	McKenzie, D., D.C.M., M.S.M.
Pte.	423076	McAuslan, J. T.
Pte.	443036	McLeod, J.
Pte.	443040	McMillan, D. D.
Pte.	422965	Nelson, R. B.
Pte.	422924	Newman, C. W.
Pte.	443067	Pearson, W. J.
Pte.	422135	Preston, J.
Pte.	423338	Richards, E. W.
Pte.	443081	Seeman, L.
Pte.	443085	Silverton, F.
Pte.	443325	Slater, T. H.
Pte.	422832	Sommerville, A. R.
Pte.	442489	Stuart, A. L.
Pte.	442800	Taylor, J. T.
Pte.	443133	Weekes, P. F.
Pte.	443112	White, N.
Pte.	423240	Wright, E. J.
Pte.	434540	Ainge, A. C.
Pte.	446925	Burchinshaw, R.
Pte.	435764	Blackwell, F. N.
Pte.	435813	Blakwell, A. J.
Pte.	446633	Buckingham, R. J.
Pte.	435737	Bennett, W. T.
Pte.	434657	Baldwin, S.
Pte.	435484	Beeton, A.
Sgt.	100075	Cameron, T. M.

2nd Canadian Mounted Rifles

Rank	No.	Name	Rank	No.	Name
Pte.	434229	Cooke, A.	Pte.	422749	McKay, R. M.
Pte.	446668	Campbell, J. T. W.	Pte.	422796	Munroe, R.
L/Cpl.	100115	Darlington, T. T.	Pte.	58125	Ouimet, P. A.
Pte.	434262	Dower, W.	Pte.	422665	Phillips, R. D.
Pte.	435809	Edward, W. B.	Pte.	423373	Phillip, T.
Pte.	435524	Edwards, J.	Pte.	423094	Parsons, T. H.
	16-3-16		Pte.	423114	Simmons, P. W.
Pte.	435577	Fowler, H.	Pte.	422909	Sturgeon, J.
Pte.	446887	Forbes, G.	Pte.	422915	Sturgeon, J. H.
Pte.	434310	Foster, J.	Pte.	422813	Tressier, A.
Pte.	435023	Forster, E.		15-4-16	
Pte.	435819	Fraser, A. L.	Pte.	443467	Allen, W. F.
Pte.	447066	Falconer, J. S.	Pte.	443886	Barnes, F. V.
Pte.	434944	Gittins, J.	Pte.	443498	Barlow, J.
Pte.	435443	Fraser, J.	Pte.	443418	Booker, T., M.M.
Pte.	435588	Hewitt, M. H.	Pte.	443646	Burt, G. J.
Pte.	434470	Hill, W.	Pte.	442558	Cavallero, E.
Pte.	435778	Jones, G.	Pte.	443452	Dooley, J.
Pte.	446591	Manton, G. W.	Pte.	443132	Fox, G. H.
Pte.	437068	Martin, R. C.	Pte.	443430	Gibeau, P.
Pte.	435053	Moulding, F. R.	Pte.	443548	Graham, R.
Pte.	435660	Mackay, A.	Pte.	442834	Hall, S.
Pte.	446358	McLeod, J. A.	Pte.	442545	Haydock, J.
Pte.	434296	McGravey, J.	Pte.	443590	Madsen, J.
Pte.	447146	McKie, G. M.	Pte.	442600	Mason, E. H.
Pte.	434652	Reid, J.	Pte.	443796	Mazur, F.
Pte.	435402	Rhodes, W. C. F.	Pte.	443378	Menzies, R. P.
Pte.	435739	Smart, J. E.	Pte.	442576	Mowatt, W. J.
Pte.	447235	Skeffingham, F.	Pte.	442541	MacKintosh, W.
Pte.	436599	Standing, E.	Pte.	443656	McDonald, K.
Pte.	434634	Treloar, P. G.	Pte.	443038	McLeod, M. A.
Pte.	436280	Vale, A.	Pte.	443877	McMahon, J. G.
Pte.	435300	Williams, F.	Pte.	443863	Nichol, W. G.
Pte.	435233	Wilson, J.	Pte.	442760	Palmer, J. L.
Pte.	435422	Williams, R.	Pte.	442774	Robertson, F.
Pte.	435728	Woods, P.	Pte.	442780	Smith, F.
Pte.	434986	Woolley, H.	Pte.	443687	Stacey, E.
Pte.	446158	Whillans, F.	Pte.	442777	St. Eloi, D. J.
Pte.	435815	Woods, A.	Pte.	443665	Thomas, T.
Pte.	435744	McIntosh, G. T.	Pte.	443134	Trevor, H. R.
Pte.	437796	Locke, B.	Pte.	443129	Wheeler, J. E.
Pte.	437185	Donnelly, J.		25-5-16	
	26-3-16		Pte.	447011	Atkinson, J. W.
Pte.	422933	Bedford, F.	Pte.	447558	Beales, R. E.
Pte.	423188	Delury, J.	Pte.	447523	Bleaken, J. C.
Pte.	422801	Edwards, A. W.	Pte.	447461	Bridges, M. H.
Pte.	422618	Gallagher, W.	Pte.	447552	Brown, A.
Pte.	423445	Gordon, C.	Pte.	446649	Brown, J. W.
Pte.	423178	Haliday, J. F.	Pte.	447532	Brown, M.
Pte.	57550	Harris, H.	Pte.	447536	Byers, M. B.
Pte.	423038	Howat, R.	Pte.	447362	Carmichael, A. C., M.M.
Pte.	423359	Ivy, J.			
Pte.	423307	Lowe, W. J.	Pte.	447494	Clarke, E. J.

Appendix V—Nominal Roll

Rank	No.	Name
Pte.	447493	Curtis, E. T.
Pte.	447997	Downs, J.
Pte.	447573	Dargie, R. E.
Pte.	447380	Fisher, G. R.
Pte.	447454	Fisher, W. G.
Pte.	447606	Fleetwood, E. H.
Pte.	447486	Grebik, A.
Pte.	447080	Gubbins, J. L.
Pte.	446139	Hardie, J. M. O.
Pte.	447086	Harris, K. M. W.
Pte.	447513	Higgins, R.
Pte.	447639	Kenney, J.
Pte.	447499	Landry, W.
Pte.	447735	McCleary, L. P.
Pte.	447456	McFarland, J. W.
Pte.	447514	McIntyre, A.
Pte.	447518	McLeod, J.
Pte.	447590	Martin, W. A.
Pte.	447555	Martinez, A.
Pte.	487680	Penny, A. E.
Pte.	447179	Phillips, W. W.
Pte.	447169	Porter, T.
Pte.	447551	Read, F. A.
Pte.	447624	Sauve, J. P.
	26-5-16	
Pte.	446508	Scott, H. A.
Pte.	447749	Sheir, G.
Pte.	447543	Stevens, J. P.
Pte.	446421	Tabbener, A. J.
Pte.	447608	Taylor, C. J.
Pte.	447611	York, B. F.
Pte.	425198	Peggs, G.
Pte.	425279	Russell, J. E.
Pte.	425280	Russell, L. C.
Pte.	425261	Robertson, J. M.
Pte.	425282	Rutz, E.
Pte.	425293	Scott, J. R.
Pte.	425287	Sanders, G. H.
Pte.	425323	Skinner, E. A.
Pte.	425330	Smith, D.
Pte.	425335	Smith, H.
Pte.	425325	Slater, W. P.
Pte.	425368	Stickney, C.
Pte.	425341	Soan, E.
Pte.	425314	Silcox, G.
Pte.	425427	Trotter, J.
Pte.	425422	Tolver, A. T.
Pte.	425443	Venner, E. O.
Pte.	425305	Sexsmith, W.
Pte.	425447	Vincent, W. B.
Pte.	425476	Westover, N.
Pte.	425507	Wren, B. E.
Pte.	425487	Wilkinson, S.
Pte.	425461	Warner, G. W.
Pte.	461142	Wylie, T.
Pte.	425517	Youngman, E. A.
Pte.	436166	Bergeron, A.
Pte.	101138	Barnett, M. P.
Pte.	100854	Brasnett, E. H.
Pte.	402266	Bates, S. W.
Pte.	20307	Davis, T.
Pte.	435717	Davis, W.
Pte.	402751	Hayward, W.
Pte.	436900	Lillies, W.
Pte.	80128	Lyon, I. H.
Pte.	436834	Miller, D.
Pte.	446914	Moran, I. P.
Pte.	455517	Pierce, D.
Pte.	20706	Smith, E. G.
Pte.	447234	Trerise, W. J.
Pte.	100374	Wells, P. M.
Pte.	463951	Amos, A.
Pte.	464407	Andrew, J.
Pte.	463724	Appleford, G.
Pte.	464458	Baker, E. E.
Pte.	464283	Baker, F. W.
Pte.	463952	Baker, R. P.
Pte.	463726	Ball, J. W.
Pte.	464477	Barr, J. W.
Pte.	464483	Bartlett, W. J.
Pte.	464547	Boult, E. G.
Pte.	463027	Brady, W.
Pte.	463012	Brown, H. W.
Pte.	463954	Brown, R. R.
Pte.	464524	Bullock, A.
Pte.	463959	Butts, C. D.
Pte.	463961	Charnley, F.
Pte.	463252	Clark, C. F.
Pte.	463037	Clark, A. N.
Pte.	463047	Corfield, G. J.
Pte.	464049	Denbigh, A.
Pte.	464561	Diplock, C. V.
Pte.	464654	Douglas, H. R. E.
Pte.	463060	Dudley, R. J.
Pte.	464294	Edkins, S. E.
Pte.	464398	Fletcher, H. H.
Pte.	464299	Forsythe, C.
Pte.	464526	Gillies, H.
Pte.	463681	Goodship, L. A., M.C., M.M.
Pte.	463279	Gourlay, W.
Pte.	464497	Gray, H. C.
Pte.	464342	Harrison, A.
Pte.	464554	Harvey, W. F.
Pte.	464643	Hazell, E.
Pte.	463096	Highet, J. A.

2nd Canadian Mounted Rifles

Rank	No.	Name	Rank	No.	Name
Pte.	464666	Hodgkins, S. E.	Pte.	463798	Hedley, R.
Pte.	464638	Hogland, O.	Pte.	464023	Horrobin, E. G.
Pte.	464098	Hughes, H. J.	Pte.	463773	Janson, T. J.
Pte.	464557	Jousiffe, E.	Pte.	464323	Leggett, F. C.
Pte.	464560	Knox, T. F.	Pte.	464144	Millard, W. H.
Pte.	464580	Marshall, J.	Pte.	463725	McBroom, G.
Pte.	463324	Marshall, K. J.	Pte.	464146	McKay, J.
Pte.	463133	Montgomery, A.	Pte.	464403	McKenzie, J. N.
Pte.	464608	McDonald, J.	Pte.	464260	McLeod, A. J.
Pte.	464505	MacLean, J. C.	Pte.	464230	Reid, H.
Pte.	464506	McGrath, M.	Pte.	464232	Riley, J.
Pte.	463138	McPhail, J.	Pte.	464370	Rodger, W.
Pte.	463150	Newberry, G.	Pte.	464166	Spears, T. N.
Pte.	463148	Newnham, J.	Pte.	464361	Summers, V.
Pte.	463147	Noble, L. W.	Pte.	464519	Thomson, E. L.
Pte.	463152	Norris, F. J. N.	Pte.	464129	Dallamore, T. G.
Pte.	454677	Norris, H. L.	Pte.	463079	Grant, C.
Pte.	463172	Redfern, A.	Pte.	463727	Bennett, A.
Pte.	464620	Robertson, D.	Pte.	463212	Anderson, B.
Pte.	464063	Rosie, M.	Pte.	463484	Keith, N.
Pte.	463171	Ross, J.	Pte.	464536	Taylor, F.
Pte.	464437	Ross, T. C.	Pte.	464327	Jackson, A.
Pte.	464397	Scrimshaw, F.	Pte.	464402	McTaggart, C. R.
Pte.	463988	Skinner, J. W. S.	Pte.	464515	Senior, S. J.
Pte.	463579	Sprinkling, C. K.	Pte.	100569	McCormick, J. W. R.
Pte.	463180	Stansby, J. M.	Pte.	441672	Primeau, T.
Pte.	463829	Stant, H., M.M.	Pte.	440091	Pritchard, R. S.
Pte.	464634	Stant, H. S.	Pte.	440393	Probert, C. A.
Pte.	463577	Stevens, C. F.	Pte.	440090	Procter, J. B.
Pte.	463183	Stevenson, E. H.	Pte.	441492	Proport, H. T.
Pte.	463372	Stralton, J.	Pte.	440572	Proudfoot, C.
Pte.	464051	Stride, H. A.	Pte.	441896	Pybus, L. J., M.M.
Pte.	463578	Stromach, A.	Pte.	440584	Quinney, H.
Pte.	463902	Taylor, A. B.	Pte.	440626	Racicot, T. H.
Pte.	463901	Thomas, G. A.	Pte.	440862	Rafter, E. J.
Pte.	464351	Thompson, J.	Pte.	440786	Rawls, A.
Pte.	463189	Todd, C. H.	Pte.	440747	Read, W. A.
Pte.	463383	Tolhurst, C. J.	Pte.	441065	Read, E. C.
Pte.	464175	Travis, A. J.	Pte.	441400	Rees, A. L.
Pte.	463194	Urquhart, J. W.	Pte.	441574	Reid, H. W.
Pte.	463201	Ward, A.	Pte.	441338	Reid, H. W.
Pte.	464674	Williams, B.	Pte.	440587	Richardson, J. T.
Pte.	464358	Willoughby, P.	Pte.	440095	Ridgwell, B.
Pte.	464349	Wilson, T. C.	Pte.	441369	Ringrose, J. F.
Pte.	463205	Woolsey, G. G.	Pte.	441575	Robbins, L. M.
		8-6-16	Pte.	440755	Roberts, C. E.
Pte.	463733	Bolevick, J.	Pte.	441063	Roberts, T. H.
Pte.	463960	Campbell, R.	Pte.	440937	Robertson, R. C.
Pte.	464025	Axon, C.	Pte.	440149	Robinson, A. J.
Pte.	463024	Booker, R. B. D.	Pte.	441060	Robinson, A. F.
Pte.	464571	Dallamore, A. R.	Pte.	440909	Robinson, W. C.
Pte.	463884	Goode, T. W.	Pte.	441800	Robinson, W. S.
Pte.	463768	Harvey, R. M.			

Appendix V—Nominal Roll

Rank	No.	Name
	9-6-16	
Pte.	441570	Rodgers, J. J.
Pte.	441806	Rodgers, M.
Pte.	441498	Roney, H. N.
Pte.	441683	Rorison, J.
Pte.	441466	Ross, J. E.
Pte.	440588	Ross, L.
Pte.	441787	Roland, H. F.
Pte.	441183	Rollette, J. T.
Pte.	440288	Roy, J. R.
Pte.	441062	Rudden, P.
Pte.	441415	Rudolph, C. P.
Pte.	441573	Rustige, D., M.M.
Pte.	441750	Rutenburg, S.
Pte.	440988	Rutt, J. H.
Pte.	441304	Noakes, N. H.
Pte.	441305	Noakes, L. A.
Pte.	441629	Noakes, R. E.
Pte.	440857	Oates, F.
Pte.	441307	O'Brien, J.
Pte.	441568	O'Connor, B. C.
Pte.	440766	O'Connor, F. M.
Pte.	440142	Ogilvie, R.
Pte.	441660	Oleson, S.
Pte.	441391	Oliver, N. J.
Pte.	441689	Olson, W. J.
Pte.	440861	Oram, D. McH., M.M.
Pte.	440860	Ortloff, E. H. J.
Pte.	440441	Orton, F.
Pte.	440767	O'Sullivan, J. L.
Pte.	441367	Pack, E., M.M.
Pte.	441058	Paddle, W.
Pte.	441747	Page, C. E.
Pte.	441405	Pelkey, A.
Pte.	441748	Palmer, E.
Pte.	440945	Panes, H.
Pte.	441444	Pankhurst, J. C.
Pte.	440768	Parker, J.
Pte.	441025	Parkin, E.
Pte.	441721	Parkin, S. H.
Pte.	441794	Parkinson, W.
Pte.	441309	Parlee, E. P.
Pte.	441785	Parsons, M., M.M.
Pte.	440092	Parsons, W. A.
Pte.	441234	Pascoe, A. H.
Pte.	441311	Pateman, E.
Pte.	440575	Patreau, C.
Pte.	766375	Francis, A.
Pte.	441820	Patterson, J.
Pte.	441056	Patterson, P.
Pte.	440195	Patterson, S.
Pte.	473085	Paul, H.

Rank	No.	Name
Pte.	441749	Pearce, G.
Pte.	425370	Pearcey, H.
Pte.	440299	Peck, P.
Pte.	441376	Pell, W.
Pte.	440777	Pellitier, P. J.
Pte.	441479	Penney, S. S.
Pte.	441824	Penrose, M. C.
Pte.	440529	Peterson, A.
Pte.	441053	Pickard, A.
Pte.	441474	Pilkington, J., M.M.
Pte.	441406	Pilkington, W., D.C.M.
Pte.	440036	Pitt, A.
Pte.	441130	Pollard, T. E.
Pte.	441381	Pook, J.
Pte.	440906	Porter, S.
Pte.	440033	Poulton, E.
Cpl.	440621	Powell, J. A.
Pte.	440771	Power, R. F.
Pte.	440882	Pratt, A.
Pte.	440582	Pratt, C. F.
Pte.	441349	Preston, J.
Pte.	136646	Abbey, T.
Pte.	136301	Abel, H. J. T.
Pte.	135412	Abernethy, J.
Pte.	135642	Addy, R. W.
Pte.	135636	Addy, E. R. N.
Pte.	135415	Agnew, R.
Pte.	135086	Airhart, L. A.
Pte.	136448	Aldridge, C. N.
Pte.	126372	Abraham, J.
Pte.	135640	Allen, E.
Pte.	136542	Allen, F. W.
Pte.	136302	Allen, G.
Pte.	126553	Allen, W. H.
Pte.	135641	Alwen, F.
Pte.	409317	Ambrose, W.
Pte.	135418	Andrews, T.
Pte.	126324	Anderson, W. H.
Pte.	135342	Angus, A., D.C.M.
Pte.	135091	Angus, J.
Pte.	136437	Anthony, E. K.
Pte.	135274	Anthony, F. J.
Pte.	135075	Apps, C.
Pte.	135419	Argue, J. P.
Pte.	135639	Armitage, S.
Pte.	135634	Armstrong, F.
Pte.	135092	Armstrong, G.
Pte.	135420	Armstrong, J. W.
Pte.	135963	Aston, T. J.
Pte.	135093	Atkins, J.
Pte.	135635	Atkinson, T. S.
Pte.	135964	Allward, A. V.

2nd Canadian Mounted Rifles

Rank	No.	Name	Rank	No.	Name
Pte.	136248	Appleby, J. H. (Jr.)	Pte.	135436	Bothwick, J.
Pte.	135422	Bacon, T.	Pte.	126407	Bowd, A.
Pte.	135965	Bain, J. W.	Pte.	126260	Boyle, H. A.
Pte.	136196	Baker, C. W.	Pte.	127705	Bower, D. E.
Pte.	135305	Baker, G. H.	Pte.	135438	Boyd, J.
Pte.	127409	Baker, W. C.	Pte.	136312	Boyes, F. C.
Pte.	135649	Ball, R.	Pte.	135440	Boyt, F.
Pte.	135966	Bambrough, C. H.	Pte.	135441	Boyt, W.
Pte.	136451	Banfield, J. H.	Pte.	136543	Brabson, H. S.
Pte.	135424	Bannister, F. E.	Pte.	135985	Brazier, I. H.
Pte.	135425	Bannister, T. S.	Pte.	136198	Brearley, A.
Pte.	136305	Barber, E.	Pte.	136433	Enright, W. J.
Pte.	136608	Barclay, A. F.	Pte.	135105	Bridge, J. A.
Pte.	135098	Barlow, C.	Pte.	135987	Bridger, C. N.
Pte.	135426	Barlow, F.	Pte.	135988	Bridges, —
Pte.	136639	Barnaby, F.	Pte.	135986	Britton, W.
Pte.	135427	Barnes, J. G.	Pte.	135250	Brooks, H., D.C.M.
Pte.	136275	Barnes, W. E.	Pte.	127046	Brooks, R. W.
Pte.	136306	Barron, T.	Pte.	135645	Broomhead, T. B.
Pte.	135428	Barrett, A., M.M.	Pte.	135442	Brown, A.
Pte.	135655	Barron, W.	Pte.	126334	Brown, G. H.
Pte.	135971	Bartle, F. E.	Cpl.	136200	Brown, H. J.
Pte.	135972	Baxter, R.	Pte.	135958	Brown, H. J.
Pte.	135430	Beamish, B.	Pte.	135663	Brown, W. A.
Pte.	135656	Beazer, W.	Pte.	135873	Schofield, R. J.
Pte.	135106	Beckett, C. A.	Pte.	136120	Schultz, T. J.
Pte.	135974	Beckwith, J. A.	Pte.	135875	Scorgie, J.
Pte.	452542	Bell, F. J.	Pte.	126065	Scott, F.
Pte.	135651	Bell, N. D.	Pte.	135219	Sear, B.
Pte.	135976	Bennett, H. T.	Pte.	135858	Setford, A.
Pte.	135432	Berry, W.	Pte.	136376	Self, T. W.
Pte.	136197	Best, E. A.	Pte.	136298	Schackleton, W.
Pte.	136645	Bestwick, H.	Pte.	136131	Shaw, F. H.
Pte.	135978	Bewsey, B.	Pte.	126882	Shaw, J.
Pte.	136544	Beynon, G. H.	Pte.	126310	Shaw, A. H.
Pte.	135653	Bibby, W. G.	Pte.	135856	Shaw, G.
Pte.	135973	Biles, H.	Pte.	136508	Shaw, W. R.
Pte.	136637	Binsley, E.	Pte.	135565	Shearer, A.
Pte.	135100	Bird, H.	Pte.	135085	Shearer, T.
Pte.	135980	Birks, C.	Pte.	126552	Sheehan, J. W.
Pte.	136546	Bishop, H. E.	Pte.	126894	Shean, J. W.
Pte.	126209	Black, J.	Pte.	136642	Shedlock, C.
Pte.	408753	Blair, E. B.	Pte.	126261	Sherman, G.
Pte.	136309	Blake, H. G.	Pte.	135566	Sheppard, W. J.
Pte.	136277	Blakeley, J.	Pte.	135879	Sherman, W. J.
Pte.	135433	Blackhall, A.	Pte.	135877	Shields, G.
Pte.	135104	Bogg, C.	Pte.	126428	Sherwood, G.
Pte.	136312	Bolton, W.	Pte.	127043	Sherwood, G. R.
Pte.	135631	Bonser, G. H.	Pte.	126579	Sims, E. A.
Pte.	135435	Booker, H. G.	Pte.	136134	Simons, W. J.
Pte.	136621	Boorman, J. R.	Pte.	136512	Simpson, J. J.
Pte.	135983	Booth, W. J.	Pte.	135864	Small, H. M.
Pte.	135327	Borland, A. S.	Pte.	135571	Smalley, G.

Appendix V—Nominal Roll

Rank	No.	Name	Rank	No.	Name
Pte.	135087	Smith, D.	Pte.	136151	Thorpe, P.
Pte.	135866	Smith, F.	Pte.	136517	Tilbe, A. V.
Pte.	136137	Smith, H.	Pte.	136628	Tobin, J. D. B.
Pte.	136379	Smith, H. C.	Pte.	135884	Tomlinson, J.
Pte.	135224	Smith, J. A. N.	Pte.	135236	Tomsett, A. J.
Pte.	135574	Smith, J. E.	Pte.	136609	Torrey, J. F.
Pte.	136158	Smith, A. L.	Pte.	135882	Train, N.
Pte.		Smith, R. G.	Pte.	136403	Trautman, N. J.
Pte.	136634	Smith, R.	Pte.	126247	Tremain, J. R.
Pte.	136139	Smith, W. H.	Pte.	135883	Trotter, E.
Pte.	478489	Henry, W. R.	Pte.	126332	Tremain, W.
Pte.	136505	Smylie, J.	Pte.	135082	Trueman, G.
Pte.	136585	Spearing, E. J.	Pte.	136389	Tubss, F.
Pte.	135025	Spence, N. J.	Pte.	136390	Tubbs, W. G.
Pte.	135228	Spicer, F. H.	Pte.	136242	Tullett, T.
Pte.	451938	Spurgeon, F.	Pte.	136144	Turner, A. E.
Pte.	135575	Squirrell, H.	Pte.	136271	Turner, J.
Pte.	136141	Staden, J.	Pte.	135589	Turp, A.
Pte.	136586	Staley, H. F.	Pte.	135886	Twaddel, J.
Pte.	136144	Stephens, W. G.	Pte.	127029	Toms, W. G.
Pte.	126686	Stainberg, E.	Pte.	136243	Ynthank, R. P.
Pte.	135229	Stevenson, E. W.	Pte.	136400	Vandervoort, S. W.
Pte.	126731	Sterney, R. B.	Pte.	136589	Varley, E. T.
Pte.	135578	Stiff, A. F.	Pte.	135591	Veater, L. T.
Pte.	135579	Stiff, H.	Pte.	127330	Smart, F. S.
Pte.	136145	Stitt, F.	Pte.	136156	Veness, E. T.
Pte.	136146	Stollard, T. H.	Pte.	135253	Vickery, W.
Pte.	136381	Streeter, W. W.	Pte.	136392	Walker, S. S.
Pte.	127257	Stubbins, H.	Pte.	136245	Waldron, W. E.
Pte.	136302	Sullivan, J. F.	Pte.	136159	Walking, A.
Pte.	126363	Stevenson, A. A.	Pte.	136300	Wallace, G. R.
Pte.	136269	Preater, J.	Pte.	136161	Walsh, P. J.
Pte.	135553	Pugh, W. J.	Pte.	135904	Walton, A. V.
Pte.	135549	Pouge, W. E.	Pte.	135898	Ward, A.
Pte.	135550	Pollock, J.	Pte.	136163	Ward, T.
Pte.	136289	Summers, H. G.	Pte.	135902	Watson, C. J.
Pte.	136383	Summers, E. P.	Pte.	135596	Watson, G. P.
Pte.	135859	Sutton, A. N.	Pte.	409766	Watson, M. H.
Pte.	136588	Swan, J.	Pte.	135597	Watson, R. A.
Pte.	127175	Switzer, W. A.	Pte.	135598	Watt, W.
Pte.	402766	Talmage, C. E.	Pte.	437179	Bates, N. A. H.
Pte.	135584	Tanner, J.	Pte.	628479	Leask, W.
Pte.	135069	Tanner, L.	Pte.	436214	Lailey, A. W.
Pte.	775395	Tapp, A.	Pte.	436914	Marshall, J.
Pte.	136239	Tapp, F.	Pte.	441189	Hughes, C. W.
Pte.	135231	Taylor, J.	Pte.	441880	Vanderstraten, J. A.
Pte.	136240	Taylor, S.	Pte.	127324	Bridge, A. S.
Pte.	135880	Theodore, H. J.	Pte.	135463	Coulter, W.
Pte.	135585	Thomas, G.	Pte.	441139	Mourant, A.
Pte.	136385	Thomason, E.	Pte.	437045	Foreman, L.
Pte.	135233	Thompson, R.	Pte.	437634	Greenwood, R.
Pte.	136149	Thornbury, W.	Pte.	447327	Milne, R.
Pte.	453229	Thorne, R. H.	Pte.	16454	McCaffrey, J.

2nd Canadian Mounted Rifles

Rank	No.	Name
Pte.	100478	Goodwin, J.
Pte.	127015	Lynch, J. W.
Pte.	437358	Lorimer, W. K.
Pte.	126711	Pearson, S. G.
Pte.	127090	Woods, T. A.
Pte.	126273	Wright, W. G.

12-6-16

Rank	No.	Name
Pte.	441916	Whiting, J.

15-7-16

Rank	No.	Name
Pte.	117526	Shillits, C.

18-7-16

Rank	No.	Name
Pte.	447003	Austin, R. C.
Pte.	446152	Adams, J. W.
Pte.	161201	Armstrong, T. L.
Pte.	447659	Brown, C. A.
Pte.	446760	Baker, W. E.
Pte.	487660	Belton, W. G.
Pte.	160509	Butler, A. M.
Pte.	446162	Brooks, E. H.
Pte.	160131	Blake, E. I.
Pte.	446153	Caffelle, N.
Pte.	161068	Clugston, H.
Pte.	160854	Cohl, R.
Pte.	447973	Clarke, A. W.
Pte.	446922	Clark, J.
Pte.	446143	Davison, J. W.
Pte.	447863	Darlow, G. H.
Pte.	446715	Davidge, A.
Pte.	161247	Doney, A.
Pte.	160410	Dunlop, J.
Pte.	446450	Ebden, T. J.
Pte.	160789	Forrest, M.
Pte.	447577	Fearey, P.
Pte.	160280	Gleason, T. S.
Pte.	447629	Graham, T.
Pte.	160443	Gunn, J.
Pte.	160399	Hewitt, F.
Pte.	447379	Haywood, W.
Pte.	447397	Hoe, H.
Pte.	160813	Huggins, C. O.
Pte.	160007	Huggins, R. E. A.
Pte.	160195	Hesleton, G. F.
Pte.	160427	Harmer, H.
Pte.	161097	Jones, J. R.
Pte.	160466	Johnson, S.
Pte.	446936	Jempson, J.
Pte.	447617	Jackson, H. P.
Pte.	160287	Littlefield, A. G.
Pte.	160910	Littlefield, H. J.
Pte.	446030	McCarthy, L. G.
Pte.	161157	McDonald, J.
Pte.	160945	Marcey, G.
Pte.	160087	McKenzie, J.
Pte.	160809	McLean, R.
Pte.	161007	McDonald, A.
Pte.	160013	Maddison, J.
Pte.	160963	Murray, J.
Pte.	161011	Mooney, J. P.
Pte.	160404	Murray, J. C.
Pte.	160309	Nicol, J. A.
Pte.	161226	Nicholls, E. S.
Pte.	447767	O'Connor, M. J. P.
Pte.	160190	Pickard, J. R. B.
Pte.	446758	Paris, W. H.
Pte.	446439	Pym, V.
Pte.	447765	Park, J.
Pte.	161152	Reid, J. S.
Pte.	160834	Rigg, T. W.
Pte.	160991	Rutherford, G.
Pte.	446413	Sloan, A.
Pte.	446045	Stiff, O.
Pte.	447434	Stain, M.
Pte.	446485	Symons, A.
Pte.	161267	Sherman, C.
Pte.	446043	Segar, S. G.
Pte.	160107	Snook, W. K.
Pte.	446023	Slipp, L. L.
Pte.	446401	Trigg, C.
Pte.	161126	Tomlinson, H.
Pte.	446946	Torrens, W.
Pte.	447239	Withnall, A. R.
Pte.	447247	Wallace, B.
Pte.	446871	Wakelyn, H. C.
Pte.	160873	Watt, G. L.
Pte.	160438	Wilson, W.
Pte.	446080	Woods, H. B.
Pte.	158558	Cembalisty, P.
Pte.	159585	Kordack, R.
Pte.	159171	Kunaenks, G.
Pte.	159156	Nitchen, J.
Pte.	425162	Netriuk, F.
Pte.	459559	Sokolovski, V.
Pte.	159746	Tracnenko, K.
Pte.	158698	Verechik, E.
Pte.	425444	Vernaichuk, M.
Pte.	159540	Vachnovich, P.

21-7-16

Rank	No.	Name
Pte.	113057	Anderson, J.

25-7-16

Rank	No.	Name
Pte.	106004	Barrett, A.

19-7-16

Rank	No.	Name
Pte.	193299	Giddy, A. E.
Pte.	500299	Glass, J.
Pte.	408791	Hammond, B.
Pte.	136482	Jowett, F.
Pte.	150171	McWade, J. F.

Appendix V—Nominal Roll

Rank	No.	Name
	28-8-16	
Pte.	700194	Crawford, R.
Pte.	700092	Dahlbury, O.
Pte.	700304	Goulding, T.
Pte.	700975	Hamilton, G. B.
Pte.	700454	Harris, F.
Pte.	700275	Howsan, R. F.
Pte.	700068	Jackson, S. J.
Pte.	700991	Lee, G.
Pte.	701163	Lester, W.
Pte.	701275	Loaring, W. L.
Pte.	700490	Loher, W.
Pte.	700916	Miller, J. D.
Pte.	701224	McAdam, R.
Pte.	700014	McMahon, E. T.
Pte.	700554	Rance, T. F.
Pte.	700255	Renning, J. J.
Pte.	700929	Sandison, R.
Pte.	701185	Sheppard, G. E.
Pte.	700492	Thomas, E.
Pte.	701015	Thomas, J. C.
Pte.	463723	Anderson, E.
Pte.	180180	Blasson, B.
Pte.	180857	Colbert, J. L.
Pte.	180198	Cochrane, P.
Pte.	442959	Clay, C. H.
Pte.	464679	Crompton, F.
Pte.	180609	Doman, R.
Pte.	464592	Donaldson, R. L.
Pte.	135473	Duncan, T.
Pte.	180815	Easton, J. R.
Pte.	464535	Elder, W.
Pte.	180414	Goddard, A.
Pte.	464629	Hawkins, W. J.
Pte.	180071	Hitchin, H.
Pte.	180630	Herd, T. H. D.
Pte.	180254	King, T.
Pte.	180490	Kingston, R.
Pte.	464448	Martin, A. W.
Pte.	180106	Moar, W.
Pte.	463786	McEwan, J.
Pte.	180661	Parker, S.
Pte.	180701	Patterson, H. M.
Pte.	181200	Patterson, T.
Pte.	180514	Paine, J.
Pte.	180919	Palmer, N. J.
Pte.	180664	Pugh, W.
Pte.	180523	Richards, J. E.
Pte.	180525	Roberts, E.
Pte.	463364	Robertson, J. R.
Pte.	180313	Silver, D.
Pte.	180671	Simpson, C. S.
Pte.	464438	Soles, A. J.
Pte.	464168	Somerville, W.
Pte.	463893	Smythe, A. H.
Pte.	180876	Stollery, E.
Pte.	180679	Stone, W. G.
Pte.	180143	Taylor, J.
Pte.	180688	Watson, W. D.
Pte.	180979	Young, C. McP.
Pte.	180554	Young, J. E.
Pte.	180708	Young, W.
Pte.	464284	Chapman, J. F.
	16-8-16	
Pte.	414283	Smith, M. F.
Pte.	415054	Mutford, W.
Pte.	414920	Neary, P. J.
Pte.	414285	Rogers, E.
Pte.	414280	Shankley, R.
	28-9-16	
Pte.	180601	Clark, F.
Pte.	442986	Forteath, W. G. B.
Pte.	443007	Hillyard, S. J.
Pte.	181022	Irvine, C.
Pte.	463114	Lock, F. W.
Pte.	457569	Clarendon,—
	22-10-16	
Pte.	437797	Banks, E.
Pte.	57397	Fleming, W. A.
Pte.	181127	Harris, T. E.
Pte.	180235	Hastings, A. F.
Pte.	464657	Jackson, W.
	29-11-16	
Pte.	116319	Agur, P. B.
Pte.	227669	Armstrong, J.
Pte.	116812	Bennett, F.
Pte.	116477	Britton, M. W.
Pte.	116128	Burgess, J.
Pte.	116568	Bushfield, A.
Pte.	116929	Barr, A.
Pte.	116471	Beard, W. K.
Pte.	116576	Bracken, F.
Pte.	116776	Baggs, W. F.
Pte.	116980	Barnes, A. G.
Pte.	227698	Bradley, T.
Pte.	227762	Birch, O.
Pte.	227681	Campbell, W. J.
Pte.	116990	Curtin, E. H.
Pte.	116412	Cluse, E.
Pte.	227712	Cavanagh, T.
Pte.	227757	Cunningham, G. S
Pte.	116917	Clinton, J. P.
Pte.	116839	Champion, E.
Pte.	116913	Carlson, C.
Pte.	227661	Cadwallader, L. J.
Pte.	116562	Carrigan, J. T.

2nd Canadian Mounted Rifles

Rank	No.	Name	Rank	No.	Name
Pte.	116418	Dorman, G.	Pte.	782347	Hewitt, O.
Pte.	227641	Dickson, G.	Pte.	781819	Hill, W. T.
Pte.	116362	Duncan, W. A.	Pte.	782325	Hinschberger, A. C.
Pte.	116862	Dyer, E.	Pte.	782354	Holt, J. E.
Pte.	116953	Doane, H. L.	Pte.	781626	Holmes, J. H.
Pte.	116411	Ellis, C. S.	Pte.	781808	Hopkins, W.
Pte.	116569	Fielding, F. J.	Pte.	781992	Huff, P.
Pte.	227627	Funnell, A.	Pte.	781723	Johnson, C. W.
Pte.	227743	Fletcher, F. J.	Pte.	781803	Jolin, N.
Pte.	116452	Glover, W.	Pte.	781151	Killion, M.
Pte.	116723	Grant, D.	Pte.	781152	Knoll, H. M.
Pte.	227711	Gray, F.	Pte.	782326	Lindsay, W. S.
Pte.	116106	Gavin, J.	Pte.	782227	Loughray, J.
Pte.	116743	Hall, P. S.	Pte.	781645	Middler, W. H.
Pte.	116196	Hope, J. A.	Pte.	782266	McNamee, W. J.
Pte.	116930	Halksworth, A.	Pte.	781681	McNutt, S. B.
Pte.	227672	Holt, T.	Pte.	781755	Nixon, W. A.
Pte.	116343	Hicks, E. P.	Pte.	781598	Nyman, J.
Pte.	227708	Hamilton, E.	Pte.	781474	Oak, T.
Pte.	227747	Howard, F. T. D.	Pte.	781553	Oliver, J.
Pte.	227613	Innes, T.	Pte.	781930	Overy, A. W.
Pte.	116121	Johnston, W. H.	Pte.	781487	Padget, J. B.
Pte.	116782	King, J.	Pte.	781680	Pialey, A. S.
Pte.	227692	Keith, F.	Pte.	782330	Poole, A.
Pte.	227690	Knowlson, G.	Pte.	907651	Quinn, D.
Pte.	116462	Lamport, W. E.	Pte.	782433	Raymer, H.
Pte.	227628	Littlemore, F.	Pte.	781435	Robertson, L. S.
Pte.	116770	Laurent, E. St. L.	Pte.	782218	Rose, N.
Pte.	116323	Lawrence, E. M.	Pte.	781840	Ross, S. E.
Pte.	116382	Lord, O. K.	Pte.	781452	Russell, W. H.
Pte.	116809	McGibbon, D. L.	Pte.	782471	Schamahorn, B. J.
Pte.	227611	Mason, J.	Pte.	781262	Smith, R.
Pte.	116926	Matveichuk, J.	Pte.	781337	Smith, F.
Pte.	116787	McKenzie, J. G.	Pte.	781687	Squires, T. F.
Pte.	116788	McKenzie, P. G.	Pte.	781527	Steele, W. H.
Pte.	116789	McKenzie, H. V.	Pte.	782052	Stemp, H. C.
Pte.	116146	Mills, F. H.	Pte.	781276	Stoakes, L.
Pte.	116246	Mitchell, W. C.	Pte.	781316	Stribbell, D. A.
Pte.	116097	McInery, A.	Pte.	781437	Thompson, A. E.
Pte.	116737	McLean, H.	Pte.	781450	Thompson, H. F.
Pte.	116843	McQuair, J.	Pte.	782248	Wade, J.
Pte.	826523	Nelson, C.	Pte.	781849	Wales, A. F.
Pte.	227689	Neal, C. B.	Pte.	781923	Wales, A. T.
Pte.	227630	O'Connor, J. E.	Pte.	781383	Walker, G.
Pte.	227666	Olson, A.	Pte.	782074	Watkins, G.
Pte.	116985	O'Reilly, A.	Pte.	781371	Waud, W. O.
Pte.	116995	Osborne, J.	Pte.	781942	Webb, D. J.
Pte.	116592	Potts, H.	Pte.	782300	Welsh, J. R.
Pte.	116979	Park, J.	Pte.	781888	Welsh, J.
Pte.	116785	Price, A. G. F.	Pte.	782306	Wilkins, P. L.
Pte.	116249	Price, D. W.	Pte.	782411	Willey, B. E.
Pte.	781551	Herd, A.	Pte.	782352	Worle, P. C.
Pte.	781122	Heslop, J. W.	Pte.	781295	Wright, J. E.

Appendix V—Nominal Roll

Rank	No.	Name	Rank	No.	Name
Pte.	782315	Young, F.	Pte.	781422	Eley, G. M.
	29-11-16		Pte.	781085	Elliott, A. F. B.
Pte.	116179	Ross, D.	Pte.	781089	Fletcher, J.
Pte.	116950	Reid, W. C.	Pte.	782089	Flock, A. J.
Pte.	116577	Rowbottom, C.	Pte.	782379	Gillies, A. C.
Pte.	116936	Ross, C. J.	Pte.	781567	Gallagher, L.
Pte.	227664	Robins, A.	Pte.	781707	Gamble, J.
Pte.	116810	Stevenson, H. A.	Pte.	782239	Garrett, W.
Pte.	227680	Sullivan, A.	Pte.	781099	Garroch, P.
Pte.	116860	Smith, F.	Pte.	781964	Garrod, W.
Pte.	116971	Smethurst, A. G.	Pte.	781774	Goodwin, W. E.
Pte.	116744	Taylor, J.	Pte.	781106	Grendon, W.
Pte.	116567	Tunstall, J.	Pte.	781769	Grosart, J.
Pte.	227649	Terry, J.	Pte.	781481	Hall, J. A.
Pte.	116194	Vernon, E. N. M.	Pte.	782439	Harmer, O. F.
Pte.	227632	Weatherly, J.	Pte.	782438	Harmer, J. W.
Pte.	116334	Welch, J.	Pte.	781131	Harmer, G.
Pte.	116585	Wright, E. F.		14-12-16	
Pte.	227752	Walton, A. T.	Pte.	687245	Adams, L. V.
Pte.	116819	Watson, A. F.	Pte.	687287	Allan, R.
Pte.	116563	Waring, G. H.	Pte.	688070	Andrews, J.
Pte.	116701	Walker, J. G.	Pte.	687476	Bennett, A. G.
Pte.	116970	Watson, G. B.	Pte.	687039	Bolam, H. H.
Pte.	227679	Whitehead, W. R.	Pte.	688203	Briston, W. H.
Pte.	116475	Hutchinson, A.	Pte.	687500	Brown, O.
Pte.	116790	Scott, H.	Pte.	687847	Burbridge, G. J. B.
Pte.	116735	Turnill, E. S.	Pte.	687718	Buzzard, H. L.
Pte.	782045	Agar, R.	Pte.	687034	Caldwell, D. J.
Pte.	781453	Anderson, J.	Pte.	688148	Campbell, D.
Pte.	252005	Angus, W. M.	Pte.	687087	Carr, B.
Pte.	782044	Armstrong, J.	Pte.	687723	Carter, A.
Pte.	781010	Bagshaw, H.	Pte.	687606	Clark, J.
Pte.	782341	Bateman, J. McL.		14-12-16	
Pte.	781592	Beattie, J.	Pte.	687222	Clark, D.
Pte.	781021	Bellegham, E.	Pte.	688097	Coombs, J.
Pte.	781031	Bentley, H. C.	Pte.	687061	Crosetta, F.
Pte.	781804	Betson, T.	Pte.	687694	Crouch, F.
Pte.	781427	Bingley, E.	Pte.	687995	Dick, J.
Pte.	782069	Bonsteel, J. B.	Pte.	687392	Draper, S. W.
Pte.	781033	Boyle, G. A.	Pte.	688090	Erickson, F.
Pte.	781737	Brown, H.	Pte.	687707	Evans, J. D.
Pte.	781852	Bryan, L. A.	Pte.	688004	Foster, H.
Pte.	781038	Burchmore, W. F.	Pte.	688160	Francis, A.
Pte.	781372	Burgess, C. S.	Pte.	687553	Francis, H.
Pte.	781381	Clark, C. F.	Pte.	688275	Freault, L.
Pte.	781542	Claydon, P. L.	Pte.	688017	Funk, L.
Pte.	781620	Crocker, H.	Pte.	687250	Garcia, A.
Pte.	781461	Dalgleish, W. O.	Pte.	688073	Grantham, V. F.
Pte.	782220	Deeprose, J. A.	Pte.	687254	Harris, S. O.
Pte.	781541	Donaldson, H.	Pte.	687358	Hayward, C. M.
Pte.	781470	Duxbury, G.	Pte.	687891	Henderson, G.
Pte.	781473	Duxbury, T.	Pte.	687407	Hereron, G.
Pte.	781373	Eaton, H.	Pte.	688145	Higgins, M.

2nd Canadian Mounted Rifles

Rank	No.	Name	Rank	No.	Name
Pte.	688186	Huelin, P. B.	Pte.	687592	Stewart, W. B.
Pte.	687376	Janes, J. S.	Pte.	687959	Stiller, F. G.
Pte.	687450	Johnson, A.	Pte.	687051	Stocking, G. H.
Pte.	687671	Johnson, H. J.	Pte.	688140	Stroud, G. H.
Pte.	687333	Jowsey, J.	Pte.	688238	Trehearne, H. L.
Pte.	688217	Kennedy, A. D.	Pte.	687665	Tyers, S.
Pte.	687961	Lockyer, W. T.	Pte.	687129	Verity, J. C.
Pte.	688158	Macnab, A. G.	Pte.	687786	Wain, A. L.
Pte.	687064	Mahoney, W. J.	Pte.	687583	Walton, L.
Pte.	687272	Mahoney, W. P.	Pte.	687127	Watson, H.
Pte.	687447	Manery, G. F. D.	Pte.	687809	Watt, J. A.
Pte.	687119	Marchenia, A.	Pte.	687692	Wilson, T. H.
Pte.	687083	Mauk, W. H.	Pte.	687069	Wilson, R. C. A.
Pte.	687779	Monnell, J. A.	Pte.	687348	Woods, J. B.
Pte.	687838	Miller, J. W.	Pte.	227780	Adams, C. E.
Pte.	687090	Carr, F.	Pte.	227635	Borrow, E.
Pte.	688279	Millard, D.	Pte.	116487	Bellringer, A. B.
Pte.	687037	Mowat, L. G.	Pte.	116832	Banning, J.
Pte.	688133	McBeath, W.	Pte.	116786	Dawley, H. E.
Pte.	687620	McCall, H. A.	Pte.	116302	Edwards, E.
Pte.	688268	McDonald, F. C.	Pte.	227660	Evans, D. J.
Pte.	687097	McGregor, C.	Pte.	116895	Elliott, J.
Pte.	688214	McPhail, J.	Pte.	116407	Graham, R.
Pte.	687451	Olson, C.	Pte.	116639	Groves, R. E.
Pte.	688177	Page, H.	Pte.	116845	Henderson, J.
Pte.	687991	Pain, F. A.	Pte.	227626	Hyatt, W. S.
Pte.	687858	Palmer, A. S.	Pte.	116823	Harwood, G. A.
Pte.	687452	Park, R.	Pte.	116738	Hannah, C. H.
Pte.	687969	Pentland, A.	Pte.	116610	Irwin, F. A.
Pte.	687740	Phinney, B. E.	Pte.	116131	Jones, E.
Pte.	687994	Pierrish, A. R. G.	Pte.	116869	Jones, T. M.
Pte.	687751	Pizzolato, A., M.M.	Pte.	116707	Johnson, C.
Pte.	687873	Poole, W. C.	Pte.	116313	Keane, W.
Pte.	687257	Pritchard, R.	Pte.	227749	Kenyon, J.
Pte.	687413	Quinn, C.	Pte.	116297	Moore, T.
Pte.	687892	Reed, C.	Pte.	227651	Mallett, A.
Pte.	688246	Richley, G.	Pte.	217944	Mayers, H. R.
Pte.	687856	Roberts, W.	Pte.	116908	Murray, D.
Pte.	687748	Robson, O. O.	Pte.	116381	Murray, A.
Pte.	688309	Rowe, F.	Pte.	116530	Morgan, T. J.
Pte.	688057	Ruddock, E. B.	Pte.	116337	Nicholls, C. S.
Pte.	687444	Ryder, J. V.	Pte.	116691	Rennie, P. M.
Pte.	688007	Salvidge, F.	Pte.	116911	Rolls, S.
Pte.	687704	Scrimgeour, J.	Pte.	116912	Roels, E.
Pte.	687752	Sharper, J.	Pte.	116320	Stanton, H.
Pte.	687505	Skorton, W. N.	Pte.	116572	Shipley, J. W.
Pte.	678988	Smith, W.	Pte.	227629	Terhune, D. A.
Pte.	687648	Smith, J.	Pte.	116298	Walters, T.
Pte.	687485	Smith, W. C.	Pte.	116369	Warman, F. D.
Pte.	688264	Snowdon, C. N.	Pte.	227702	Wilkie, O. J. H.
Pte.	687824	Soulle, A. J.	Pte.	116749	Wasilieff, T.
Pte.	687616	Spooner, F.	Pte.	116801	Watson, T.
Pte.	687706	Stephenson, G. B.	Pte.	227701	Yool, J.

Appendix V—Nominal Roll

Rank	No.	Name	Rank	No	Name
Pte.	116256	Brind, W. F.	Pte.	707213	Franklyn, E.
Pte.	116153	Bridgeman, W. 23-12-16	Pte.	706343	Frew, J.
Pte.	454053	Joliffe, H. H.	Pte.	706936	Funk, J. G.
Pte.	454159	Elliot, J. E.	Pte.	707199	Gatti, C.
Pte.	469131	Martin, A. J.	Pte.	706813	Gillan, F. H.
Pte.	470144	McDonald, E. R.	Pte.	706854	Gilbert, R.
Pte.	469444	Owens, W.	Pte.	706495	Gould, L.
Pte.	470165	Stevens, L. D.	Pte.	706798	Harper, C.
Pte.	706424	Allen, C. B.	Pte.	706801	Handlen, J. W.
Pte.	706523	Allard, F.	Pte.	706861	Haycroft, C. E.
Pte.	707157	Anderson, W. A.	Pte.	706665	Halliday, T. W.
Pte.	707096	Arden, J. A.	Pte.	706556	Hickman, E.
Pte.	707254	Arundel, J.	Pte.	706487	Jackman, A.
Pte.	707242	Armstrong, W. R. C.	Pte.	706644	Jancowski, W. J.
Pte.	706719	Augustine, V. C.	Pte.	706590	James, T.
Pte.	707133	Baldie, R.	Pte.	706579	John, J.
Pte.	208247	Banister, J. M.	Pte.	707032	Johnson, S.
Pte.	707021	Blackburn, G.	Pte.	707102	Jones, F.
Pte.	707220	Blackwell, A.	Pte.	826057	Judd, J. H.
Pte.	707156	Bowler, P. J.	Pte.	707640	Kelly, D. E.
Pte.	707209	Boskovich, V.	Pte.	706524	Kenning, G. A.
Pte.	706805	Bobbott, T.	Pte.	116769	Lambert, J.
Pte.	707173	Brown, H. A.	Pte.	706616	Lang, W.
Pte.	706693	Brown, J.	Pte.	706761	Liddell, W. K.
Pte.	706335	Brough, R. C.	Pte.	707211	Lipscomb, C. H.
Pte.	706759	Burgess, G.	Pte.	707101	Loudon, W. D.
Pte.	707178	Burns, R. M.	Pte.	707171	Lubbe, W. T. H.
Pte.	707208	Burn, R. S.	Pte.	707195	Matheson, B.
Pte.	706493	Cooley, R.	Pte.	706821	Maxwell, D.
Pte.	706951	Butcher, E. J.	Pte.	116295	MacDonald, R. W.
Pte.	706565	Butters, W.	Pte.	706460	Mankin, G.
Pte.	826029	Canning, P.	Pte.	707025	MacDonald, A.
Pte.	706980	Cardwell, J. M.	Pte.	706956	Margetts, P.
Pte.	706161	Carley, S. W.	Pte.	706446	Martin, J. H.
Pte.	706594	Carter, E.	Pte.	706325	Martin, J. W.
Pte.	706697	Casey, J.	Pte.	706475	Maynard, F. H.
Pte.	707141	Charlesworth, M. M.	Pte.	706566	Mitchell, A. M.
Pte.	706673	Cheslyn, W. N.	Pte.	706704	Montgomery, J. D.
Pte.	706490	Copas, R.	Pte.	706953	McColl, J.
Pte.	707067	Coddington, A. D.	Pte.	706762	McIntosh, G.
Pte.	707099	Cobble, W. S.	Pte.	706390	McIntosh, H.
Pte.	707169	Creber, H. H.	Pte.	706505	McKay, J.
Pte.	706667	Cunningham, R. H.	Pte.	706548	McKinnon, A.
Pte.	706536	Dawson, C. E.	Pte.	706586	McNeill, F. J.
Pte.	706632	Dee, J. W.	Pte.	706997	McNeill, J. R.
Pte.	706455	Dean, A.	Pte.	706800	Nairn, J.
Pte.	706468	Duffield, J.	Pte.	706928	Neill, J.
Pte.	181039	Eaton, W. M.	Pte.	706481	Orchard, L.
Pte.	706900	Elkerton, W.	Pte.	707030	Parker, A. H.
Pte.	706544	Evans, C. S.	Pte.	707123	Hurst, H. J.
Pte.	706624	Evans, E.	Pte.	707158	Sinclair, R. C.
Pte.	706690	Flett, A. L. M.	Pte.	706733	Parlee, G. M.
			Pte.	706527	Pike, E.

2nd Canadian Mounted Rifles

Rank	No.	Name	Rank	No.	Name
Pte.	706477	Porter, J. F.	Pte.	931035	Forbister, F. W.
Pte.	707223	Purser, J.	Pte.	931642	Fuller, J. W.
Pte.	707237	Purser, E.	Pte.	931438	Furneaux, T. R.
Pte.	707217	Reardon, H.	Pte.	931008	Gaskell, R.
Pte.	706489	Riley, W. G. S.	Pte.	931208	Gilmour, R.
Pte.	706526	Roberts, E.	Pte.	931584	Gordon, H. McG.
Pte.	707212	Rourke, W.	Pte.	931289	Grant, J.
Pte.	706551	Gough, G.	Pte.	931142	Green, A. O.
Pte.	707261	Ruebery, E.	Pte.	931116	Greenough, J.
Pte.	706414	Rule, A.	Pte.	931148	Halliday, J. G.
Pte.	706815	Scott, G. M.	Pte.	931146	Hamblin, F. G.
Pte.	707225	Scott, J.	Pte.	931509	Hammond, J.
Pte.	706757	Scott, J. A.	Pte.	931379	Hare, J. J.
Pte.	707210	Sivertz, G.	Pte.	931150	Hillyard, C.
Pte.	707191	Sivertz, H. G.	Pte.	931800	Hogan, S.
Pte.	706629	Sloman, H.	Pte.	931266	Holland, W. M.
Pte.	707130	Smith, E. T.	Pte.	931213	Hollis, C. E.
Pte.	706626	Snape, P. B. P.	Pte.	931206	Holmes, J. W.
Pte.	706914	Stilwell, W. B.	Pte.	931783	Hornsey, R.
Pte.	706611	Sutton, G. F.	Pte.	931694	Hubberstey, R.
Pte.	706606	Sweeney, W. H.	Pte.	931446	Hyde, H. N.
Pte.	706729	Taylor, W. W.	Pte.	931550	Ion, J. A.
Pte.	706484	Thompson, R. T.	Pte.	931155	Jesty, M.
Pte.	706485	Thompson, T. A. J.	Pte.	931570	Joy, J.
Pte.	706126	Walton, A.	Pte.	931260	Kana, J.
Pte.	706930	Watkiss, G.	Pte.	931159	Kennedy, C. H.
Pte.	706912	Watkins, A. D. J.	Pte.	931726	Kent, G. S.
Pte.	706858	Watkins, M. W.	Pte.	931846	Kerr, J.
Pte.	706554	Webster, D.	Pte.	931465	King, B. MacM.
Pte.	706635	Cowie, J.	Pte.	931818	Kinney, F.
Pte.	707253	Dasher, A. J.	Pte.	931198	Krall, A. A.
Pte.	706708	Earl, A. E.	Pte.	931197	Krall, L.
Pte.	706585	Griffith, W. J.	Pte.	931161	Laughton, W. M.
Pte.	706448	Howe, J. E.	Pte.	931160	Lindblad, H. J.
Pte.	706906	McKeon, P.	Pte.	931755	Little, J.
Pte.	706804	Peck, T. E. L.	Pte.	931319	Lunn, J. F.
Pte.	707234	Spracklen, D. A.	Pte.	931455	MacDonald, C. R.
Pte.	706680	Thornton, D. R.	Pte.	931122	Mansfield, J.
Pte.	707187	Downie, G.	Pte.	931095	McDonald, A.
	19-4-17		Pte.	931458	McDonald, R. L.
Pte.	931259	Anderson, C. B.	Pte.	931835	McCallum, M.
Pte.	931449	Billsborough, R.	Pte.	931686	MacGregor, F. H.
Pte.	931014	Buly, J.	Pte.	931270	McGuire, W.
Pte.	931205	Blaney, W. B.	Pte.	931612	McIlwraith, P. H.
Pte.	931133	Bourne, C. S.	Pte.	931353	McIntosh, W. P.
Pte.	931020	Buxton, E.	Pte.	931165	McLaughlin, C.
Pte.	931603	Chrishop, R.	Pte.	931117	McRae, A. F.
Pte.	931541	Church, C. W.	Pte.	931294	Murdoch, W.
Pte.	931552	Clease, W. J.	Pte.	931838	Nickelby, T. P.
Pte.	931716	Coles, P. F.	Pte.	931692	O'Connor, W. P.
Pte.	931121	Couillard, H. E.	Pte.	931533	Pavlos, A.
Pte.	931421	Dixon, J. T.	Pte.	931215	Perry, M.
Pte.	931374	Elliott, T. J.	Pte.	931429	Peter, O.
Pte.	931717	Folliard, W.			

Appendix V—Nominal Roll

Rank	No.	Name	Rank	No.	Name
Pte.	931114	Phillips, T. A.	Pte.	931216	Freer, E. E.
Pte.	931247	Pinkerton, J.	Pte.	931376	Gane, G. B. M.
Pte.	931278	Podrasky, A.	Pte.	931600	Geddes, E. R.
Pte.	931078	Precious, F.	Pte.	931300	Goulding, W. P.
Pte.	931668	Ptashnik, J.	Pte.	931378	Greenwood, F.
Pte.	931328	Ramsden, C. H.	Pte.	931143	Gridley, H. C.
Pte.	931058	Raven, J.	Pte.	931401	Harrison, F. E.
Pte.	931569	Reade, W.	Pte.	931241	Harrison, S.
Pte.	931737	Rice, W.	Pte.	931789	Hatt, C.
Pte.	931773	Rock, E. P.	Pte.	931505	Healey, H.
Pte.	931743	Roper, W.	Pte.	931606	Hugh, L.
Pte.	931740	Rowe, T. H.	Pte.	931012	Jenkinson, H.
Pte.	931248	Roycroft, F.	Pte.	931840	Kay, W. B.
Pte.	931317	Ryckman, J. A.	Pte.	931157	Keatley, G. E.
Pte.	931074	Sampson, C.	Pte.	931484	Kemball, A.
Pte.	931839	Skaale, K.	Pte.	931693	Knowles, J.
Pte.	931665	Spinkins, E.			19-4-17
Pte.	931749	Smith, H. T.	Pte.	706568	Anderson, S. R.
Pte.	931681	Stow, J. P.	Pte.	707207	Baker, W.
Pte.	931435	Strossi, D.	Pte.	102887	Buxton, B. W. J.
Pte.	931391	Tanner, H. W. G.	Pte.	707001	Cuthell, G. W.
Pte.	931843	Taylor, H. J.	Pte.	116029	McDonald, F.
Pte.	931577	Trewhelle, J.	Pte.	102868	Price, W. E.
Pte.	931535	Wade, J.	Pte.	706144	Province, G.
Pte.	931032	Wallwork, J.	Pte.	707227	Sizertz, C.
Pte.	931291	Womack, T. W.	Pte.	463829	Staut, H.
Pte.	931057	Woodley, A.	Pte.	116388	J'Anson, N.
Pte.	931432	Woods, T.			22-4-17
Pte.	931731	Yates, A.	Pte.	926039	Burch, A. F.
		22-4-17	Pte.	706028	Calvert, D.
Pte.	931775	Allen, T. H.	Pte.	706933	Clark, W. S.
Pte.	931345	Anderson, C.	Pte.	160754	Dayton, A. G.
Pte.	931411	Appleby, T.	Pte.	101552	Faulkner, H. F. N.
Pte.	931046	Atherton, W. D.	Pte.	706127	Halstead, A.
Pte.	931844	Battershall, W. G.	Pte.	706239	Mathews, R. N.
Pte.	931265	Brooks, C. H.	Pte.	760175	McIntyre, W.
Pte.	931634	Brooks, J. R.	Pte.	707153	Penwell, S. J.
Pte.	931595	Campbell, L. O.	Pte.	707093	Platt, F. C.
Pte.	931037	Carlson, E.	Pte.	706533	Sun, E. R.
Pte.	931491	Croquette, J. W. A.	Pte.	760360	Smith, X. C.
Pte.	931501	Cobb, E. R.	Pte.	707138	Stewart, L.
Pte.	931496	Conrad, J.			4-5-17
Pte.	931334	Cookson, T.	Pte.	707145	Wilson, W.
Pte.	931277	Cotter, J.	Pte.	706812	Goldie, F.
Pte.	931497	Crosskey, J. F.	Pte.	706552	Knox, F.
Pte.	931302	Danielson, D. M.	Pte.	460746	Richardson, W. G.
Pte.	931368	Davidson, W.	Pte.	706625	Sherman, D. H.
Pte.	931560	Deverall, G. H.	Pte.	760942	Whaley, J.
Pte.	931559	Deverall, S. J.			12-5-17
Pte.	931346	Dickson, C.	Pte.	706971	Armstrong, F.
Pte.	931137	Dill, A. W.	Pte.	625294	Clicteur, H.
Pte.	931290	Dolstra, C.	Pte.	704093	Colomiyi, P.
Pte.	931763	Donegan, R.	Pte.	688009	Cornis, J. E.
Pte.	931047	Ferguson, J. M.			

2nd Canadian Mounted Rifles

Rank	No.	Name
Pte.	687298	Hall, F. S.
Pte.	811695	Kenney, W. H.
Pte.	811921	Magee, W.
Pte.	180100	Mann, J. J.
Pte.	180113	Palmer, R.
Pte.	687120	Sokoloff, T.
Pte.	790500	Sullivan, T.
Pte.	687386	Wall, W.
Pte.	180916	Ward, J. C.
Pte.	704090	Wassil, A. F.
Pte.	688157	Wood, C. B.
Pte.	117077	Lewis, R.
Pte.	931179	Slater, H. G.

22-4-17

Rank	No.	Name
Pte.	931279	Kotek, J.
Pte.	931468	Laderoute, C. E.
Pte.	931819	Lavigueur, D.
Pte.	931829	Lee, R.
Pte.	931443	Lewis, W. H.
Pte.	931431	Leyland, J.
Pte.	931635	Manning, J.
Pte.	931267	Markland, D. F.
Pte.	931460	Marnoch, A.
Pte.	931068	Meinster, F.
Pte.	931697	Morgan, D.
Pte.	931447	Morris, W. A.
Pte.	931164	Murray, J. M.
Pte.	931544	McCammon, T.
Pte.	931563	McDonald, H. D.
Pte.	931816	McGuire, J. C.
Pte.	931305	McIntyre, M.
Pte.	931112	McNicholas, J. M.
Pte.	931388	Nicholls, S. J.
Pte.	931169	Oliver, W. J. G.
Pte.	931721	Palmer, T. G.
Pte.	931051	Peet, W.
Pte.	931735	Philips, W.
Pte.	931220	Ratcliffe, S. H.
Pte.	931450	Reed, I.
Pte.	931067	Regan, J.
Pte.	931022	Robichaud, M. F.
Pte.	931324	Roscrans, J. A.
Pte.	931651	Schupe, G. T.
Pte.	931520	Seaman, F.
Pte.	931660	Shaw, J.
Pte.	931007	Stephens, F. W.
Pte.	931287	Thompson, R. E.
Pte.	931372	Thorburn, W. A.
Pte.	931187	Waldie, W.
Pte.	931320	Walker, H.
Pte.	931189	Wallace, G.
Pte.	931363	Watson, J. M.
Pte.	931101	Watt, C. F.

Rank	No.	Name
Pte.	931821	White, W.
Pte.	931338	Williamson, E.
Pte.	931439	Wood, J. W.
Pte.	931327	Lehman, J.
Pte.	931630	Penson, E. F.
Pte.	931640	Arnold, R. I.
Pte.	931641	Barnes, E. E.
Pte.	931021	Clark, C.
Pte.	931771	Garbutt, R.
Pte.	931611	Greenwell, J.
Pte.	931275	Greenwell, N. A.
Pte.	931144	Greyson, R.
Pte.	931362	Watson, I. M.

12-5-17

Rank	No.	Name
Pte.	826066	Abbott, L.
Pte.	826520	Allard, J.
Pte.	826634	Allardice, R.
Pte.	827045	Anderson, F.
Pte.	826195	Armstrong, W. H.
Pte.	826136	Artus, W.
Pte.	826158	Attwood, F.
Pte.	826372	Bagos, J.
Pte.	826636	Balcarras, J.
Pte.	827139	Barnes, J.
Pte.	826742	Barnes, W.
Pte.	827064	Barham, L.
Pte.	826036	Barrett, E.
Pte.	827181	Beldham, E.
Pte.	826642	Barra, C.
Pte.	826033	Biggan, J.
Pte.	826786	Bleckley, J. W.
Pte.	826624	Bodys, J.
Pte.	826938	Bolton, N.
Pte.	826086	Bonach, J.
Pte.	826153	Boudon, C. A.
Pte.	826427	Bowie, C.
Pte.	826061	Bownes, F.
Pte.	827001	Boyden, R.
Pte.	826716	Brock, C.
Pte.	826649	Brodie, G. P.
Pte.	827040	Brown, J.
Pte.	826310	Brown, S. J.
Pte.	826983	Brune, C.
Pte.	826725	Bryenton, C. N.
Pte.	826814	Bullock, A.
Pte.	827036	Burnio, R.
Pte.	826650	Burns, J.
Pte.	826527	Butters, J.
Pte.	826878	Campbell, F. O.
Pte.	826637	Campbell, L. N.
Pte.	826392	Canary, J. N.
Pte.	826185	Cantwell, F. W.
Pte.	827011	Chapman, G.

Appendix V—Nominal Roll

Rank	No.	Name	Rank	No.	Name
Pte.	826518	Churchill, T. S.	Pte.	826045	Grove, R.
Pte.	826201	Clark, G.	Pte.	826989	Gurling, S.
Pte.	826065	Clifford, G.	Pte.	826312	Hanwright, E.
Pte.	826597	Cochrane, J.	Pte.	931799	Dyer, K. W.
Pte.	826138	Collins, J.	Pte.	180721	Fairhurst, W.
Pte.	826088	Cooke, A. E.	Pte.	826155	Hardy, A.
Pte.	826137	Connelly, J.	Pte.	826190	Harker, H.
Pte.	826697	Cowan, J.	Pte.	826917	Hart, R.
Pte.	826585	Coyle, T. J.	Pte.	826809	Hart, S. S.
Pte.	826038	Crombie, J. G.	Pte.	286093	Harwood, A. A.
Pte.	826580	Cumberland, J.	Pte.	826087	Harwood, C. N.
Pte.	826030	Cummings, J.	Pte.	826940	Hoath, C.
Pte.	826526	Davidson, J. C.	Pte.	826934	Hensill, R.
Pte.	826274	Davies, T. E.	Pte.	826764	Hencher, L.
Pte.	826837	Delaney, J.	Pte.	826602	Hennesy, E.
Pte.	826760	Denicola, A.	Pte.	826606	Henshaw, W. H.
Pte.	826437	Dimock, G. W.	Pte.	826332	Henshaw, E.
Pte.	826850	Disley, T. W.	Pte.	826084	Henry, J. R.
Pte.	826449	Dougherty, P.	Pte.	826032	Heron, R. L.
Pte.	826262	Dowell, W. W.	Pte.	827017	Horton, R.
Pte.	826331	Downie, J.	Pte.	826360	Howard, W. H.
Pte.	826041	Dransfield, H.	Pte.	826784	Hurst, H. L. R.
Pte.	826672	Duke, W. H.	Pte.	826822	Irving, A.
Pte.	826861	Dunn, J.	Pte.	826489	Jack, G.
Pte.	826173	Durham, A.	Pte.	826807	Jefferson, R.
Pte.	826901	Dysart, G. M.	Pte.	826718	Jenkinson, J. W.
Pte.	826507	Eaton, A. J.	Pte.	826931	Jessop, P.
Pte.	826686	Erickson, A.	Pte.	826343	Jones, D.
Pte.	826504	Evans, F. E.	Pte.	826953	Kelley, F. D.
Pte.	826252	Evans, R.	Pte.	826942	Kellow, R. T. M.
Pte.	827050	Fennel, G.	Pte.	826048	Kirkham, J.
Pte.	826265	Ferguson, J. S.	Pte.	826324	Kyle, R.
Pte.	826720	Field, J.	Pte.	826854	Lane, C.
Pte.	826826	Finnigan, W. J.	Pte.	826632	Lavery, F. T.
Pte.	826458	Klick, F.	Pte.	827034	Lane, J. R.
Pte.	826141	Forrester, N. B.	Pte.	826267	Laybourne, H.
Pte.	826969	Franklin, J.	Pte.	826977	Lazenbury, C. J.
Pte.	826530	Fraser, W. B.	Pte.	826012	Lee, A.
Pte.	826851	Frewin, F.	Pte.	827087	Lee, R.
Pte.	826496	Fukushima, Y.	Pte.	826638	Leibert, J.
Pte.	826746	Garrett, R.	Pte.	826711	Lewis, W.
Pte.	826835	Gascoigne, C.	Pte.	826125	Lindner, F.
Pte.	826910	Gauthier, J. R.	Pte.	826336	Lindsay, W. H.
Pte.	827120	Glauser, W. A.	Pte.	826236	Louch, C. T.
Pte.	826738	Glazebrook, J. G.	Pte.	826313	Lowe, T. W.
Pte.	826916	Gops, A.	Pte.	826796	Luffman, H. J.
Pte.	826046	Gorgon, W.	Pte.	826568	Maley, T. V.
Pte.	826860	Gordon, W.	Pte.	826560	Maloney, W.
Pte.	826756	Graham, R.	Pte.	826370	Marr, W. N.
Pte.	826169	Grant, J. M.	Pte.	826692	Marrington, T. F.
Pte.	826472	Gray, A.	Pte.	826175	Mason, J. L.
Pte.	826196	Greaves, J. C.	Pte.	826144	Mathewa, G. W.
Pte.	826157	Greer, T.	Pte.	826516	Mercier, R. J.

2nd Canadian Mounted Rifles

Rank	No.	Name	Rank	No.	Name
Pte.	826713	Meunier, C.	Pte.	826393	Thew, F. W.
Pte.	826008	Mills, J.	Pte.	826481	Thrippleton, A.
Pte.	826377	Morse, S.	Pte.	826147	Tose, P.
Pte.	826064	Moss, W. C.	Pte.	931113	Tripp, L. E.
Pte.	826535	Moyles, F.	Pte.	826412	Turner, T. S.
Pte.	826173	Murdoch, L. S.	Pte.	826781	Ward, H.
Pte.	931013	Murray, H.	Pte.	826384	Waterman, E. S.
Pte.	826133	McGinnie, F.	Pte.	826896	Watson, H. J.
Pte.	826145	McGuire, W.	Pte.	826025	Watson, J. W.
Pte.	826379	McLuckie, J.	Pte.	826769	Watt, E.
Pte.	826329	McNaughton, R. E.	Pte.	826913	Webb, F. S.
Pte.	826302	McWilliam, L.	Pte.	826190	Webber, F. W.
Pte.	826050	Nicholson, R.	Pte.	826254	Wigham, R.
Pte.	826483	Nickerson, H. S.	Pte.	826363	Whipple, K. G.
Pte.	826019	O'Connor, S.	Pte.	827072	White, A. D.
Pte.	826259	Padgham, A.	Pte.	826928	Wilcox, W.
Pte.	826536	Partington, J. L.	Pte.	826381	Wilkie, M.
Pte.	826304	Phillifant, F.	Pte.	826303	Wilson, J.
Pte.	826202	Pitello, G.	Pte.	826664	Wilson, J.
Pte.	826821	Plimmer, W. J.	Pte.	826698	Wilson, J. R.
Pte.	826270	Potter, H.	Pte.	826357	Wilson, P.
Pte.	827071	Prager, W.	Pte.	826542	Wright, J. S.
Pte.	826160	Proctor, S.	Pte.	826997	Zink, J.
Pte.	826163	Rand, J. G.	Pte.	827134	Watson, J.
Pte.	826446	Robertson, A.	Pte.	826448	Morrison, G. E.
Pte.	826522	Ross, G.	Pte.	826305	Ashe, A. E.
Pte.	826703	Rutherford, T.	Pte.		Cross, W. W.
Pte.	826496	Sakinyama, M.	Pte.	826054	Fulton, G. J.
Pte.	826677	Salous, P. L.	Pte.	826231	Geldard, G. F.
Pte.	826599	Sanders, W.	Pte.	826090	Hoita, R.
Pte.	826436	Saunders, F.	Pte.	826870	Collier, L.
Pte.	826561	Scorgie, A.	Pte.	826069	Kenning, G. E.
Pte.	826406	Shaw, G.		13-5-17	
Pte.	826186	Shaw, H. W.	Pte.	826651	Ferguson, D. K.
Pte.	826205	Shaw, J. G.		20-6-17	
Pte.	826462	Sherman, W. C.	Pte.	931757	Bolton, C. W.
Pte.	826631	Simpson, A. W.		5-7-17	
Pte.	826321	Skinner, D. S.	Pte.	200165	Woods, T. S.
Pte.	826626	Skolberg, A.		16-8-17	
Pte.	826277	Slater, H. A.	Pte.	255830	Harmer, A. R.
Pte.	826376	Smith, A. G.		8-7-17	
Pte.	826432	Smith, H. C.	Pte.	4302586	Burt, F.
Pte.	826794	Sovereign, W.		19-9-17	
Pte.	826463	Spencer, G. P.	Pte.	1049293	Anderson, L.
Pte.	826875	Spicer, W. P.	Pte.	2025193	Bailey, D. J.
Pte.	826572	Stearns, J. N.	Pte.	931132	Ball, J.
Pte.	826833	Stephens, H. B.	Pte.	790397	Ballard, N. S.
Pte.	826286	Stephenson, H. N.	Pte.	760256	Baxter, C. J.
Pte.	826505	Stride, L. C. W.	Pte.	2015199	Bergman, A.
Pte.	826022	Sutherland, W. J. S.	Pte.	2025177	Brass, J.
Pte.	826184	Syer, W. S.	Pte.	687755	Brett, F. J.
Pte.	826562	Taylor, J. S.	Pte.	931574	Bridger, J.
Pte.	826666	Taylor, W. LaV.	Pte.	790487	Brock, K.

Appendix V—Nominal Roll

Rank	No.	Name
Pte.	931131	Buckingham, A.
Pte.	2025136	Carson, J.
Pte.	2015159	Carter, E. R.
Pte.	2025157	Davison, T.
Pte.	2020211	Dobie, F. G.
Pte.	2015196	Ekmenko, J.
Pte.	430144	Fisher, N. E.
Pte.	790078	Fox, W. A.
Pte.	931359	Fuller, T. C.
Pte.	931053	Giddings, M. E.
Pte.	200118	Groves, S. G.
Pte.	408791	Hammond, B.
Pte.	294844	Jacobsen, T. E. H.
Pte.	2137311	Johnson, J. B.
Pte.	294879	Kruger, A.
Pte.	761282	Kynoch, A. E.
Pte.	294832	Lamon, E.
Pte.	707091	Mastin, W.
Pte.	706409	McKitrick, C.
Pte.	294833	Moore, E.
Pte.	2142365	Robbins, J. W.
Pte.	2142321	Ryan, W.
Pte.	294863	Starr, S.
Pte.	931466	Twaddle, J. B.
Pte.	2020168	Usaloff, J.
Pte.	294862	Webb, O. M.
Pte.	912032	Webber, J.
Pte.	931202	Webster, J. T.
Pte.	645691	Wilson, J.

15-10-17

Rank	No.	Name
Pte.	2025211	Bunting, J. A.
Pte.	2025210	Dorman, W. K.
Pte.	2142341	Paul, R.
Pte.	2142312	Russell, J. L.
Pte.	2142346	Small, E. C.
Pte.	2142311	Tetreault, A.

18-10-17

Rank	No.	Name
Pte.	2137535	Charters, R.
Pte.	2025229	Gray, C.
Pte.	2020212	Davis, W. J.
Pte.	2142301	Husband, C. W.
Pte.	2142357	Johnson, H. J.
Pte.	2015588	Kinnear, E. L.
Pte.	294262	Larsen, J. B.
Pte.	103415	Marman, H.
Sgt.	135613	Manders, H. J.
Pte.	2142329	Richards, E. S.
Pte.	931185	Talbot, G. J.

2-11-17

Rank	No.	Name
Pte.	707094	Bassett, R. H.
Pte.	2137303	Bronson, A. T.
Pte.	2015167	Davidson, A.
Pte.	2142319	King, W. McK.

Rank	No.	Name
Pte.	2137313	Lenzin, J. G.
Pte.	200101	Robinson, J. J.

6-11-17

Rank	No.	Name
Sgt.	430474	Humphrey, T.

9-11-17

Rank	No.	Name
Pte.	261054	Barrett, J. R.
Pte.	2137332	Fisher, C.
Pte.	2025164	Hampton, H. T.
Pte.	2142350	Martin, F. A.
Pte.	706885	Priest, C. F.
Pte.	706002	Wren, J. A.

11-11-17

Rank	No.	Name
Pte.	2137304	George, A.
Pte.	2137305	Lulu, H.
Pte.	931264	Pollard, E. J.
Pte.	2142325	Phillips, D.
Pte.	760668	Renwick, E. J.
Pte.	200210	Taylor, N.

14-11-17

Rank	No.	Name
Pte.	102584	Bayley, T. A.
Pte.	489659	Eustace, W. D.
Pte.	103127	Perry, H. H.

24-11-17

Rank	No.	Name
Pte.	116723	Alexander, A. H.
Pte.	931063	Barton, G.
Pte.	760146	Chipperfield, H. H.
Pte.	760410	Cullen, J.

30-11-17

Rank	No.	Name
Pte.	931369	Hadden, W. E.

15-12-17

Rank	No.	Name
Pte.	2137321	Anderson, O. M.
Pte.	103106	King, J. H.
Pte.	705086	Wren, W. E.

28-12-17

Rank	No.	Name
Pte.	706709	Parkinson, I.

6-1-18

Rank	No.	Name
Pte.	826264	Dean, J.
Pte.	706342	Ferrabee, G. T.

12-1-18

Rank	No.	Name
Pte.	531132	Barrie, C.
Pte.	295002	Barclay, W.
Pte.	2015158	Cartier, R. E.
Pte.	2015194	Isdal, S.
Pte.	2137331	McLennan, R. W.
Pte.	525214	Nixon, S. L.
Pte.	527055	Provost, D.
Pte.	2004150	Quilty, C. R.
Pte.	2115330	Reid, G.
Pte.	428884	Trenholme, F. M.

18-1-18

Rank	No.	Name
Pte.	844212	Carey, A. E.
Pte.	2015175	Emery, E. G.
Pte.	200164	Howse, F.
Pte.	2223304	Kerr, W. McL.

2nd Canadian Mounted Rifles

Rank	No.	Name	Rank	No.	Name
Pte.	525015	McArdle, B.	Pte.	916893	Burgess, W. F.
Pte.	706001	Miller, R.	Pte.	916475	Broughton, E.
Pte.	2004185	Murphy, J. W. R.	Pte.	916424	Cahill, T. J.
Pte.	525203	Phillips, H. W.	Pte.	916369	Campbell, P.
Pte.	529303	Summerville, E. C.	Pte.	916306	Cantwell, W.
Pte.	527089	Surman, J.	Pte.	916515	Caruk, P.
Pte.	706816	Travis, A. W.	Pte.	916170	Cast, G.
Pte.	1012725	Webster, G.	Pte.	916595	Cotton, H.
	26-1-18		Pte.	916204	Chalmers, J.
Pte.	2223310	Archer, I.	Pte.	916205	Conacher, A.
Pte.	525308	Galbraith, H. W.	Pte.	916795	Coope, E. L.
Pte.	1042123	Hedges, H.	Pte.	916563	Conacher, R. B.
Pte.	525309	Rines, L. A.	A/Cpl.	916182	Coop, F. R.
Pte.	502552	Barry, J. W.	Pte.	916450	Currie, J.
	7-2-18		A/Cpl.	916254	Dent, J.
Pte.	177793	Bourgeau, V.	Pte.	916766	Dynski, F.
Pte.	200043	Reid, J. L.	Pte.	916855	Ellis, H. C.
Pte.	2147327	Jackman, G.	A/Sgt.	916097	Ellison, J. W.
	8-2-18		Pte.	916429	Evanizski, F.
Pte.	525326	McDiarmid, G. S.	Pte.	916416	Francis, J.
	15-2-18		Pte.	916622	Forrest, J.
Pte.	525197	Allen, T.	Pte.	916445	Gibson, D.
Pte.	529086	Broderick, W. J.	Pte.	916778	Godfrey, C.
Pte.	931436	Burkman, C. H.	Pte.	916933	Goodall, W. J.
Pte.	525144	Galbraith, S. A.	Pte.	916267	Hamilton, A. E.
Pte.	524530	Gibson, G.	Pte.	916185	Harman, F. J.
Pte.	524696	Hatch, R. W.	Pte.	916807	Harris, G. W.
Pte.	931061	Lane, R.	Pte.	916230	Harrison, A.
Pte.	400439	Mewha, W.	Pte.	916941	Haya, W.
Pte.	514422	Michael, M.	Pte.	916591	Holora, F.
Pte.	2223318	Plows, F. T.	Pte.	916619	Honchoruk, S.
Pte.	526964	Robertson, J. E.	Pte.	916143	Hopkins, R. G.
Pte.	200193	Thomson, W.	Pte.	916685	Hunter, I. D.
Pte.	2142338	Wilkinson, E. W.	Pte.	916506	Hunter, S. J.
Pte.	2223311	Walker, H. V.	Pte.	916734	Johnston, E.
Pte.	464240	Wright, A.	Pte.	916928	Karaka, N.
	20-2-18		Pte.	916596	Kotik, W.
Pte.	525190	Barnes, W.	Pte.	916433	Mandichura, Y.
Pte.	294796	Grant, E.	Pte.	916819	Marchant, W.
Pte.	524880	Magnall, B.	A/Cpl.	916044	Martin, C. McK.
Pte.	707148	Norton, M. O.	Pte.	681104	Mason, G.
	2-3-18		Pte.	542093	Mitchel, A. T.
Pte.	916771	Allard, H. J.	Pte.	916473	Muringer, F. C.
Pte.	916139	Allen, S.	Pte.	916604	Nolloth, W. R.
Pte.	916331	Armour, W. J.	Pte.	916647	Osadchy, L.
Pte.	916662	Baby, A.	Pte.	916362	Pearson, C.
Pte.	916618	Bailey, A. H.	Pte.	916626	Pearson, G. D. E.
Pte.	916849	Barnes, W. T.	Pte.	916980	Petherick, W. H.
Pte.	916872	Bones, A. A.	Pte.	916737	Phillips, H. J.
Pte.	916373	Bradbury, W. T.	Pte.	916592	Polistchick, N.
Pte.	916392	Brinkworth, G. A.	Pte.	916437	Reid, A. W.
Pte.	649406	Brown, B. H.	Pte.	916389	Robb, H.
Pte.	916308	Brown, F.	Pte.	916359	Roberts, G.

Appendix V—Nominal Roll

Rank	No.	Name	Rank	No.	Name
Pte.	916644	Rollins, P.	Pte.	916089	Egan, S. M.
A/Cpl.	916160	Rowe, J. A.	Pte.	916484	Emery, T. W.
Pte.	916391	Saddler, A.	Pte.	916032	Evis, A. A.
Pte.	916061	Sayer, A. S.	Pte.	542446	Gale, F. J.
Pte.	916664	Scott, J. C.	Pte.	916225	Greenland, R. E.
Pte.	916879	Simpson, J. M.	Pte.	916241	Gray, F. G.
Pte.	916641	Skirving, J.	Pte.	916047	Hogan, G. E.
Pte.	916564	Slipenko, I.	Pte.	916852	Hall, J. H.
Pte.	916624	Smith, J. A.	Pte.	916066	Hill, W. J.
Pte.	916996	Smith, N. O.	Pte.	916420	Hansuld, J. H.
Pte.	916427	Snider, W.	Pte.	916700	Harwood, A. E.
Pte.	917000	Steele, W.	Pte.	916738	Holding, C.
Pte.	916760	Speirs, R. E.	Pte.	228283	Houseberger, I. L.
A/Cpl.	916135	Stephenson, H. G.	Pte.	228540	Houston, J.
Pte.	916094	Strathdu, J.	Pte.	228491	James, R. G.
Pte.	916531	Stubbington, W. L.	Pte.	916218	Jeffereys, A. N.
Pte.	916658	Swenpitzki, J.	Pte.	916035	Johnston, G. F.
Pte.	916825	Switzer, W. G.	Pte.	228370	Kimmons, W. H.
Pte.	264495	Thornton, E.	Pte.	916063	Kinkaid, A.
Pte.	916486	Thrush, F.	Pte.	916698	Kenny, F. C.
A/Sgt.	916108	Toms, J. F.	Pte.	514144	Light, W. A.
Pte.	916324	Tomlins, W. S.	Pte.	916605	Livernois, A. J.
Pte.	916430	Vasiliachuk, M.	Pte.	228463	Ledlie, G. C.
Pte.	916335	Verity, H.	Pte.	916190	May, C. P.
Pte.	916642	Wallace, J. R.	Pte.	916730	McCann, W. A.
A/Sgt.	916407	Watson, C. F.	Pte.	916245	McLellan, D.
Pte.	916031	Whalen, G. J.	Pte.	916039	McKenzie, H.
Pte.	916261	Wilcock, L.	Pte.	916988	McMahon, A. L.
Pte.	916120	Williamson, R.	Pte.	916147	Mein, E.
Pte.	916128	Wilson, A.	Pte.	916212	Mulhern, J. B.
Pte.	916544	Wilson, P. H.	Pte.	285324	O'Rourke, M.
Pte.	916716	Yates, H. P.	Pte.	542495	Potts, V. C.
Pte.	916646	Zhoko, M.	Pte.	228198	Rowsell, R. W. R.
Pte.	916906	Zivior, P.	Pte.	542493	Ruddick, T. W.
A/Cpl.	916889	Lord, E. F.	Pte.	916757	Ryan, N. J.
A/Cpl.	916547	Paton, T. A.	Pte.	542413	St. Onge, J. J.
	9-3-18		Pte.	542299	Scales, C. G.
Pte.	916826	Allman, S. S.	Pte.	228448	Seeds, H.
Pte.	916566	Baller, G.	Pte.	916021	Sharp, G. F.
Pte.	916319	Binks, W. C.	Pte.	916714	Sherry, G. J.
Pte.	524809	Batten, W. B.	Pte.	916812	Shook, R. C.
Pte.	228504	Benzie, J.	Pte.	916067	Smith, A. V.
Pte.	542505	Blackshaw, R.	Pte.	542414	Smith, F. L.
Pte.	541235	Booth, W. G.	Pte.	916780	Speight, A.
Pte.	916083	Boulton, H. W.	Pte.	916323	Stevens, M. H.
Pte.	916338	Bradley, N. W.	Pte.	2334316	Stidolph, S. H.
Pte.	916423	Butler, H. S.	Pte.	916978	Stocks, C.
Pte.	916074	Cane, A. R.	Pte.	916620	Stroud, H. W.
Pte.	228261	Cockerill, E. C.	Pte.	2134833	Sykes, F. J.
Pte.	916521	Coe, F. W.	Pte.	542303	Tighe, J. E.
Pte.	228459	Coxwell, E. G.	Pte.	541250	Williams, A. J. L.
Pte.	228320	Dover, M. F.	Pte.	916027	Wise, R.
Pte.	228481	Dunstan, J. R.	Pte.	228497	Wilson, J.

2nd Canadian Mounted Rifles

Rank	No.	Name	Rank	No.	Name
Pte.	228108	Young, T. C.	Pte.	228296	Purdue, A. E.
		17-3-18	Pte.	210778	Rogers, W. R.
Pte.	273986	Brandreth, W. H.	Pte.	916149	Rutherford, A. C.
Pte.	1027540	Campbell, L.	Pte.	916106	Spyer, S.
Pte.	1063118	Gunter, W. G.	Pte.	916100	Sanders, P.
Pte.	784073	Husk, W. G.	Pte.	916215	Toms, H.
Pte.	1027476	Jarvis, G. S.	Pte.	401139	Mayne, T. D.
Pte.	1063004	Miller, H. J.			29-3-18
Pte.	1063101	Richards, C. A.	Pte.	1027499	Best, T. F.
Pte.	902187	Smith, G. H.	Pte.	916191	Brabbs, L.
Pte.	507372	Staples, J. T.	Pte.	514135	Bridges, H.
Pte.	274085	Strebig, D. L.	Pte.	916845	Busby, C. D.
Pte.	853436	Windle, C.	Pte.	916784	Cairns, D.
Pte.	853408	Williamson, H. L.	Pte.	507598	Chapman, W.
Pte.	784319	Woodward, H. J.	Pte.	853036	Donaldson, J. E.
Pte.	642862	Whale, A. F.	Pte.	916749	Hanson, J.
Pte.	916367	Kerr, J. A.	Pte.	916033	Hughes, J.
		26-3-18	Pte.	602580	Knighton, R. A.
Pte.	916179	Benjamin, A.	Pte.	916783	Lancaster, G. H.
Pte.	228321	Baker, R.	Pte.	916796	Morgan, F. E.
Pte.	916692	Cordner, W. E.	Pte.	796059	MacNab, O. S.
Pte.	542374	Cournoyer, P.	Pte.	916464	Robertson, W. G.
Pte.	264392	Cowan, A.	Pte.	916834	Rumsey, R. W. E.
Pte.	916854	Edgler, G. W.	Pte.	916368	Stanley, P.
Pte.	2751035	Heyd, F.	Pte.	784149	Stonehouse, G. M.
Pte.	916477	Gardner, W. C.	Pte.	1027669	Van Hedegen, R.
Pte.	916283	Harrod, S. A.	Pte.	916077	Lang, F. G.
Pte.	916142	Hollocks, F.	Pte.	273329	Kinmond, C.
Pte.	916523	Hollingsworth, G. R.	Pte.	916188	Perrin, W. J.
Pte.	916781	Lumb, H.	Pte.	228380	Rudd, J. H.
Pte.	2245503	Lundeborg, F. H.	Pte.	1027498	Best, T. F.
Pte.	2245504	Lundeborg, J. A.	Pte.	1063041	Anderson, D. R.
Pte.	228301	Osborn, J.			30-3-18
Pte.	916065	Royce, W. H. M.	Pte.	916451	Ainsworth, T.
Pte.	65911	Smith, H. J.	Pte.	228210	Airth, I. T.
Pte.	916330	Smith, H.	Pte.	916742	Anderson, J. M.
Pte.	228450	Tolcher, E.	Pte.	916510	Ansell, H. G.
Pte.	916984	Walmsley, J.	Pte.	916827	Barker, E.
Pte.	868165	Rowe, N. V.	Pte.	163788	Bloomfield, E.
		30-3-18	Pte.	916193	Bosanquet, H. E.
Pte.	916862	Knight, A.	Pte.	916072	Cavers, A.
Pte.	916949	Lambie, G.	Pte.	916611	Collins, A. A.
Pte.	916790	Lowry, T. R.	Pte.	916259	Douglas, G.
Pte.	916071	Maddeaux, R.	Pte.	540102	Dwyer, A. J.
Pte.	916963	Maxwell, J.	Pte.	739303	Duffy, P. E.
Pte.	192269	Maddeaux, W. A.	Pte.	228288	English, W. B.
Pte.	916718	Mackerell, R. R.	Pte.	407114	Fenton, H. S.
Pte.	228193	Murray, J. P.	Pte.	228128	Green, R. F.
Pte.	916499	McLellan, A.	Pte.	916305	Harbord, R. J.
Pte.	916723	Patterson, D. B.	Pte.	228530	Harrison, A. H.
Pte.	916736	Patterson, A.	Pte.	916105	Hay, J. G.
Pte.	916877	Paterson, W. C.	Pte.	916395	Heyes, S.
Pte.	916852	Pidduck, E. W. R.	Pte.	135488	Hoili, J. R.

Appendix V—Nominal Roll

Rank	No.	Name
Pte.	916697	Howarth, W. R.
Pte.	916456	Hunter, T.
Pte.	916379	Hitchman, E. C.
Pte.	916729	Jones, E.
Pte.	228234	Jordan, S. J.
Pte.	1027688	Jennings, A. W.
Pte.	139181	Singh, H.
Pte.	916263	Sellors, J. R.
Pte.	228242	Kieran, M. H.

9-4-18

Rank	No.	Name
Pte.	602389	Allen, H.
Pte.	491372	Bennett, J. W.
Pte.	273020	Brooks, H. J.
Pte.	681062	Butler, W.
Pte.	491323	Borrowman, W. W.
Pte.	407003	Burgess, W. A.
Pte.	751319	Blackmore, F. C.
Pte.	778846	Carney, R. J.
Pte.	126911	Cogger, E.
Pte.	274002	Crane, P.
Pte.	1263337	Creak, W. F.
Pte.	862256	Dewey, A. G.
Pte.	1063018	Faulkener, J. A.
Pte.	862848	Freeman, C. H.
Pte.	406721	Gibson, W.
Pte.	1027040	Greenfield, V. R.
Pte.	916725	Gibson, A. W.
Pte.	451994	Grant, J. T.
Pte.	853457	Hibberd, H. J.
Pte.	853479	Johnson, E.
Pte.	1027057	Laugher, A. J.
Pte.	510285	Lee, J.
Pte.	853323	Lockhart, W. C.
Pte.	274141	Lunn, A. W. J.
Pte.	814708	Mason, M.
Pte.	644668	McIndoo, I. J.
Pte.	739433	McGregor, C. J.
Pte.	7620	Mannan, A. F.
Pte.	739576	Pettigrew, C. E.
Pte.	273990	Thompson, W.
Pte.	142514	Tourtel, E. J.
Pte.	527901	Wilkerson, J. E.

2-5-18

Rank	No.	Name
Pte.	226072	Cummings, J. J.
Pte.	642804	Atkison, A. J.
Pte.	643830	Ball, D. R.
Pte.	916557	Bethell, A.
Pte.	916198	Bentley, F. A.
Pte.	400706	Brown, R.
Pte.	135265	Breeze, J. L.
Pte.	406690	Carey, A. A.
Pte.	853622	Chalmers, R. A.
Pte.	784040	Cross, B. W.

Rank	No.	Name
Pte.	868294	Craig, G. J.
Pte.	916948	Delahunty, C. J.
Pte.	1063139	Dixon, W.
Pte.	274155	Grandin, H. D.
Pte.	602582	Hubbard, S.
Pte.	814572	Holden, P.
Pte.	814447	Harnden, W. G.
Pte.	916525	Harrington, H. C.
Pte.	814424	Kirkpatrick, N.
Pte.	27411	McFarlane, E.
Pte.	797201	McClung, H. R.
Pte.	928833	Reesor, A. E.
Pte.	916396	Riddagh, A. B.
Pte.	1263345	Richardson, H.
Pte.	916042	Sharp, R.
Pte.	916355	Shier, W. H.
Pte.	796659	Slade, F.
Pte.	195206	Smith, T.
Pte.	916573	Seredink, J.
Pte.	1263344	Llowarch, T. E.

11-5-18

Rank	No.	Name
Pte.	3032369	Bulger, W. B.
Pte.	3032513	Colbert, T.
Pte.	797667	Dickson, P.
Pte.	1263350	Fletcher, A.
Pte.	3032247	Jacques, F.
Pte.	3032273	Lawson, T. W.
Pte.	3032291	Lillicrop, E.
Pte.	3032313	Litt, R. H.
Pte.	3032380	McDougall, W. J.
Pte.	3032362	McLean, G. J.
Pte.	3032332	O'Hara, S.
Pte.	3032460	Parkes, M. H.
Pte.	3032303	Potter, E. H.
Pte.	3031953	Prendergast, J. W.
Pte.	3031954	Primrose, A.
Pte.	3032282	Ritchie, R. M.
Pte.	3032318	Searles, P. O.
Pte.	3032258	Skingle, B. F.
Pte.	3032564	Skinner, A. F.
Pte.	3033038	Smith, A.

16-5-18

Rank	No.	Name
Pte.	2528367	Anderson, F. A.
Pte.	3032808	Boott, H.
Pte.	285459	Heeps, J. E.
Pte.	3032230	Higgins, J. P.
Pte.	3032876	Lane, R. F.
Pte.	3032488	Levi, C.
Pte.	3031458	Nerpaw, W. A.
Pte.	3032644	Murless, G. H.
Pte.	3032616	McCorry, T. G.
Pte.	3032599	Newson, E.
Pte.	3032523	Perry, W. J.

2nd Canadian Mounted Rifles

Rank	No.	Name
Pte.	3032149	Plate, M. J.
Pte.	3032146	Reede, R. H.
Pte.	2562370	Sineyr, A. E.
Pte.	3231272	St. Amour, A.
Pte.	3033444	Tochey, E. J.
Pte.	3032713	Turner, F. M.
Pte.	3032853	Veitch, G. H.
Pte.	3032001	Wood, F. J.
Pte.	3033553	Morris, A.

30-5-18

Rank	No.	Name
Pte.	3231096	Alderson, J.
Pte.	2378520	Beauchamp, L.
Pte.	3033450	Berg, L.
Pte.	3032946	Bond, C. J.
Pte.	3231541	Bouchard, J. P.
Pte.	853376	Bressette, M. J.
Pte.	3032352	Brown, A.
Pte.	3231330	Burton, J. H.
Pte.	3231289	Cook, S.
Pte.	3231344	Delane, H.
Pte.	2355421	Delane, G.
Pte.	3230836	Erb, W. O.
Pte.	3033430	Faris, T. W.
Pte.	225266	Fennelly, T.
Pte.	3032959	Freshour, C.
Pte.	3231038	Hanna, W. C.
Pte.	3033205	Hass, A.
Pte.	2378346	Hopley, O.
Pte.	2378609	Isaac, E.
Pte.	3030072	Kane, J.
Pte.	3231217	LaFontaine, S.
Pte.	3231153	Laframboise, A.
Pte.	3231082	LeBlanc, H.
Pte.	3032143	Lolle, M.
Pte.	3231152	Lundmark, A.
Pte.	3031786	Lyle, A. R.
Pte.	3231032	Maxted, W.
Pte.	3230986	McKelvey, E. R.
Pte.	2751216	Ogden, R. A.
Pte.	3032977	Osbaldstone, W. H.
Pte.	3231070	Pronlx, F.
Pte.	3032367	Sanders, F.
Pte.	3033443	Schuler, P.
Pte.	3231251	St. Onge, B. J.
Pte.	3230998	White, R.
Pte.	3030592	Wotherspoon, T.

7-6-18

Rank	No.	Name
Pte.	3231663	Haynes, N.
Pte.	739676	Henry, E.
Pte.	3231500	Higgins, H. G.
Pte.	916028	Ingram, A.
Pte.	3033483	Jackson, J. H.
Pte.	3231510	Johnston, T.
Pte.	3031474	Kliskey, S.
Pte.	3231472	Laderoute, A.
Pte.	3231212	Lalonde, A.
Pte.	3231637	Lemaire, W.
Pte.	3231279	Lavigne, G.
Pte.	3230956	Levesque, H.
Pte.	916195	Long, J.
Pte.	3032965	Luxford, W.
Pte.	739939	Maracle, D.
Pte.	3231026	Miller, J.
Pte.	3230923	Molan, H.
Pte.	3033286	Mullin, J. K.
Pte.	648661	Myers, H. G.
Pte.	3231560	Moor, C. E.
Pte.	228374	Baber, H.
Pte.	228271	Davey, H.
Pte.	228309	McFarquhar, A. J.

22-6-18

Rank	No.	Name
Pte.	3230493	Baker, C. F.
Pte.	3231083	Bazinet, L. D.
Pte.	3030669	Bertelsen, V. L.
Pte.	3033500	Buttonshall, J.
Pte.	3231481	Boulger, T.
Pte.	2392311	Corless, J.
Pte.	3031441	Courtier, C. S.
Pte.	3230225	Curnow, M. H.
Pte.	3231094	Dubie, L.
Pte.	3231609	Dubois, A.
Pte.	3230999	Durrell, W. L.
Pte.	3032288	Dyer, J. H.
Pte.	2393335	Lazenby, A. B.
Pte.	3231548	Mallette, J.
Pte.	3231559	Mask, A.
Pte.	3230971	Morris, G. F.
Pte.	3031736	McKeown, R.
Pte.	3033073	Oates, R. J.
Pte.	3033136	Pigeau, A.
Pte.	3231205	Primeau, O.
Pte.	3231502	Ritchie, D. S.
Pte.	3033442	Roberts, S.
Pte.	3231278	Rochefort, J.
Pte.	3231714	Scafe, F.
Pte.	3033318	Sherratt, O.
Pte.	3231554	St. Marseille, A.
Pte.	3033138	Thibedan, P. L.
Pte.	3030979	Voight, W. C.
Pte.	3032534	Wallace, J. F.
Pte.	3033329	Woods, W. J.
Pte.	916086	McGilivray, A. D.
Pte.	228164	Robertson, W. E. G.

5-7-18

Rank	No.	Name
Pte.	3230851	Allen, R. C.

Appendix V—Nominal Roll

Rank	No.	Name
Pte.	3230478	Altavista, J. P.
Pte.	3231500	Armitage, R.
Pte.	3231256	Bezley, C.
Pte.	3031924	Bourier, J. H.
Pte.	1069510	Boyce, E.
Pte.	3033076	Brown, F. R.
Pte.	3130094	Cowell, C.
Pte.	3032953	Dukes, G. A.
Pte.	916490	Exley, C. E.
Pte.	651090	Gillen, W. L.
Pte.	3231048	Jacklin, D.
Pte.	3231562	Matheson, D. A.
		19-7-18
Pte.	757478	Cochrane, L. G.
Pte.	514417	Lewis, C. H.
Pte.	928787	Bramhill, W. R.
Pte.	1045829	Biggs, E. F.
		1-8-18
Pte.	916100	Sanders, P.
		3-8-18
Pte.	916051	Bullock, W. E.
Pte.	2517377	Higgins, J. E.
Pte.	273130	Jamieson, F.
		13-8-18
Pte.	3033805	Pegg, F. J.
Pte.	3231329	Piper, R. S. K.
Pte.	3031544	Powell, C. L.
Pte.	3033757	Puterbaugh, W.
Pte.	3031500	Rentner, A. A.
Pte.	2355382	Rigdon, C. E.
Pte.	3032983	Robinson, O. R.
Pte.	3033549	Rodger, T. A.
Pte.	3231243	Savard, R. J.
		10-8-18
Pte.	853676	Banks, W. T.
Pte.	928111	Black, D.
Pte.	3497934	Bloomberg, J.
Pte.	3033428	Brown, J. R.
Pte.	3031581	Closs, R. A.
Pte.	3230996	Crawford, J.
Pte.	1007000	Dove, H.
Pte.	3231057	Frazer, E. P.
Pte.	1063136	French, J.
Pte.	3033458	Fuller, W. F.
Pte.	513969	Gagnon, J. H.
Pte.	853459	James, H.
Pte.	273821	Jones, W.
Pte.	853663	Paxton, A.
Pte.	916613	Pirie, W. A.
Pte.	3030915	Purves, C. W.
Pte.	3231037	Robinson, C. E.
Pte.	273360	Shea, E. T.
Pte.	3230988	Shields, P. C.

Rank	No.	Name
Pte.	3033665	Whitney, A. R.
		13-8-18
Pte.	3231005	Anderson, R. G.
Pte.	3033474	Bissen, J. L.
Pte.	3033666	Cameron, J. T.
Pte.	3033717	Daubney, W.
Pte.	3033845	Dewdney, S. P.
Pte.	3033846	Down, A. M.
Pte.	3034062	Durnin, J. E.
Pte.	3033331	Dyer, A. R.
Pte.	3032956	Fawcett, J. H.
Pte.	3032997	Feldman, J.
Pte.	3033164	Ferguson, S. J.
Pte.	3033509	Fisher, W. R.
Pte.	3032957	Fitzgerald, M.
Pte.	2562338	Food, F.
Pte.	3033917	Gardner, F.
Pte.	3032249	Geall, J.
Pte.	3034065	Givins, F. M.
Pte.	2529321	Goodyear, T. L.
Pte.	3033810	Goddard, E. W.
Pte.	3033919	Gomme, P.
Pte.	3033636	Harman, H. E.
Pte.	3032905	Heron, A. L.
Pte.	3033171	Hicks, T. W.
Pte.	3033926	Hobson, H. F.
Pte.	3231084	Hussey, J. A.
Pte.	3033695	Johnson, W. D.
Pte.	3032588	Johnston, H.
Pte.	3033174	Lecocq, J. T.
Pte.	3032971	Munslow, S.
Pte.	3032262	Murphy, J.
Pte.	3033555	Munro, H.
		18-8-18
Pte.	3032542	Knife, S. W.
Pte.	3033862	McNicols, C.
Pte.	3033821	Webster, W.
Pte.	3035568	Ladoncour, H.
Pte.	3033625	Wilson, A.
		15-8-18
Pte.	2355378	Brooks, B.
Pte.	739892	Buck, R.
Pte.	183316	Burke, W. L.
Pte.	772250	Burley, A. C.
Pte.	772526	Burrows, J. E.
Pte.	651824	Campbell, D. E.
Pte.	654602	Carpenter, R. H.
Pte.	823780	Caton, W.
Pte.	651126	Carson, J. E.
Pte.	405731	Chatterton, E. J.
Pte.	491245	Chettleburgh, R.
Pte.	163807	Clark, P. M.
Pte.	2355577	Colitz, J.

2nd Canadian Mounted Rifles

Rank	No.	Name
Pte.	657101	Collins, T. H.
Pte.	651875	Craig, G. B.
Pte.	805030	Currie, J. H.
Pte.	2355352	Davis, G.
Pte.	2355349	Davison, H.
Pte.	644008	Day, J. S.
Pte.	651995	Dobson, W. M.
Pte.	2334307	Doig, P.
Pte.	928015	Dunn, J.
Pte.	2334364	Elliott, W. H.
Pte.	2355497	English, L. D.
Pte.	2355591	Faulkner, J. R.
Pte.	2355717	Fauste, J. J.
Pte.	2517356	Flower, A. W.
Pte.	657165	Forde, W. H.
Pte.	2355381	Fry, C. R.
Pte.	2355408	Gilmore, P.
Pte.	651898	Greig, A. J.
Pte.	2453313	Gunn, W. C.
Pte.	652270	Hodge, R.
Pte.	675504	Holmes, H.
Pte.	739545	House, A.
Pte.	788938	Huckabom, P.
Pte.	651771	Kennedy, A. W.
Pte.	2355351	Kerrigan, F.
Pte.	3130260	La Marsh, F.
Pte.	282382	Lantz, A. C.
Pte.	2355809	Lee, H. E.
Pte.	1045301	Love, G. H.
Pte.	1013653	Martin, L.
Pte.	2355566	May, J. P.
Pte.	2355448	Meirthew, A. H.
Pte.	126051	Merrill, A. S.
Pte.	2334335	Miller, G.
Pte.	651025	Moore, W. G.
Pte.	651388	Moore, M.
Pte.	2355727	Moore, J.
Pte.	2463311	MacDonald, S.
Pte.	651178	McLeod, A.
Pte.	651010	McWhinney, C. E.
Pte.	845056	Nicholls, L.
Pte.	2448432	Normandy, P.
Pte.	405097	Osborne, E. R.
Pte.	2517395	Ott, C. M.
Pte.	823050	Pulham, W. D.
Pte.	2334378	Reynolds, E. N.
Pte.	2355442	Rider, D.
Pte.	2355639	Robinson, H. F. T.
Pte.	405846	Rogers, H. E.
Pte.	2448447	Ryan, R. J.
Pte.	2517380	Schiebel, G.
Pte.	730443	Shoesmith, A.
Pte.	2448384	Skinner, E. B.
Pte.	189439	Smith, R. S.
Pte.	2334379	Strachan, A. McL.
Pte.	928041	Tate, J. S.
Pte.	802499	Taylor, H.
Pte.	2458366	Thompson, J. S.
Pte.	651236	Threndyle, H. A.
Pte.	654372	Tonkin, W. E.
Pte.	651555	Tulock, H. V.
Pte.	651994	Watchter, F. J.
Pte.	2448374	Walcarins, H.
Pte.	845437	Ward, C. M.
Pte.	654567	Westlake, W. M.
Pte.	657771	Wice, R.
Pte.	651145	Willaujham, H. B.
Pte.	602993	Williamson, H.
Pte.	928055	Winston, G. D.
Pte.	823550	Wood, J. C.
Pte.	654658	Wray, G.
Pte.	2109815	Young, H.

22-8-18

Rank	No.	Name
Pte.	2691139	Hogg, S. J.
Pte.	853729	Holden, A.
Pte.	3231062	Johnston, C. J.
Pte.	2498654	Johnston, J.
Pte.	3033597	Keeton, W. B.
Pte.	3230977	Kirkpatrick, C. R.
Pte.	3231471	Lansep, F.
Pte.	2499335	Leaks, C. H.
Pte.	1003981	Lemap, L.
Pte.	853441	Lightfoot, M.
Pte.	3033348	Lindquist, H. A.
Pte.	3032993	Masterson, J.
Pte.	3033840	Meagher, C. M.
Pte.	3032493	Machow, J.
Pte.	3033661	Montgomery, C. W.
Pte.	3033611	Mooney, J.
Pte.	3032208	Morrison, R. E.
Pte.	3032884	Murray, A. H.
Pte.	3230973	McCartney, C. W.
Pte.	3033527	McDonald, C. E.
Pte.	853182	McGill, J. E.
Pte.	3039648	Roberts, A. B.
Pte.	3032170	Prendergast, E. D.
Pte.	3033796	Rider, W. E.
Pte.	3033884	Shank, R.
Pte.	3030022	Sullivan, R. E.
Pte.	3031485	Wade, J.
Pte.	3231653	Watson, R. E.
Pte.	406879	Vance, F.

15-8-18

Rank	No.	Name
Pte.	2355336	Acker, E. J.
Pte.	2448456	Adams, E. C.
Pte.	2355586	Armfelt, O. M. W.

Appendix V—Nominal Roll

Rank	No.	Name	Rank	No.	Name
Pte.	644554	Anderson, F.	Pte.	3232134	Donovan, L.
Pte.	651112	Arnold, J.	Pte.	3233874	Flesher, S.
Pte.	651680	Arnold, M.	Pte.	763051	Glass, R.
Pte.	178042	Ball, J.	Pte.	3231072	Hamilton, W. R.
Pte.	201536	Barker, W.	Pte.	642818	Hardy, W.
Pte.	190096	Barnes, W.	Pte.	3233452	Heard, G. T.
Pte.	225525	Bell, W. H. F.	Pte.	3233429	Hillyard, J. W.
Pte.	189795	Billings, F. H. J.	Pte.	3234225	Hunter, H. P.
Pte.	437737	Bowsher, A. W.	Pte.	3108333	Kidd, W. E.
Pte.	2355537	Boyd, J. D.	Pte.	3036217	Lachance, G.
Pte.	2448495	Brennan, W. J.	Pte.	3039364	Long, S.
	22-8-18		Pte.	3230229	Allin, W. J.
Pte.	3032391	Agios, J.	Pte.	3233443	Baker, E.
Pte.	643382	Anderson, T. H.	Pte.	3232406	Bortheamus, A. H.
Pte.	1063006	Avery, G.	Pte.	3039358	Burberry, W.
Pte.	3231119	Bailles, W. N.	Pte.	3107820	Chadwick, A.
Pte.	1102601	Boyd, M. S.	Pte.	3035514	Cochran, J. W.
Pte.	863134	Breeden, W. H.	Pte.	3232604	Coolan, E. J.
Pte.	3031009	Caron, R.	Pte.	3106340	Eaglesham, J. H.
Pte.	2304440	Clark, J.	Pte.	3036442	Gardiner, F.
Pte.	829422	Cole, A. E.	Pte.	3233446	Guirl, C. J.
Pte.	3033157	Contvin, J. H.	Pte.	3039361	Hanna, R. G.
Pte.	2590979	Doyle, E. J.	Pte.	3037492	Harrison, W.
Pte.	3033822	Fenech, G.	Pte.	3035847	Hedican, T.
Pte.	3032070	Flear, T. J.	Pte.	3037495	Hogan, J. D.
Pte.	3033166	Glore, D. R.	Pte.	3233902	Jolliffe, A. F.
Pte.	3033209	Harris, J. M.	Pte.	3234369	Lachance, E.
Pte.	3034067	Harvey, H.	Pte.	3037702	Larsen, G. L. S.
Pte.	3031470	Hill, E. G.		3-10-18	
	29-8-18		Pte.	3230047	Adams, J.
Pte.	916790	Lowry, T. R.	Pte.	3233790	Allingham, N. G.
	5-9-18		Pte.	3037753	Argue, H. H.
Pte.	805091	King, F.	Pte.	3037920	Bentcliff, J.
Pte.	751320	Sexton, P. H.	Pte.	3233581	Belanger, P.
Pte.	3032392	Bogya, S.	Pte.	3034191	Cunningham, D.
Pte.	3031327	Conyan, J.	Pte.	3233756	Etherington, G. A.
Pte.	2537338	Curry, W.	Pte.	3233778	Ganteaume, P.
Pte.	3033649	Dennis, W. R.	Pte.	3230394	Hayman, A. L.
Pte.	3031762	Sandford, F. R.	Pte.	3234112	Mahoney, J. F.
Pte.	3032378	Sullivan, D.	Pte.	3034523	McDonnell, J. F.
Pte.	853633	Sykes, F. A.	Pte.	514088	Squires, F. E.
Pte.	2250741	Thompson, F. A.	Pte.	3107401	Wortley, C. J.
	10-10-18		Pte.	3233577	Adams, H. P.
Pte.	1013181	Gustafson, H.	Pte.	3036993	Anderson, A. M.
Pte.	1013250	Pilling, N.	Pte.	3233556	Bedford, V.
Pte.	1013117	Van Duren, H.	Pte.	3231490	Belanger, V.
Pte.	3037305	Allen, C. E. F.	Pte.	3230369	Bewell, E. C.
Pte.	3233865	Argent, F.	Pte.	3031227	Dault, A.
Pte.	3234505	Barbeau, P.	Pte.	3037791	Frappier, L.
Pte.	273782	Begg, J. L.	Pte.	3035603	Gladn, R.
Pte.	273695	Buxton, W. B.	Pte.	3233557	Knight, A. W.
Pte.	3107451	Clarke, W.	Pte.	3234165	McAllister, J. A.
Pte.	3233553	Cochrane, W. H.	Pte.	3035605	Pare, A.

2nd Canadian Mounted Rifles

Rank	No.	Name	Rank	No.	Name
Pte.	220168	Thompson, R. C.	Pte.	3036166	O'Connell, J.
Pte.	2218334	Crowther, D. B.	Pte.	3036790	Parsons, W. E.
	18-10-18		Pte.	3234067	Perryman, T. A.
Pte.	507366	McNamara, S.	Pte.	3107056	Pritchard, R. C.
Pte.	507584	Verity, C. R.	Pte.	3230854	Rennison, G.
Pte.	505349	Jones, R. T.	Pte.	3035790	Ross, W.
Pte.	1048657	O'Shea, J. A.	Pte.	3037937	Scharf, H. E.
	5-10-18		Pte.	3031166	Shanley, T. H.
Pte.	1013153	Watkinson, A. B.	Pte.	3106751	Sollman, C. C.
Pte.	1049036	Stewart, F.	Pte.	3037880	St. Pierre, L. F.
Pte.	2204360	Russell, H. A.	Pte.	3234036	Studholme, N. E.
Pte.	498521	Watts, H.	Pte.	3035532	Tench, J. A.
Pte.	1013089	Wheeler, D.	Pte.	3233562	Thomson, D.
Pte.	1013113	Roberts, E.	Pte.	3231041	Tittensor, W. F. J.
Pte.	1012812	Nicholson, T.	Pte.	3107397	Vail, C. L.
Pte.	1048258	Zrzan, A.	Pte.	3037501	Van Hoesen, H. T.
Pte.	1048247	Powell, G. N.	Pte.	838203	Wall, J.
Pte.	1048240	O'Brien, C.	Pte.	2378384	Waters, F. E.
Pte.	1048260	Wass, G.	Pte.	3035845	Waugh, W.
Pte.	1048320	Simard, J. N.	Pte.	2650510	Whitton, R.
Pte.	1048550	Skellett, W.	Pte.	3034537	Wilkie, V. L.
Pte.	1013178	Smith, R.	Pte.	3035533	Williams, D. R.
Pte.	1048231	Sime, T.	Pte.	3233538	Young, E. J.
Pte.	1048549	Shortt, D.	Pte.	770284	Honeywell, J. J.
	10-10-18		Pte.	3106549	Rousseau, H.
Pte.	2203440	Merriman, L.	Pte.	3233873	Gillespie, F.
Pte.	1012710	Curran, F. J.	Pte.	3035846	Barnes, G.
	17-10-18		Pte.	3233971	Collins, J.
Pte.	3230227	Baker, A.	Pte.	3031177	Cyr, L.
Pte.	3031201	Black, A.	Pte.	3231328	Eastwood, C. A.
Pte.	3035660	Colville, J. F.	Pte.	3035265	Ferguson, J.
Pte.	3231124	Diggins, H. J.	Pte.	3031357	Fitzpatrick, R. R.
Pte.	3035517	Findlay, W.	Pte.	3232000	Ferris, R. H.
Pte.	3233761	Fourlong, G. H.	Pte.	3233566	Garcia, I.
Pte.	3035887	Gareau, E.	Pte.	3233504	Gawley, R.
Pte.	3233682	Gauci, P.	Pte.	3231703	Gies, W.
Pte.	3233491	George, R.	Pte.	3230438	Grayer, E.
Pte.	3036161	Gilmartin, M.	Pte.	3234199	Harpe, W. G.
Pte.	3233441	Hansen, N. K.	Pte.	3036318	Harvey, A.
Pte.	3037806	Harrison, J. F.	Pte.	3233456	Higgins, J.
Pte.	3234218	Harvie, R. G.	Pte.	3107908	James, A. C.
Pte.	3233842	Jezeph, E.	Pte.	2355930	Keezer, C. H.
Pte.	3032631	Keetch, C. S.	Pte.	3233886	Lehane, J. F.
Pte.	3030473	Kelly, T.	Pte.	3036342	Lindsay, G. J.
Pte.	3037380	Lepard, A. C.	Pte.	2500402	Lloyd, C. E.
Pte.	3233812	Little, A.	Pte.	1027358	Locey, R. S.
Pte.	2537437	Lovell, J. B.	Pte.	3234448	Mason, W. W.
Pte.	3233276	Machin, B.	Pte.	3233623	Magnan, G. J.
Pte.	3233899	Matson, I. O.	Pte.	3233459	Mink, N. A.
Pte.	3233895	Mildrew, J.	Pte.	3232859	McAuley, K. S.
Pte.	3037006	Moran, W. J.	Pte.	3037847	McDonald, W.
Pte.	3234182	McCausland, T. R.	Pte.	3035577	McNulty, G. H.
Pte.	3037007	MacIsaac, D.	Pte.	828768	Oxford, J. M.

Appendix V—Nominal Roll

Rank	No.	Name	Rank	No.	Name
Pte.	3232359	Peal, J.	Pte.	3037429	Thomson, W. J.
Pte.	3035654	Poirrier, S.	Pte.	249369	Timpson, G. J.
Pte.	3233552	Radford, W.	Pte.	3038454	Todd, H. W.
Pte.	3230284	Robertson, C.	Pte.	3040093	Tridone, R.
Pte.	3107619	Santary, W. G.	Pte.	3039414	Turgeon, A. A.
Pte.	3233524	Scott, W. T.	Pte.	3038467	Vasey, J. A.
Pte.	3234962	Sherk, H.	Pte.	644847	Vessair, F.
Pte.	3231454	Stewart, R.	Pte.	3038475	Walker, W. J.
Pte.	3036753	Streeter, G. L.	Pte.	3039046	Webster, H. D.
Pte.	3036222	Sullivan, J. C.	Pte.	3038650	Wilton, E. C.
Pte.	3234359	Thompson, A. A.	Pte.	3039419	Yeo, R. J.
Pte.	3233476	Thorp, A. E.	Pte.	3036999	Keenan, P. J.
Pte.	3233013	Trimmingham, J. E.	Pte.	3032923	Batten, B.
Pte.	3233647	Vaillancourt, F.	Pte.	515139	Betts, A. H.
Pte.	3036160	Vaughn, T. F.	Pte.	3108083	Brownlee, S. W.
Pte.	3233463	Walton, J.	Pte.	3036216	Des Lauriers, W.
Pte.	3037023	Watson, L.	Pte.	3032960	Gamble, C. M.
Pte.	3034688	White, J. H.	Pte.	3032225	Jenkin, A. J.
Pte.	3037016	Wildgust, F.	Pte.	3231516	Kenshol, A. R.
Pte.	782306	Wilkins, P. L.	Pte.	3039165	Leroux, O.
Pte.	3230273	Wise, H. F.	Pte.	2591087	Preston, A.
Pte.	3233558	Wood, W. M.	Pte.	3233434	Ralph, J.
Pte.	3107504	Hayden, R. J.	Pte.	3037405	Rennick, R. J. R.
	21-10-18		Pte.	3107367	Robertson, W.
Pte.	3107417	Albert, C.	Pte.	3040164	Samson, C. W.
Pte.	3107805	Beatty, S. A.	Pte.	3035730	Scoones, F. G.
Pte.	3033798	Bond, F.	Pte.	3039679	Sexton, G. S.
Pte.	3034159	Burns, J. E.	Pte.	3230357	Simpson, F. W.
Pte.	3107863	Fettes, J. A.	Pte.	3039038	Sutton, H. J.
Pte.	3107257	Gordon, M. F.	Pte.	3037899	Sloss, M.
Pte.	3107293	Kennedy, A.	Pte.	3108306	Smith, G.
Pte.	3107540	McClintock, R. L.	Pte.	3037414	Smith, J. G.
Pte.	3131709	Pipter, I. W.	Pte.	3037416	Snider, A. E.
Pte.	3040086	Price, V.	Pte.	3231007	Stenhouse, J.
Pte.	190125	Ramey, C.	Pte.	3033416	Strand, C.
Pte.	3038508	Robertson, A. P.	Pte.	3036445	Sweeney, D.
Pte.	3040211	Sage, E. W.	Pte.	797108	Terry, H. W.
Pte.	3037239	Sawyer, L. R. J.	Pte.	3232455	Thinn, H.
Pte.	853281	Service, J.	Pte.	3233565	Thompson, J. E.
Pte.	2250825	Shannon, J.	Pte.	3033031	Tilley, G.
Pte.	3031204	Smith, H. G.	Pte.	3038462	Tonkin, A. S.
Pte.	3037234	Simpson, H.	Pte.	3034349	Tremblay, C. A.
Pte.	3040125	Smith, C.	Pte.	3039882	Trimble, R. H.
Pte.	3032275	Smith, H. J.	Pte.	3033674	Vanderbeck, W. J.
Pte.	3040293	Smith, S. G.	Pte.	3040037	Villa, S.
Pte.	3031993	Spencer, A. B.	Pte.	3039876	Vyse, N.
Pte.	3233642	Stevens, C.	Pte.	3038491	Walsh, J. J.
Pte.	3039945	Stone, L. D.	Pte.	3039926	White, J.
Pte.	3233461	Sulkes, B.	Pte.	3037256	Woods, L. H.
Pte.	3038461	Taylor, J. G.	Pte.	3233464	Tribbick, S. G.
Pte.	3234766	Thibault, A.	Pte.	3033412	Padbury, P. N.
Pte.	3039284	Thomas, T. J.		29-10-18	
			Pte.	3033429	Davis, H.

2nd Canadian Mounted Rifles

Rank	No.	Name	Rank	No.	Name
Pte.	303999	Grech, J.	Pte.	3233630	McFadden, E. M.
Pte.	3040157	Harney, L.	Pte.	3040243	MacFarlane, A.
Pte.	3235380	Harper, C. G.	Pte.	3036723	McGowan, W.
Pte.	3040207	Hastings, W. A.	Pte.	3037219	McInnes, J. N.
Pte.	3038068	Hearn, W. A.	Pte.	3037392	McKinnon, A. W.
Pte.	2500294	McShane, J.	Pte.	3040047	McMullen, J. C.
Pte.	3039281	Perry, P. C.	Pte.	3038851	McNichol, D.
Pte.	853359	Calvert, J. L.	Pte.	3231466	McPhee, G.
Pte.	853340	Plunkett, F. R.	Pte.	3039521	Potter, J.
Pte.	3231195	Sprickerhoff, H.	Pte.	3107984	Redcliffe, A.
Pte.	3035272	Guthrie, J.	Pte.	2498326	Reynolds, W. A.
Pte.	3039895	Gregory, L. A.	Pte.	3033194	Rodgers, J. A.
Pte.	3040306	Harper, G.	Pte.	3039963	Hall, A.
Pte.	1024281	Hastings, P. A.	Pte.	3040196	Ross, E. L.
Pte.	3037359	Hayes, C. R.	Pte.	3033887	Keenan, T. V.
Pte.	3036319	Helm, H.	Pte.	514062	Middleton, L. F.
Pte.	3035602	Potts, W. A.	Pte.	2591095	Talbot, F. G.
Pte.	853744	Benn, A. E.	Pte.	3040352	Barlow, A.
Pte.	3231028	Fogler, A.	Pte.	3040494	Baulaurier, J. H.
Pte.	916264	Penrose, W. C.	Pte.	3040444	Berwick, J.
5-11-18			Pte.	3040424	Blair, L.
Pte.	3039516	Groome, J. F.	Pte.	3040431	Breen, M.
Pte.	3040219	Guild, W. A.	Pte.	3032898	Capp, W.
Pte.	3040077	Hansen, G. J.	Pte.	3040409	Cocking, S. W.
Pte.	3039565	Hardy, C. S.	Pte.	3040474	Colhoun, S.
Pte.	3034285	Harris, O.	Pte.	3039562	Collins, F. M.
Pte.	3039152	Hatherley, H. C.	Pte.	3040069	Cox, J. M.
Pte.	3037355	Hawes, G. C.	Pte.	3040126	Craig, F.
Pte.	3035087	Hellowell, W. H.	Pte.	3039640	Cuttell, G. W.
Pte.	3039511	Hellwig, E. W.	Pte.	3035761	Davidson, O. M.
Pte.	3040239	Hill, B. L.	Pte.	3039810	Daldonne, L.
Pte.	3039750	Hille, W. J.	Pte.	3040412	Gagnon, R.
Pte.	3040315	Hummell, J. C.	Pte.	3037051	Gilliland, S. C.
Pte.	3232912	Hurst, J.	Pte.	3037178	Gillespie, D. V.
15-11-18			Pte.	3039919	Graham, W.
Pte.	654114	Wells, R.	Pte.	3035987	Heitzner, J. H.
18-11-18			Pte.	3040381	Smith, F.
Pte.	3039707	Hall, C. W.	Pte.	3040623	White, J. N.
Pte.	3039453	Larson, J. M.	Pte.	3040379	McNeill, W.
Pte.	3235115	Lye, H.	Pte.	3040580	Simmons, T.
Pte.	3040166	Morin, R.	Pte.	3040109	Somerville, J. W.
Pte.	3107934	MacDonald, G.	Pte.	3039093	Beasley, A.
Pte.	3038234	McDougall, T. R.			

APPENDIX VI

Glossary of Abbreviations

a.	Acting.
attd.	Attached.
Bde.	Brigade.
B. M.	Brigade Major.
Bn.	Battalion.
Btty.	Battery.
C. A. M. C.	Canadian Army Medical Corps.
C. A. P. C.	Canadian Army Pay Corps.
C. E.	Canadian Engineers.
C. E. F.	Canadian Expeditionary Force.
C. F. A.	Canadian Field Artillery.
Capt.	Captain.
Cpl.	Corporal.
Col.	Colonel.
Coy.	Company.
D. C. M.	Distinguished Conduct Medal.
Div.	Division.
D. S. O.	Distinguished Service Order.
d. w.	Died of wounds.
Far.	Farrier.
G. H. Q.	General Headquarters.
H. Q.	Headquarters.
K.	Killed in action.
L/	Lance.
Lieut.	Lieutenant.
M. C.	Military Cross.
M. M.	Military Medal.
M. G. C.	Machine Gun Company.
M. S. M.	Meritorious Service Medal.
Maj.	Major.
o/c	On command.
p. o. w.	Prisoner of war.
Pte.	Private.
R. A. F.	Royal Air Force.
R. Q. M. S.	Regimental Quarter Master Sergeant.
R. S. M.	Regimental Sergeant Major.
Sad.	Saddler.
Sig.	Signaller.
S.	Squadron.
S. o. d.	Still on duty.
Sgt.	Sergeant.
T. M. B.	Trench Mortar Battery.
Tpr.	Trooper.
Tpt.	Trumpeter.
t. o. s.	Taken on strength.
V. C.	Victoria Cross.
w.	Wounded.

2nd Canadian Mounted Rifles

Additions

2nd Canadian Mounted Rifles

Additions

2nd Canadian Mounted Rifles

www.ingramcontent.com/pod-product-compliance
Lightning Source LLC
Chambersburg PA
CBHW071819230426
43670CB00013B/2506